27.11.01

To ?

With great affection
from

Teddy

Moossia

Edward Graham.

Moossia

A true story of survival and triumph through the horrors of revolutionary Russia

Edward Burnham

ISBN 978-1-456-59265-3

Designed and edited by Tim Burnham

Printed in the United States of America

To Dagmar. This is your story, and it must be told

Author's Note

I first met Moossia around 1980, by which time she had become Mrs Dagmar Cooper-Jeeves, twice married and twice bereaved. She must have been nearing seventy and I was ten years younger.

She was then living in our own village in the English countryside. Her family, the Dvorskys, owners of a pickle factory, had fled for their lives from the brutality of the Russian Revolution; from St Petersburg, first to Finland, then Denmark, and eventually to England.

When I met her, Dagmar was teaching Russian in a school in Brighton. She told me the extraordinary and very moving story of her life as a small girl in the troubles, and we decided to work it into a book. It took about two years to gather the material and fashion it into a narrative.

That was about thirty years ago. I didn't know how to sell it to a publisher and the manuscript was put away in a drawer for almost three decades.

But it seems that Moossia's history had to be told. So I have dusted it off so that you are now at last able to read her true story.

I am now 94 years old. It intrigues me that a man of my years should be narrating the account of a seven-year-old girl, whose story begins in St Petersburg in the year of my own birth.

Chapter 1

Late Winter 1916

The crystal ball lived on its little black fretted stand on the top of the china cabinet in the drawing room of our apartment on the corner of Fourteenth Avenue. Once I heard Agasha say that some people could look into it and see what was going to happen in the future. I never could, however hard I tried, not even when I peered into it with Mama's black Spanish shawl draped over my head, and waved my arms about the way Agasha said the fortune-teller did. Perhaps it was just as well. Perhaps even the pure gold of my early happy childhood would have been tarnished if I had been able to conjure up the black days ahead.

When I stood on the embroidered footstool which was usually in front of the handsome armchair which Granny sat in when she came round to visit us from her house in the grounds of the family pickle factory round the corner, I could just reach up to lift the crystal ball off its stand. But my seven-year-old hands were only just big enough to grasp it, and it was so heavy that it came down with quite a bump on to the front of my pinafore. I loved to put the ball on the ledge of the wide bay window, and to lean against the warm, bumpy, cast-iron radiator below the double glazing and, since our apartment was on the first floor, I could put my face quite close and see wonderful squashed pictures up and down the usually busy avenue with its two cobbled roads, one on either side of the tree-lined promenade which ran down the middle.

Agasha once told my little brother, Koka, that you only had to sit in the window long enough and, sooner or later, all the people of St. Petersburg would be sure to pass by. But I think she may only have said

1

this because Koka was being fidgety and a bit of a nuisance at the time, the way boys are, just to keep him quiet for a few minutes. Anyhow, it didn't work with Koka because he just didn't have the patience. Then, he was only about four and three quarters and had never been very strong, so nobody blamed him much.

On sunny days I could catch the sun's rays in the crystal ball and throw rainbows over the drawing room walls, but today the colours were dimmed by the mist rising from the river Neva a short walk away. It was the very beginning of the spring thaw. I could see a group of sailors walking smartly in step along the promenade, their hat ribbons flapping, maybe going on leave from the fortress of Kronstadt. A wounded soldier struggled along on crutches some distance behind, one leg heavily plastered. Then the soft clop-clop of a horse and the slither of runners announced a sleigh jingling by in the other direction. The driver was swathed up to the eyebrows, and had a heavy fur hat pulled right down to meet his turned-up collar. You could tell they were on their way home because the reins were slack in his hands, and the little horse was trotting briskly and obviously knew the way as well as the driver did.

On the other side, plodding along with a great effort, a flat-capped figure bearing a heavy grindstone in a rickety wooden stand over his shoulder looked about him for possible but not very likely customers. I could just hear his cry through the two layers of glass, "Knives and scissors to sharpen, knives and scissors." They all swam in and out of the crystal ball like different coloured goldfish in a goldfish bowl. A sudden flash of light across the curved glass made me look closer to see a ball of white doggy fur hurtle right across the road towards the knife-grinder, and then slide out of control along a patch of ice, unable to stop itself, so that I burst out laughing, it looked so funny.

"Moossia! Moossia! Where are you, my dove?"

"I'm here in the drawing room, Agasha. I shan't be a minute."

I picked up the crystal ball and, hurrying slowly so as not to drop it, ran the obstacle course past great-grandfather Nord and Aunt Alexandra smiling stiffly from the walls, in front of Granny's armchair, behind Mama's grand piano and over the polar-bear rug which tickled your feet when you came in shoeless sometimes to be kissed goodnight, and up onto the footstool by the china cabinet. I had just put the crystal ball back on its stand and was returning the footstool to its rightful station

2

when Agasha came through the drawing-room door. She could see at a glance what I'd been up to.

"Come along, my little gypsy. Time for us to go for our walk."

Her dark blue eyes were warm with affection, and her fresh young face crinkled with merriment. She already had her padded jacket on over her white blouse and red-flowered sarafan, and was tying a many-coloured kerchief round her head.

"Let's go and fetch Koka!" And down the corridor we went, past the closed door of Papa's study, past Mama's and Papa's bedroom, and the spare room, and then turned left to the nursery at the other end of the apartment. I chattered to her about the sailors all in step and the poor wounded soldier and the knife grinder and the skating dog that was so funny.

"Come along, Kokochka, time for our walk. You can finish building your castle when we come back. Now sit down and get your feet into the gaiters."

"Oh, no, Agasha! Not gaiters today!"

"Oh, yes, Koka, certainly gaiters today. You must have gaiters to keep your legs and your tummy warm."

Funny face from Koka, but he sits down and holds his feet out stiffly.

"Where are we going today, Agasha?"

"Where would you like to go, my sparrows? Stand up, Koka." Shouts of laughter when Agasha's strong arms lift Koka right off his feet to settle him into his gaiters. Then buttonings with button hooks, tying on of mittens, pulling on of warm fur hat and galoshes. Then the same process for me, with more shouts of laughter. All carried out expertly, firmly, lovingly.

"Agasha, can you tie my ear-flaps down, please?"

"There, Kokochka, you look just like your Papa when he goes hunting. Now, Moossia, take your muff to keep your hands warm."

"Do I have to? It only gets in the way when I run."

"Merciful Heavens. 'I don't want this. I don't want that.' Whatever next?" and the muff string is popped over my head before I can say another word. "Off we go!"

And, hand in hand, Agasha in the middle of course, we march off down the corridor, sally from the front door of the apartment, climb down several short flights of stairs, still rather steep for our young legs so we hang on to the cast iron balusters and the mahogany banister when we can. Now we confront the great doors leading to the world outside.

"Egor isn't here to open the doors!"

"Never mind. I can open the doors."

"You can do everything, Agasha!"

A broad smile from Agasha, who says, "I expect Egor is drinking tea in his little room." The doors are very heavy but Agasha is very strong.

Outside, we take a deep breath to brave the sharp air, and find ourselves in the Avenue. Not only did the coming thaw show itself in the thick mist shrouding everything around us, but the faint music of the melting snow and ice was just beginning. Water tinkled in the downpipes, babbled in the gutters and gurgled down the drains. An occasional icicle shattered tunefully on a bared patch of window-ledge, and there was the crunch, crunch, crunch, occasional splash, splash made by the feet of the few passers-by.

"Let's walk along the promenade; it's not so slushy there." More straightening of ear-flaps, buttoning of undone buttons come adrift in the intrepid climb down the long stairway. Then hand in hand across the pavement.

"Wait!" Hands held very tightly.

Two heavy horses with shaggy feet loomed out of the mist, followed by a great dray with huge iron-shod wheels and laden, as we well knew, with giant-size barrels full of vinegar on their way to Granny's pickle factory down the road to pickle the onions and the cucumbers and the cabbages. We waved to the horses and the driver. The driver waved back. When the road was clear again we trotted, all three, over to the promenade. There was still too much snow on the roadway for us to feel the knobbly cobbles under our feet.

As we plodded towards the river, down the promenade between the rows of snow-covered trees and benches, Koka suddenly got a little devil in him, and began to skip and caper about like a lamb.

"Spring is coming", said Agasha, smiling down at him. But then he broke loose from her hand and stamped about a few steps in front of us, from one little puddle of melting snow to another, arms and legs turned outward, like a puppet on strings. Both Agasha and I tried to keep our faces straight because he was so funny and we didn't want him to get any wilder; but when he skipped too close to the road, we ran after him and took him by the hands between us.

"Let's all keep our eyes open and see if there any rooks about", suggested Agasha. "When the rooks come then the power of winter is broken. When the rooks come then Spring is really on its way."

Koka saw rooks everywhere. "There's a rook!"

"No, no, that's not a rook. It isn't big enough. It's only a starling."

"There's lots of rooks over there!"

"Silly billy. Rooks aren't that colour. Rooks are black, aren't they, Agasha?"

"Black as chimney sweeps." By then we had reached the walk by the river Neva, and Agasha let us run about freely.

"Now remember what Mama said. Breathe through your noses. You don't want to get sore throats."

Koka and I ran up to the railings by the edge of the river to look at the cracks in the ice. Koka tried to climb over.

"Kokochka, come down. You'll fall in!" Hanging half up, half down, like a little fur-hatted monkey, Koka chattered, "Can't we go down and walk on the ice?"

"Certainly not. It isn't safe any more. Look at all the cracks!"

"Where's a crack, Agasha?"

"Over there's a crack!" and then in chorus, "There's a crack, and there, and there, and there!"

"Now we're being silly", smiled Agasha.

"There's a rook, anyway." A black bird had lighted on the railings.

"Ugh, no. That's not a rook. That's a crow, a horrid old crow, Kokochka." Agasha hunched her shoulders and pretended to shiver, then she crossed herself. I looked up at her troubled face. "Don't you like crows, Agasha?"

"Oh, yes, I do, if they just keep their little beaks shut, but not if they caw at you. Then they bring you bad luck."

"Caw, caw, caw", went Koka, wickedly, and flapped his arms high in the air. "Caw, ca-a-aw, ca-a-a-a-aw."

"Stop it; that's just asking for trouble!"

Although this was a dull grey day, with the sun no more than an enormous orange low in the sky, we so loved our walks with Agasha that we turned back home with bright eyes and shining faces.

As we came close to the factory gates, I said, "Let's go inside and talk to the horses, Agasha."

"Not today, Moossinka."

"Granny said we could, if you are with us."

"Your Papa wouldn't want us to bother the stableman."

"But it's Granny's factory, Agasha."

"Yes, Moossinka, I know, but you must do what your Papa says."

"But…"

"No buts, my little ones."

And there were no buts.

Egor was back at the main door when we got home, and opened it when we rang. When he saw who was there he half closed the door again, and then peeped round with his peaked cap, heavy beard and strawberry nose, and, very politely in his deep bass voice, asked, with a very low bow to each of us in turn,

"Good day, Barin, good day, Barinya; what is your wish?"

Koka and I giggled helplessly, and looked at each other, unable to speak. Then Egor straightened up to his full height, towering above us.

"I think you must have come to the wrong house." Agasha stood patiently by for a while, waiting for this oft-repeated ritual to run its course. We couldn't restrain our giggles any longer, exploded into loud laughter, and chorused,

"But, Egor, we live here!"

"No-o-o-o, I think there must be some mistake", and his hand moved as if he was going to close the big door again. Here Agasha intervened.

"Now stop your nonsense, Egor, and let us in. The children will catch cold standing here." She moved forward.

"This is Moo-oo-ssia!"

"This is Ko-o-o-ka!" Pointing to ourselves.

"Upon my soul", in complete amazement, "so you are! Bless my old eyes, how big you are growing!" Then, busily, he jerked down his long blue uniform coat, straightened his peaked cap, stepped back and opened the door as wide as it would go.

"Please come in." Straight back and feet together like a soldier in a sentry-box, and with his right hand to his forehead quivering in an ecstatic salute, he let us pass to scamper up the stairway, racing to be first, totally out of breath, racing to be first to pull the bell by the apartment door, and making such a hullabaloo, pulling the bell, first one and then the other, over and over, even after snub-nosed Masha in her neat white apron, blonde hair caught back in her pink and white kerchief, even after she had opened the door to us. She clapped her hands over her ears and stepped nimbly back to avoid being knocked over.

Off came hats and coats and galoshes in all directions, making splashes of wet snow on the polished floor of the hall as we raced towards the welcome warmth of the nursery.

"Masha, please take the children's things into the kitchen to dry. Goodness, just look at the mess they've made here!"

"It doesn't matter, Agasha. Barinya says that the floor polishers are coming tomorrow."

We stopped in our tracks and doubled back into the hall as fast as our legs would carry us.

"Agasha, do you think one of them will let me ride on his brush?"

"Ride, indeed, Kokochka. You must let them get on with their work!"

"Well then, can we watch them?"

"We'll see!"

"Agasha, I won't get in their way, I promise. I'll sit here on the settee." He landed with a thump on the settee, but was off again in a moment, having pulled off his shoes. I could read his mind, and did the same.

"They look like skaters when they slide about the floor with their brushes tied to their feet!"

"Just like skaters." I followed Koka, and we glided haltingly about the hall in our stockinged feet with our hands behind our backs, chanting,

"Just like skaters!"

"Just like skaters!"

Chapter 2

March 1916 – Agasha

I think I'm very lucky to have been working for the Dvorskys all these years. They weren't obliged to keep me on after Moossia was weaned. I know it happens a lot but not to all girls. They're just good people and understand how unfortunate I'd been and wanted to help me. They're just good people.

My family, the Abramovs, had lived in our village for generations. My father, Josip, told stories that his grandfather had told him about the war against a French soldier called Napoleon and he had got his stories from his grandfather who was a soldier in a big battle against the French.

The Abramovs always seemed to have been the poorest family in the village. On the other hand, the Brodskys always seem to have been the top dogs. They owned a lot of land around the village. They weren't gentry but they were very well off. My father used to look after Oleg Brodsky's cows. My mother, Katya, did some of the milking and housework, too, for the Brodskys. My sister Tanya used to help me look after the children Oleg had had by his second wife. His first wife had died of a fever about seven years before. I had charge of little Lena and little Valya. Everybody thought they were twins because they looked so alike but they weren't. Actually they had been born a year apart.

Oleg Brodsky had a son, also named Oleg, by his first wife. He was tall and fair-haired and had the beginnings of a moustache on his upper lip. All us girls in the village were secretly in love with him. He was the handsomest young man for miles around and I was very pleased when he started to notice me. We fell head over heels in love. My parents thought I was a bit young, at sixteen, to think of getting married, but didn't make any objections. They were really very flattered by the thought of a union between our two families. It meant a step up in the world for the Abramovs. So they encouraged us to go for walks in the woods and quite soon I found I was pregnant. Both Oleg's parents were happy about it and preparations were started for our wedding on Easter Day.

My Oleg was an adventurous young man and joined the army, hoping to be stationed not too far from me. But things didn't go well. Just before Palm Sunday he was transferred to the Caucasus which have always been a trouble spot. He had to leave at once and there was no time for us to get married. He told me to name the little boy (he was sure I would have a boy) after him and his father. So my son would be the third Oleg in his family. Oleg the third you might call him.

We were very sad to have to part so soon. He couldn't take me with him because of some army regulation and promised to send for me as soon as he was settled wherever he happened to find himself. He promised to write to me and he kept his promise. But I only got one letter from him. The next letter was from his commanding officer telling me a lot of stuff about what a good soldier Oleg had been and that he had been killed by a sniper.

I think I cried solidly for a week but decided I must pull myself together for the sake of the baby. It actually was a little boy. A very sweet little fellow he was and I loved him with all my heart. But little Oleg only lived three weeks. Doctor Panov did his best but he had no idea what was the matter with my little boy who died after only three weeks. After his father's death this second disaster completely numbed me. I didn't know what to do. Here I was, with a dead baby, and no husband to look after us. I was at my wits' end.

Doctor Panov came to the rescue. He had had to go to St. Petersburg for some sort of conference and went to stay with some people named Dvorsky. Mrs Dvorsky was pregnant and would be giving birth in the next few days. The Dvorskys were looking for a wet-nurse and Doctor Panov told them of my situation and how reliable and hard working I was. They said they would give me a trial so I went to St. Petersburg. I wasn't at all sorry to leave the village. It was freezing cold in the Winter, mud up to your ankles in the Spring and all dust and nasty smells in the Summer. I'd never been to St. Petersburg and hoped it would make a change. Most of my friends had stuck by me but there one or two spiteful voices raised because I'd had a baby out of wedlock. They just didn't stop to think. What would Lydia Granin and Lera Shvartz have done in my place? On the other hand some people were very kind and Dmitri Joffe gave me a lift in his cart to St. Petersburg and left me right outside the apartment on St. Basil's Boulevard.

It was horrid leaving the family. Mamochka hugged me and cried her heart out. Tanya hugged me and couldn't utter a word. Papachka kissed me three times and told me not to get into mischief.

I had been very unhappy but my life changed when I joined the Dvorskys. I've been with them ever since and very content from the moment I put Moossia to my breast.

Chapter 3

March 1916

"Agasha, may I have something to drink please?"

Koka and I had got quite out of breath skating about the hall, and our faces were flushed with the exertion.

"No, Moossia, not yet; you're too hot to drink just now. Little horses must cool down a little before you take them to the water."

"But I'm not a little horse."

"It's the same thing."

So we put our shoes on again and went on building Koka's castle for a few minutes.

"I've cooled down now, Agasha, I know I have! May I have some Mors to drink, please?"

Agasha came over and put her hand to my forehead.

"Yes, all right; you can have some now, just a little. It'll be supper time soon, you know."

But when she came back from the kitchen she had a glass of cold tea with a spoonful of jam in it.

"Here, drink this, my precious."

"But I wanted some Mors, Agasha!"

"The cranberries didn't come today so Masha couldn't make it. She says she'll get some tomorrow when she goes to market. Now be a good girl and drink it up. Cold tea makes you beautiful, my little dove." And she brushed my hair gently from my face.

"Oh, does it, Agasha, does it… really?" I went over to the mirror on the wall and began to sip the tea with relish and to watch developments. A curious thought came to me.

"Agasha, is it true that Cook washes her face in the washing up water?"

"Whoever told you that, Moossinka?"

"Mama was talking about it to Granny when I went into the drawing room to say goodnight."

"I don't think you could have heard it right, my little one." Agasha was clearly embarrassed.

"Oh, yes, Granny said that Cook had a beautiful complexion and Mama told her how she got it."

For a moment Agasha didn't know what to say.

"And that's why her face is so shiny."

Agasha recovered and took charge of the situation.

"Well, we don't have any washing up water here so it doesn't concern us, does it?" Which firmly put an end to that little piece of tittle-tattle. "Koka, I can hear Masha getting the supper ready. Do you want to do pee-pee first?"

"No thank you, Agasha. What are we going to have for supper?"

"Something to eat, I shouldn't wonder."

"Bitki?"

"Pancakes?" We let our imaginations wander.

"Piroshki?"

"Meat balls?"

"Sit up at the table, Moossia. Come along, Kokoshka."

Agasha had just lifted Koka up into his high chair when Masha came in with the supper tray. Koka screwed his face up.

"Oh, no! Not semolina! Semolina, semolina, always semolina."

"Eat it up, Koka. Semolina is good for you. Look at Moossia. She loves it. Why can't you?"

"No, she doesn't. Not really. She only likes playing rivers with the milk." Agasha took up the spoon and tried to feed Koka but he pressed his lips together and shook his head obstinately. "No, I don't want it. I'll starve and then you'll cry and be sorry. You'll see."

"Don't make fun of God's good food!" Agasha was quite sharp. "It's a sin!" Koka changed his tactics at once and looked up at her winningly.

"Well, could I have some kissel with it then, Agasha?" She recognised what he was up to but couldn't resist him and a slight smile hovered round her lips. "I'll see if there's some left over in the kitchen." She came back almost at once with a small dish of slightly thickened red currant juice which she ladled in equal shares on to our semolina.

"There. Now you make all the red rivers and lakes you want to, but mind you eat it up."

"Why can't we have pancakes?"

"Everything at its proper time. It isn't pancake time yet. I'll get your warm milk for you."

She left the room and that matter was settled, too. So for a little while we contented ourselves with making patterns with the kissel and eating a very little semolina with it. The murmur of conversation between Cook and Masha and Agasha came from the kitchen with the clink of the milk saucepan on the kitchen range. In the distant drawing room Mama began to play a lilting romantic tune on the piano.

"I've finished first", triumphed Koka and started to climb out of his high chair. But somehow he caught his foot, toppled over and, as he fell, caught his head a glancing blow on the radiator and lay still and white-faced on the nursery floor.

I was very frightened and burst into tears. The noise of Koka's fall and my outcry brought Agasha rushing into the room with the two glasses of warm milk in her hands.

"What is it? Whatever happened?"

Then, as she saw Koka lying still on the floor, her hands, not mindful of what she had in them, went up to her face so that the milk spilled on her sleeves. "Dear God, Kokoshka. Dear God!" She went to put the glasses on the table but was so distressed that she missed the table entirely and they fell to the floor splintering and splashing the milk in all directions. She knelt by the little boy and gathered him tenderly into her arms. Rocking him to and fro as if to breathe life into Koka's limp body Agasha whispered endlessly over his chalk white face, "Almighty One have mercy, Almighty One have mercy…"

All this time we could hear Mama playing rippling passages on the keyboard. Obviously she hadn't heard a thing.

"Agasha, look, his eyes are closed," I breathed over her shoulder, "is he going to die?" Koka chose that moment to open his eyes and utter a little mew of indignant protest.

"No, no, of course not, of course he isn't. Don't talk such nonsense, my little dove… There, you see! He's opened his little eyes." Her sympathetic crooning prompted Koka to start wailing loudly.

"Hush, my darling, hush, it's all right. Agasha has got you. What a bump it was, what a nasty bump!" Then, to Masha who was standing in the door, helplessly, turning this way and that, the picture of indecision, not knowing the least how to deal with the sudden crisis, "Masha, go and tell the Barinya. She can't have heard. The drawing room door must be closed and she's playing the piano. No! Wait!", as Masha started to dash off, "Tell her gently! Don't frighten her! Don't upset her!" Then Agasha turned to me.

"Moossinka, give me that big spoon on the table, will you?"

She gently pressed the cold metal bowl of the spoon to the swelling bump on Koka's forehead. Koka's wailing gave way to a shout of pain.

"Don't cry, don't cry, my little chickabiddy. You'll soon be better."

"Agasha, it hurts when you do that. Mama, Mamaa-a. Where's Mama?"

Mama came rushing through the doorway pale with anxiety and out of breath with running from the drawing room. She knelt on the floor by Agasha and Koka.

"Agasha, what is it? Whatever happened? Why were they left alone?" Mama was always upset when anything happened to Koka, who had been ill many times.

"Barinya, I only went in to the kitchen to fetch the warm milk…" I tried to help. "Mama, he was climbing down from his chair and he fell down and bumped his head and Agasha put a spoon on it to make it better."

"Agasha, carry him to my bedroom while I send for the doctor."

"Something like this would happen when the Barin is away hunting."

"Mama, where is Papa?"

"I'm not quite sure, Moossia. He's away hunting bears. Come along, Agasha." I went to follow them but Agasha stopped me.

"No, Moossinka, you wait here with Masha. I'll be back soon. Masha, don't let Moossia out of your sight."

Koka was carried off in Agasha's strong peasant arms and I was left with the cold semolina and Masha standing sentry over me. By now any appetite I had had for my supper had been quite banished by the anxiety for Koka and I aimlessly made red rivers and red lakes with the semolina and the kissel, just waiting for Agasha to come back. Masha picked up the pieces of broken glass and mopped up the spilt milk, nervously glancing up at me to watch my slightest movement. She sniffed with emotion from time to time but had nothing whatever to say.

"Masha, I'd like to have my warm milk now, please."

"I can't get it for you now, Moossia, I can't. Agasha told me not to let you out of my sight. You heard what she said." Masha was determined to carry out her instructions to the letter.

Then Agasha billowed into the room and I couldn't bear it any longer. I got up from my chair and hurled myself into her arms. She just held me quietly for a while as I shook and sobbed, stroking my hair soothingly.

"There, there, don't cry, my angel, don't cry, my chick. It's going to be all right. It's all right."

"Is it, really and truly? Will Koka get better?"

"Oh, yes, but when your Mama brings him back we shall have to be quiet as mice, mind. Now let's go and wash your hands and face, shall we?"

We crept into the bathroom practising to be quiet as mice and not raising our voices above a whisper.

"Here's the toothpowder."

"Can't I just do them with water this time?"

"I should think not indeed. Mama says to clean your teeth with tooth powder and tooth powder it must be. Here it is."

Back in the nursery Agasha helped me to get ready for bed and I knelt by my bed in my nightie to say my goodnight prayer. As I went to get up Agasha said, "Let's say a special prayer for Koka."

So she led me over to the other side of the room, and we knelt by her bed looking up at Agasha's ikon of the Mother of God and the Christ Child.

"Blessed Mother of God, look down upon me, a sinner, and don't let the little boy suffer, and…" she looked at me.

"Bless Mama and Papa."

"And…?"

"And bless everybody else."

"And…?"

"And may your will be done for ever and ever. Amen."

"Amen."

I was still frightened to Koka's accident and I couldn't sleep very deeply that night, although I didn't hear Mama bring Koka back and put him to bed. But after that it seemed that the least noise made me wake with a start, but I was instantly reassured when I looked over and could see the outline of Agasha's figure sitting quietly by Koka's bed, her hands busy with her sewing. Her white apron gleamed in the semi-darkness where it lay crumpled on one of the chairs, and the glass beads she usually wore round her neck glittered as they lay in a heap on the table where the oil lamp, which had been brought in specially to give a dim light to this all-night vigil, was turned low so as not to disturb us.

On one occasion, when I woke up to hear the bells ringing to tell the hour in a nearby church, Agasha looked across at me, aware by instinct that I wasn't sleeping.

"Agasha!" I whispered.

The little meadow of coloured flowers on her sarafan skirt rose without haste and floated towards me. Agasha still had her sewing in her hands as she sat by me on the bed.

"Yes, my little dove?"

"I can't sleep, Agasha. Can you tell me a story?"

"It's very late, Moossinka."

"Then can I have a cup of tea?"

"Close your eyes and sleep will come." She began to get up but I wouldn't let her go.

"I'm hungry, Agasha." To my relief, she sat down on the bed again.

"Hungry? Merciful Heaven, what a stupid woman your Agasha is! Of course you're hungry. You didn't finish your semolina. You were upset because of Koka, weren't you? Now don't you fret; I'll find you something to eat and I'll make us some tea. The samovar is still on the table. Just you wait a little while."

She clucked scolding to herself as she lifted the lid of the samovar to see how much water was left, and then went off to the kitchen, to return with some pieces of charcoal with which she stoked the samovar. A match flared red in the shadows, then the white cloth over the loaf of bread whisked into the air and settled down again, and I could dimly see and dimly hear Agasha preparing a slice of bread and butter which she brought to me in her hand. I was difficult to satisfy.

"Can I have some jam on it, please, Agasha?"

"I'll give you the next one with jam. Eat this one first, little one. Tea will be ready soon." I couldn't let her go.

"Agasha!" in the stealthiest whisper. She tiptoed back again and, so as not to raise her voice, bent over me.

"Tell me the story of the rolling Kilibak. How he rolls away and the fox eats him up."

"Not tonight, my little sunshine. We might wake Koka up. Agasha will tell you in the morning."

Contentedly, I munched my slice of bread and butter, sitting up in bed. Agasha was keeping an eye on the fire in the samovar.

"Agasha, the samovar is singing."

"I can hear; but we must wait for the steam to push up the little lids on the top to tell us that the water is boiling. Here, eat this."

This time there was jam on the bread and butter.

There was no sound from the world outside, and the room was quiet as quiet. The lamplight cast an amber glow on Agasha's serene face. The warm light, the stillness broken only by the signing of the samovar, and even the unusual delight of the feast-in-the-middle-of-the-night, all spoke of Agasha's love and care which constantly surrounded us. But it spoke most clearly of all to me because Agasha was mine and I was hers. I wished then that nothing would ever change; that it would always go on and on like this forever.

"Agasha, now the samovar is hissing."

"Sh-h-h-h. Not so loud." She pointed towards a sleeping Koka.

Then the beloved ritual of tea-making. The teapot from the top of the samovar. The teaspoon of tea from the lacquered caddy. The rising sound of boiling water bubbling and hissing into the pot. The small noise of the pot going back on to the top of the samovar to draw for a while.

"Oh dear, the sugar basin is empty. I won't go out into the kitchen again. Never mind, Agasha will put a teaspoonful of strawberry jam into our glasses. Then it will be nice and sweet."

"Put in two teaspoonfuls, Agasha."

"No, my dove, that will make it much too sweet. Here you are. Mind, it's very hot. Be careful how you drink it." But sleep suddenly overtook me and, after only a few sips, I gave my glass back to Agasha and snuggled down into the warmth of my bed.

"I don't want any more, thank you, Agasha."

And I just remember Agasha pulling up the bedclothes around me.

Chapter 4

April 1916

"Masha," Mama said, "Lay places for the children at the dining room table today. The old Barinya and Barinya Dorothea are coming as well so we shall need an extra chair for Barinya Dorothea's dog. The old Barinya is sending her cook, Fedotya, across to help you in the kitchen. You know she likes her pancakes hot, just out of the pan."

"All right, Barinya, I'll tell them in the kitchen." Masha went busily off.

Today was pancake day and Koka and I were always allowed to have lunch with the grown ups. "The old Barinya" was Mama's Mama and she lived in a house in the grounds of the pickle factory behind our apartment building. Granny was the owner of the factory and her house had a garden of its own and a pond, too, where we used to skate in the winter. She was small and plump, a good businesswoman, and her word was law. I never knew my grandfather because Granny had divorced him when Mama was little.

Aunt Dorothea, who lived with Granny, came from Denmark and spoke hardly any Russian. Koka and I had nothing much to do with her. She was tall and gaunt and very reserved. Mostly she wore grey clothes with a high ruffled lace collar. She thought that all Russians were barbarians and she always had her little dog with her. As Aunt Dorothea always carried the dog, which gloried in the unusual name of Kroshka-Crumb, tucked under her arm or else resting on her lap, we hardly ever saw his feet.

When Granny arrived with Aunt Dorothea and Kroshka-Crumb she was dressed for a party with a corded silk skirt and dark blouse and a cream lace jabot fastened with her ruby brooch. She was in high spirits and very mischievous.

"I'm hungry as a horse. Lead me to the pancakes!"

They were still in the hallway so Papa darted over to the kitchen door and opened and closed it two or three times to waft the tantalising smell out towards us. Granny played up to him and trotted over to his side as if drawn by a magnet and stood by his side with her eyes closed and one hand on her bosom, savouring the delicious aroma.

"They're almost ready, Mamochka." Then he threw down his challenge.

"I bet you won't be able to eat more pancakes than I can." Granny drew herself up, fished for the lorgnette hanging round her neck on a silken cord, flicked it sharply open and, looking Papa straight in the eye in mock outrage,

"Who lost the bet last year? You did. I warn you. I've had nothing to eat for two days to prepare me for this feast."

Papa took her by both hands laughingly and drew her so quickly towards the dining room that she had to break into a little run and she squeaked in protest. Papa burst out laughing as she pretended to beat him with the lorgnette.

"Lilya, I want you to be the witness. I bet Mamochka that I shall eat more pancakes than she will."

"All right, Karloosha, I'll be the witness. You must shake hands on it properly then."

Papa and Granny clasped their two hands together like two peasants selling geese in the market place, very serious and, at the same time, bubbling with laughter.

"There!" Mama struck their two clasped hands lightly with one of her own and they parted under the blow. Everybody, even Aunt Dorothea, laughed out loud because they knew that Papa was bound to let Granny win in any case.

Just then Masha came out of the kitchen to tell us that the pancakes were ready and we all bustled into the dining room. Koka sat between Mama and me and Agasha stood behind us. The meal started with clear soup and then the pancakes started to come in, piles and piles of them brought by a scurrying glowing-faced Masha in constant relays from the kitchen. A plateful would disappear as if by magic when it was passed round the six of us sitting at the table. First we had the thick pancakes made with yeast for the savoury part and then the thin ones made with batter for the sweet fillings. Because we didn't only have pancakes to eat. The whole table was spread with dishes containing all kinds of fillings. There were dishes of sour cream, of chopped herring in a sauce or caviar for the first course, and after we could have jam or sugar or lemon juice or any combination of the three which took our fancy.

"Mama, can I roll my pancake up like Granny does?"

"Yes, Koka, you may, but see that you eat it up, won't you." Koka spread his pancake liberally with strawberry jam, rolled it up with his fingers and picked it up and ate it like a squirrel. He was blissfully happy as the jam was squeezed out in all directions and he munched on. Agasha was hovering a little anxiously behind us, ready to come to the rescue when Koka or I got into too much of a mess.

"That's it. I can't eat any more. That's my last one." Papa leaned back in his chair in make-believe exhaustion.

"How many?" crowed Granny, scenting another victory.

"Six."

"This is my eighth." Triumphantly chewing away. A small cheer rose from the company and there was scattered, mock applause and cries of "Granny won, Granny won!" from Koka and me. Granny rubbed her success in.

"I told you your eyes were bigger than your belly."

"Oh! Emilie!" Aunt Dorothea had hardly said a word until now and had been eating very sparingly as if to express her disapproval of the Russian barbarians. "You really are overdoing it. You'll be poorly tomorrow for sure."

"Fiddlesticks, Dorothea. Tomorrow can look after itself."

"Kokochka, Moossia!" cried Mama, half despairing, half in laughter, "Just look at you, just look! You're covered in jam." She turned appealingly to Agasha just behind us.

"Come along Koka, come along, Moossia." She took us carefully but firmly by the wrists to stop the jam spreading any further. Koka made a last effort to rescue some of his jam and Mama let out another despairing cry.

"Koka, dear, don't. Don't lick your fingers like that."

Everybody in the room suddenly became very jam-conscious. People got up out of their chairs, chairs were edged away, doors were opened to allow our messy little procession to find its way to the bathroom without doing any further damage. As Agasha washed our hands and faces, Koka, still undefeated:

"I want to go back. I'm still hungry."

"So you shall. When you're clean again. But I think you've had enough pancakes, haven't you?"

I was not so sure of myself.

"Aga-a-a-sha-a-a. I feel sick."

"I thought you might." Agasha was amused. Koka crowed,

"Look, Moossia's gone all green."

"You be back off to the dining room, Koka. Agasha and Moossia will come in a minute. Now just you sit still, my little one. I'm not at all surprised. You're not used to all that rich food. Here, now, have a few sips of cold water."

In a short while I felt a bit better and we made our way back towards the dining room, but everyone was in the drawing room by now so we followed them in there.

"Agasha, we'll look after the children. You go and have some lunch yourself." I still felt a bit wobbly and I didn't like the idea of being without Agasha so I clung to her skirt. She gently freed herself.

"I won't be long, my little heart." And she left the room.

The gaiety of the party had now subsided somewhat. Koka had edged near Aunt Dorothea and had both hands round Kroshka-Crumb's middle. He was squeezing the little dog thoughtfully. Suddenly Aunt Dorothea saw what he was up to and snatched the creature up to her bosom out of harm's way.

"Leave Kroshka in peace Koka," said Granny, "He's not a teddy bear."

"What does Koka want, Emilie? I don't understand what he's saying."

This led to a long conversation in Danish between Granny and Aunt Dorothea... Danish was the language they always spoke when they were together which was, perhaps, why Aunt Dorothea never did learn to speak much Russian. Or maybe it was just one of the reasons.

There was a sad story which Papa liked to tell, when she wasn't there, of course, and which I believe is quite true but the children were not supposed to know. It's a funny thing how grownups like to think that children are deaf sometimes, not all the time, to be sure, but just when it suits them. When she first started to live in Russia, the story goes, Aunt Dorothea decided to go into the market to get some milk. She hunted round for something to put the milk in and, on opening a cupboard in the house in which she lived, she found a row of suitable-looking pots, each with a single handle. She chose one of them and went marching off to the market only to return soon after, flustered and very put out at the barrage of ribald remarks and the hilarious reaction she had had from the down to earth stall keepers. After this upsetting experience her interest in shopping came to an abrupt end, she kept herself to herself, looked upon all the Russians as a race of ill-mannered oafs and never bothered to learn more than a smattering of their language.

"I do feel sleepy, Mama," Koka yawned.

"Will you call Agasha, Papa-a-a-a-achka." Mama was almost nodding off, too.

"No, Lilya, it's not necessary. Let them have their lunch in peace. I'll put him on the bed in Granny's room. He can have a little nap in there. Up you come, old chap."

Papa lifted Koka up in his arms and carried him out of the room. There was a general atmosphere of sleepiness. Mama idly turned the pages of a magazine on a table by her chair. Aunt Dorothea crooned softly in Danish to Kroshka-Crumb. Granny stretched her arms above her head and said,

"Moossinka, come and sit over here by me. Then we can both have a little rest." She edged along the settee to make room for me. I sat well back in the settee to avoid leaning against the hardness of her corsets and settled myself against her comfortable bosom. With her arm encircling me I soon closed my eyes and went to sleep.

Chapter 5

April 1916

Quite suddenly St. Petersburg broke into its raucous spring song. The padded white quietness of winter gave way in a few days to a whole Babel of living sounds. The ice of the Neva split apart with gunshot sounds; steamers began to move along the river, hooting like great joyful birds. Horses clattered along the streets and the carts behind some of them rattled like side-drums over the cobblestones.

Although many of the walkers on the promenade still kept to their galoshes because of the slush and the puddles left by the melting snow, they began to leave off their dull winter clothes, and blossomed into brighter spring colours. Everybody moved about more quickly, more lightly, more optimistically.

"When are the rooks coming, Agasha?"

"Quite soon, you'll see."

"Where are they now?"

"Now they're in the country. First they're in the country. Then they come to the town."

The new mood could be felt in our apartment just as strongly as on the streets. One Sunday morning, just as Koka and I had begun to dip our corners of bread and butter into our soft-boiled eggs, Mama appeared early in the nursery, clear-eyed and sparkling, and dressed to go out. Her whole appearance, from the little pointed buttoned shoes, the long grey silk skirt, the frilly white blouse high about the neck, to the profuse black hair piled high and held in place with tortoiseshell combs – all this said to us that something special was afoot. The broad-brimmed hat gaily trimmed with flowers which Mama held in her hands make us quite sure.

"Good morning, Agasha."

"Good morning, Barinya."

The warmth in their voices at their daily greeting made us realise how glad Mama and Agasha were to see each other. Then there was a pat on his fair tousled head as Mama bent over Koka.

"Good morning, Koka, are you eating all your breakfast up?" Koka's mouth was much too full to allow him to answer so he turned his eggy face up to be kissed on the cheek. "That's a good boy. Good morning, my great big daughter." And a pat and a kiss for me. For a moment the room was full of smiling suspense, then,

"It's such a lovely day, Agasha. The old Barinya and I think we'll take the children to the Verba Fair."

Koka jumped up on his stool, tottered, and was caught just in time by Agasha.

"To the Verba? Did you hear, Moossia, we're going to the Verba?"

"Is Agasha coming, Mama?"

"Of course she is, Moossia. How could we go without Agasha?" Giving a warm smile to Agasha.

"I think you'd better take Moossinka on the tram again, Agasha. You know how sick she was in the cab last time. Koka and I and the old Barinya will meet you at the fair."

"Very well, Barinya. But suppose we miss you? With all those crowds of people…"

"Just stay at the first stall you come to when you get off the tram."

"Yes, Barinya, we'll wait there till you come."

Mama floated to the door. Then, as an afterthought,

"Agasha, do see that the children eat a lot of butter, won't you? They say that it contains iodine and that's very important."

"Yes, yes, Barinya, of course, I always give them plenty."

"Let the children have an early lunch and come and see me. I shall be back from church by then. I will give you enough money for the tram fares and something extra just in case we should happen to miss each other at the fair."

"We won't miss you, Barinya. We'll be sure to wait until you come."

"That's right. If you have Moossia dressed I'll see to Koka myself. Be good, children, and eat up all your breakfast." Mama's dainty figure whisked out of the room. I had a horrid thought.

"Do you know, Agasha, I think that one day Mama will break in two pieces."

"What do you mean? What nonsense you talk, my little snow-white."

"Well, she's so thin in the middle. She's just like a wasp."

"A wasp, indeed? Let me tell you that your Mama has a very beautiful figure. Not like your poor Agasha!"

I put my arms round her and snuggled close.

"But you aren't Mama, Agasha. It wouldn't be nice at all if you were like a wasp."

Although very proud of myself in my blue spring coat with its matching bonnet as I walked hand in hand with woolly jacketed and kerchiefed Agasha, down the avenue to the tram stop in the main street, my pride was mixed with some qualms. It was always an ordeal for me to travel on most kinds of transport, because of travel sickness. This was why Agasha was given the task of taking me to the fair on the tram. For some reason trams upset me less than cabs or buses. Trains, on the other hand, hardly bothered me at all.

"I can hear the tram bell. Here it comes, here it comes. Quick, Agasha, quick."

"There's plenty of time, Moossinka. No need to hurry. Up you go. Hold on tight."

"Can I sit on a seat of my own, Agasha?"

"Let's see if we can find two together. We're lucky. Here we are."

The tram jerked forward and we were thrown back in our seats. It rocked from side to side. It racketed over junctions in the lines. It stopped suddenly and threw us towards the seats in front and we had to save ourselves by throwing our hands out. It lurched forward and threw us back into our own seats again. Every little slope up or down made the tram seem like a boat cresting the waves of the sea. It screeched loudly every time it turned a corner. It hummed and clicked and clacked and rattled and the bell rang all the time and it had a disagreeable electrical kind of smell.

"Agasha, I feel sick."

"It isn't far now, my little dove. We'll soon be there."

"Can I come and sit on your lap?"

"Of course you can. That's right. Just lean against me and close your eyes."

Even that didn't help a great deal. CLICK CLACK STOP START. Would it never end? UP DOWN SCREECH LURCH. On and on and on.

CLICK RING CLACK STOP START RING RING. My head was spinning and my tummy was in turmoil and we only just got there in time. Agasha stayed quite calm and lifted me down mercifully to dry land. Once I felt the firm ground underneath my feet I began to recover from the whirling nightmare.

"Take a deep breath! Then you'll feel better. Now another one. That's right. Now again."

Regardless of the curious and amused glances of passers-by on their way to the fair I went through the tried and tested drill with Agasha watchful over me, breathing in and out as deeply as I could, my nostrils sucked in by the effort.

"Now take my hand. It isn't far. All this jolting and twisting and turning upsets your tummy. Of course it does. No wonder. I'm not at all surprised. Now I wonder if your Mama and Koka and the old Barinya have got there before us…" And so on, and so on… Agasha's endless flow of comforting chatter took my mind off feeling sick as it was meant to and, by the time we reached the outskirts of the fair I'd forgotten all about it.

"Here's the first stall. We seem to have got here first."

It was quite hard work to stop ourselves being swept into the fair by the tide of people coming from all directions but we managed to find a little sheltered spot where we could be safe from the flood for a few minutes. Everyone seemed happy and excited. Some were bareheaded, some wore flat caps, some had coloured kerchiefs like Agasha's. There were bonnets like mine and hats covered with flowers and shawls and uniform hats of all descriptions. Lots of children like Koka and me had been brought by their parents and nurses and governesses and were holding on to their grownups' hands very tightly while mischievous ragged urchins burrowed through the crowd in complete abandon laughing and shouting to each other, here, there and everywhere. The confusion was even greater inside the fair itself. Shouts and bells and peals of wild laughter and the sounds of many different kinds of music were all mixed up together and a gentle breeze brought a mixture of smells of sweets and tobacco and alcohol and fishy things and perfume and smells you just couldn't describe to puzzle your nose.

"There you are! Where have you been? We've been looking for you all over the place!" We could hear Koka's voice close by although we couldn't see him. He had caught a glimpse of us though the crowd and was parroting things he'd heard Agasha say at some other time. Then, there they were!

There were Koka and Mama and Granny, small and plump but very active and with great authority, who at once became the leader of the expedition.

"No harm done, Koka," she said, furling her long sunshade into a walking stick so that she could take my other hand. Agasha was anxious.

"We did what you said, Barinya. We didn't move once we got here."

"It's quite all right, Agasha. That was just Koka making jokes. We've only just got here ourselves."

When we got into the fair the crowd was very thick in places and the grownups surrounded us so that we wouldn't be swept off our feet. Then all we could see were people's legs and billowing skirts and top boots and sometimes bare feet and every now and then a mischievous face would pop out through the crowd at our level, take a close look at us and promptly disappear again. When the crowds did thin out here and there we could see women, some remarkably fat and some very scrawny, and pale bearded men and foreign looking people of different kinds behind the stalls selling all kinds of things to eat, all kinds of loaves and even live, clucking hens and piles of eggs and biscuits and baskets full of red and yellow roses and brightly painted wooden eggs of all sizes, one inside the other, and piles of coloured shawls and carved wooden boxes lacquered over, and wooden toys, and a stall full of painted round wooden spoons.

"Just look at these, Koka, Moossia." Agasha, who was enjoying the fair just as much as were, managed to make a way for us to a stall full of little bottles just big enough to hold in your hand. They were full of water and each one had a little devil inside it. When the stall keeper took one of the bottles in his hand the little devil in it swam up to the top and then down to the bottom again.

"Granny, can I have a little devil in a bottle, please?"

"Of course you can. Would you like one, too, Koka? Then we'll have two little devils, please."

Granny pulled open the cords of the little velvet bag which hung round her left wrist and got the money out to buy the two little devils from the rosy-faced stall keeper.

"Thank you, Granny." She placed the little bottles ceremoniously into our outstretched hands.

"So that's one for you, Moossia, and one for you, Koka." Then, to our disappointment she had second thoughts and took them back from us again. "Perhaps I'd better keep them for you until we get home. You could easily drop them in this crowd and you might never find them again." In a trice the two little devils disappeared into Granny's bag. This made me very unhappy.

"Granny, could I just try mine, please? Just once... now?"

"I don't see why not. Here you are then."

But I didn't have the magic touch of the stall keeper and, although I jerked the bottle up and down and shook it from side to side my little devil just sulked and stayed at the bottom of the bottle. I was almost in tears with frustration.

"It's no good. He won't swim for me."

"Let me show you, little lady." The rosy-cheeked stall keeper had been watching me with a broad smile on his face. He took my bottle into his own hand.

"Now, when you press the cork with your thumb... like this... the little devil gets angry and he swims up the top to bite your thumb... Then, when you take your thumb away again he gives up and dives down to the bottom."

"Now you know, Moossia." Granny pressed another small coin into the man's hand and he bowed low to her in gratitude.

Back we went into the thick of the crowd again. On all sides came the cries, loud and piercing, gruff and hoarse, some lilting like the snatch of a song, some sharp and quick like the bark of a dog, some with the accent of St. Petersburg, some with peasant voices from out in the country, some Gipsy voices from nowhere in particular but a sound all of their own and some with accents so strange that they sounded like foreign languages.

"Look, Mama, that boy has some sooshki on a string round his neck. Can we have some, too? Look, there's a stall."

"What do you think, Granny, Agasha?"

"I don't think they look very fresh on that stall, Barinya. They look to me as if they had been there since this morning. There will be lots of others, Moossia," quickly, as she saw my face fall, "Agasha will find you some."

"Pooh, what a smell." Koka held his nose as we passed a stall with barrels on it and around it.

"It's only pickled herrings in the barrels over there. The sun makes them smell a bit, that's all."

"Mamochka," said Mama to Granny, "Perhaps we should go home soon. These crowds are very tiring."

"We'll go home soon, Lilichka. Look, Agasha, there are some more sooshki over there. They look very nice. Here is some money. Get the children two rings."

I tore my hand away from Granny's and hung on to Agasha while she carefully picked out two necklaces of round biscuits.

"Can I wear them round my neck, Agasha?"

"Certainly not. Whatever next! I'll put them in my bag." And she pulled a small net bag from the pocket of her skirt, much to our annoyance.

"There's a tumbler-man, Granny!" shouted Koka, pulling Granny over to a stall full of wooden men and spoons.

"But Koka, you've already got one at home", said Agasha.

"Listen! I can hear someone playing a barrel organ!" I said to Agasha.

"Oh, Granny, do look over there!" Koka was pointing to a huge bunch of balloons some way off, floating above the heads of the crowd. "Can we have some balloons, please, Granny?"

"There, look, Agasha, one has got loose; it's floating right up into the sky!"

"Mamochka, I don't really like the children to have balloons. They burst so easily and make such a noise."

"But we've come to the fair, Lilya! Who ever heard of a fair without balloons?"

Delighted, we threaded our way through the crowd, following Agasha, who made a way for us. The man with the balloons, which floated high above him, straining at their strings as if they were trying to get away, was very small with a dark face, slanting eyes and a long pigtail down his back. He gave us a broad smile and spoke rapidly in a language we couldn't follow.

"He's a Chinaman", whispered Agasha.

"Which one do you want, Moossinka?"

"That white one with a cockerel, please. Look, Granny, there's another little balloon inside it!"

"Give that one to the little girl. And what about you, Koka?"

"The blue one with the bird, please."

"And give that one to the little boy", pressing some money into the Chinaman's hand. "Hold it tight, Koka, or it will float off up into the sky like the other one."

It wasn't very easy to get through the crowd with our balloons. We had to hold the strings high up over our heads so that the balloons were above the crowd and out of harm's way. Agasha put out her arm to protect Koka, and he walked like a chick under the wing of a mother hen.

The excitements of the balloons, the little devils and the sooshki, the noise and the fun and the buffeting of the crowd began to make us tired, but Koka and I were determined to stay at the fair as long as we possibly could.

"Can I eat one of my sooshki, Agasha? I'm hungry."

"No, Agasha, no. certainly not. Eating in the street! I never heard of such a thing." Granny had overheard me; she brought her sunshade down with a sharp tap onto the ground. We knew better than to argue with Granny.

"Listen, Agasha, there it is again, the music."

"Yes, my dove. It's the barrel-organ man."

"Will there be a monkey?"

"Perhaps."

"Can we go and see him, Agasha?"

"We must ask your Mama first. Where did they go? Ah, there they are, over by the lace stall. Let's go and find out."

"All right. Just take Moossia. Koka can stay with us. There's sure to be a big crowd."

"If Moossia goes I want to go as well." Koka was on the verge of tears. "I want to go as well. I want to…"

"I think somebody is getting tired", murmured Mama to Granny.

"Never mind, Lilichka." Granny took our side again, as she so often did. "Let Agasha take them both. She can manage, and they won't be long."

"Two children are a lot to handle in this crowd."

"Don't worry, Barinya. I'll carry Koka if I have to." Agasha took us by the hand and headed for the music.

"Agasha!" called Granny, "We shall wait for you over there." And she pointed to an empty bench not far away.

"Come on, Agasha." I was impatient. "He might go away!" We made our way slowly through the crowd and the stalls and barrows and piles of sacks, towards the space where the music came from.

The organ was a squarish sort of box standing on a wooden leg, and had a leather belt over the organ-grinder's shoulder. He had masses of black curly hair and big turned-up moustaches and gold earrings. A ragged dark curly-headed boy about my size was moving through the bystanders with a greasy flat cap, shaking it up and down to encourage people to add to the little hoard of copecks inside it.

Agasha's hands tightened on ours, as if someone might run off with us.

"He's a gipsy."

The whining, grinding tune of the organ sent shivers down my spine.

"Look, Moossia, look, Koka, can you see the monkey on top of the organ?"

"He's got a red hat with a tassel!"

"Doesn't he look nice, Agasha?"

"His little jacket is nice, but I think his eyes are very sad."

"Perhaps the long chain is hurting him."

"He is probably feeling cold. Where he comes from the sun shines all the time."

"How did he get here?"

"The gipsy brought him to work for him."

"Look, he's dancing now!"

"Agasha, here comes the boy with the hat."

"He wants us to give him some copecks to buy food for them all."

"Give me a copeck, Agasha. Let me put it in his cap."

"Certainly not, Moossia. Look how dirty it is. I'll do it." Agasha gave some money to the boy, who looked very tired and didn't even smile.

"Come along then."

"Just a bit longer, Agasha."

"Your Mama will be thinking we're lost. Come along now."

"I'm tired, Agasha", decided Koka.

"Agasha will carry you back." She picked Koka up as if he weighed nothing at all, and, taking my hand, led us off to look for Mama and Granny, the balloons still waving above our heads.

Chapter 6

April 1916

The sun was still only the colour of pale lemonade, but now it was strong enough to have melted all the snow; and bold enough to set fire to all the touch-paper buds on the trees lining the promenade down the middle of the avenue. It seemed that the Russian spring would explode all around us at any moment.

From my post at the drawing room window I could look down on the intricate lace patterns thrown by the watery sun through the branches of the trees onto the cobbles and paving stones.

A familiar movement caught my eye through the branches. Pressing my nose to the window I could make out a tall dark man walking jauntily down the middle of the promenade. His hat was slightly to one side, and his handsome moustache fluttered slightly in the breeze. He held something white and frothy and fragile in his left hand, and in his right was swinging a light walking stick. Every few steps the stick would pause in the air, and move horizontally to and fro. I could be sure that he was conducting the band which was playing in his head.

I watched him until he crossed from the promenade over the cobbles towards the door of our apartment building. When I was quite sure that it really was Papa I turned to tell Mama he was on his way. But she was sitting on the settee with her feet up on a footstool, deeply immersed in the novel she was reading.

So I changed my mind about telling her, walked slowly out of the room so as not to disturb her, and then fairly scampered down the hallway to open the door for him, just as he was getting his key out. We studied each other for a moment or two conspiratorially, and then he formally handed me his hat, then the gloves he held in his hand, and then his walking stick; and then he walked down the hall towards the drawing room, with me following. Somehow a secret message seemed to have run like electricity round the apartment, for by the time Papa and I had reached the drawing room door, Koka and Agasha and Masha had crept silently from their places, and had gathered round expectantly.

Papa opened the door very quietly and walked softly over to Mama, who heard nothing, being still engrossed in her reading. Then he took the branch of cherry blossom into both hands as he stood just behind and slightly to one side of her, and lowered it so that it fell gently on her lap, across the book she was reading.

Mama came to with a slight start, picked up the branch of cherry blossom into both hands and, smiling, swung her feet down from the footstool on to the ground. She abandoned her languid reading posture and sat up straight, with the cherry blossom raised slightly in her hands, and her eyes gazing down on it, waiting for the next stage of the ceremony.

Papa had been bending over her, waiting for this reaction. Now he stood up straight and held his hands up almost as if bestowing a blessing, and spoke the well-known words.

"I have come to you with a greeting
To tell you that the sun has risen
And that Spring is here!"

"Thank you, Karloosha", said Mama with infinite tenderness.

"Yes, thank God. It's Spring again." He brushed back his dark wavy hair, so very like mine, smoothed his handsome moustache with a forefinger, and bent down to kiss Mama.

There was a sigh from the doorway as Agasha and Masha went back to their domestic tasks and Koka and I ran over to Papa with cries of inexplicable delight. Koka got to him first and Papa picked him up under the shoulders, lifted him high into the air and twirled across the room with him. Round and round and round.

"All the birds in the air flying high, high, high."

"Karloosha! Calm down, calm down! You're making my head spin." Mama was still smiling at us but she raised her hands to her head.

"Sh! Sh-h-h--!" A finger to his lips. "We shall play very quietly." The three of us sat down on the rug together. Papa took one of my hands, palm up, and drew circles on it with his long forefinger.

"The Magpie cooked some porridge and she invited some guests to share it. She gave some to this one, some to this one, some to this one." He tickled each of my fingers in turn as Koka and I suppressed our giggles. But when he reached my little finger,

"But this one had been very lazy and so it got nothing at all." There was always a slight pause here.

"And all the birds flew away."

All our arms went high above our heads with fingers fluttering as we repeated,

"And all the birds flew away."

Chapter 7

April 1916

"It's Palm Sunday tomorrow," I heard Mama say one evening when she came into the nursery to kiss us goodnight.

"Oh, Agasha!" wailed Koka in dismay, "We don't have any palms. Can you get us some for tomorrow, please?"

"And some for me, too, Agasha."

"All right, all right; it's late but I think I know where I can find some."

"You won't forget, will you, Agasha?"

"I promise they will be on your chairs waiting for you when you wake up in the morning."

"Agasha," Koka edged close to her and whispered in her ear but I heard distinctly what he said, "will you wake me up first, please?"

"I can hear what you're whispering, Koka. That sort of thing isn't allowed, is it Agasha?"

"I should say not indeed. I wouldn't dream of waking you up in any case. It's very bad for you to wake up too early. It's when you're asleep that you grow. You should be asleep now, both of you. Look how late it is. Off you go, my little ones." We said our prayers; she tucked us in; kissed us and made the sign of the cross over us and then sat down at the table to get on with her sewing. For a time all was quiet.

"Agasha?"

"Why aren't you asleep, Kokochka?"

"In a minute I will be... Agasha... How do you know we grow at night?"

"What a question! I just do know, that's all. Everything grows at night. In the evening there aren't any mushrooms in the fields. Next morning you can find them everywhere. They grow in the night. It's quite simple. Now be a good boy and go to sleep."

He thought this over… "Oh… I see… Goodnight, Agasha."

"Goodnight, my precious."

Koka turned over towards the wall and there were a few moments more of silence. Then he turned back again quickly,

"Agasha?"

"What is it now?"

"You do know ever such a lot of things."

"Goodnight, my cherub. Look! Moossia is already asleep."

In spite of Koka's attempt to get Agasha to help him steal a march on me I was the one who woke up first next morning. I looked at my bedside chair and, sure enough, there was the branch of pussy-willow palm just as Agasha had promised. I picked it up and crept softly on tiptoes over to Koka's bed. Then I vigorously beat the huddled figure under his bedclothes with the palm branch, crying out victoriously,

"Beat him, Palm! Beat him, Palm!

I'm the first today."

Little squeaks and cries came from under the bedclothes.

"Careful, Moossia, not too hard! He's still asleep," said Agasha as she came into the room. When he heard her voice Koka assumed he was safe from a further beating and popped his head above the blankets.

"Don't Moossia, don't. You're hurting me!"

"No I didn't. I was only smacking the blanket. Cry-baby. Koka oversle-e-ept. Koka oversle-e-ept."

"What if I did. I don't care. It's a silly game anyway." He disappeared under the bedclothes again.

"Now you two, don't squabble. Time to get up. Moossinka, you haven't got a stitch on. You'll catch your death of cold."

"Agasha, when are we going to paint the eggs?" I asked as I started to put my clothes on. Koka flung back the bedclothes and shot right out of bed onto the floor.

"The eggs? Are we painting the eggs? I want to get up."

"Not today nor tomorrow nor the next day, nor the next day, but the day after that."

"Not today! Then I'm not going to get up." He got back into his bed and flung the blankets over himself and stuck his bottom in the air like an ostrich.

"Don't be naughty, Koka. Up you get. Look, here's Masha with your breakfast."

"Good morning, Agasha."

"Good morning, Masha."

"Good morning, children."

"Good morning, Masha. Good morning, Masha."

"What have you brought us for breakfast, Masha?" I asked.

"There's soft-boiled eggs and warm milk and booblichki rolls", she answered, holding the tray low so that I could see for myself.

"Hurrah, booblichki. I'm up. I've got up." In a twinkling Koka was out of bed and scrambling on to his high stool.

"Careful, Koka, careful!" cried Agasha who had taken the tray from Masha and now swung it deftly out of danger and up on to the table.

"Hm-m-m, the booblichki are nice and warm," approved Koka holding one of the rolls between his palms like a proper little connoisseur. "Aga-a-a-sha, would you cut it in the middle, please, and put the butter on?"

"Oh, it's milk again, Agasha. Couldn't I have some tea?"

"The samovar isn't on yet. In the morning we drink milk. Come along now, eat up your egg."

"Couldn't you get me some tea from the kitchen?"

"No, your Papa and Mama aren't up yet so tea won't be made until later. Drink up your milk like a good girl."

After breakfast Koka pressed his nose to the window. "Oh dear, it's raining again." I joined in with the complaint.

"What a pity! Now we can't go for a walk. Why can't the sun shine?" But Agasha believed in looking on the bright side of things and had little patience with our grumblings.

"The rain may not always be nice for us. But if the rain didn't fall then the corn wouldn't grow and then we'd have no bread, little ones."

"What shall we play, Moossia?"

"Let's play Mothers and Fathers!"

"No, not Mothers and Fathers. All I have to do is sit still and read a newspaper. I'd rather be a doctor."

"But I don't need a doctor. My children aren't ill."

"Then I'll be the yard-keeper, Ivan."

"Whatever for?"

"Well, at least I can sweep the yard and bring the logs in and talk to everybody. 'Good morning, Barin, good morning, Barinya.'" He bowed very deeply to his right and then his left.

"I think that's stupid."

"Why is it stupid?"

"Because Ivan lives somewhere in the yard. He doesn't live up here where we live. So you can't possibly be him." Fortunately Agasha intervened.

"What is all the argument about? Look, the rain has stopped. Let's go for a walk."

Next day the rain had quite disappeared and the sun was shining again. Mama decided that she would go into town and take us all with her. But Koka wasn't pleased.

"I don't want to go into town. I want to go to the park or down to the river."

"Well, we're all going. Come along, Kokochka. Just imagine! You'll see the trams and the cabs and all the horses and the street sweepers and perhaps even a fire engine or a chimney sweep."

"Agasha, are the children ready?"

"There, your Mama is calling. Come on. Let me put your coat on." Agasha tried to get Koka's arms into his coat but he awkwardly made his arms all stiff and she had some difficulty. Then Mama came in.

"Egor has called a cab so don't be too long, my dears." Now it was my turn to be difficult.

"Oh, no, Mama, not a cab!"

"You'll be all right, Moossia. It isn't all that far. Whatever's the matter with Koka?"

"He doesn't want to come with us, Mama."

"Nonsense, give me your hand, Koka." An unwilling Koka was led, still mutely protesting, down to the waiting cab.

When we got to the town, somewhere along the Nevsky Prospekt, we left the cab and continued on foot. Mama marched in front with the rest of us hurrying to keep up with her. Then she would stop and chat with all sorts of people she knew or look endlessly into shop windows. Koka and I quickly grew tired of this and invented a game for ourselves to while away the time. We pretended that the separate shadows thrown by the sun blinds were our houses.

"This is my house", claimed Koka, jumping into one shadow.

"And this one is mine." Then Koka would pass me and go on to the next one. We wandered some distance quite absorbed in what we were doing till Agasha came running down the street calling our names and rounded us up.

"Just a minute, children. Your Mama wants to go into this dress shop."

"Can we go in, too?"

"No, Moossinka. You had better stay with Agasha. There are lots of people in that shop. The air won't be good for children." Koka had had enough already.

"Oh, Agasha, let's go home. I'm tired."

"Presently. Presently. We must wait for your Mama."

"They didn't have the colour I wanted." Mama came out on to the pavement. "They are going to send me some to choose from when the new stock comes in. Come along, children, let's go home."

"I'm ever so tired, Mama." She stooped over Koka anxiously. "Yes, you do look pale Kokochka. What a pity we let the cab go, Agasha." This was no problem to Agasha. She went down to the edge of the pavement and waved vigorously to the first empty cab which came along. No cab driver would have dared to pass her by.

"Tr-r-r-r-r" went the cabman, pulling tightly on his reins to stop the horse. He climbed down obligingly off his seat and unbuttoned the leather apron covering the seat behind. We climbed in and he hoisted himself back up on to his perch.

"Where to, Barinya?"

"To Fourteenth Avenue on St. Basil's Island. We'll tell you where to stop." The cabman touched his cap and flicked the horse lightly with his whip. It broke into a sharp trot.

"Try not to jolt us so much", Mama called to the cabman with an anxious look in my direction. But her request didn't make a lot of difference. Both the cabman and his horse seemed determined to get us home as quickly as they could and, since the hood of the cab was folded back to take advantage of the welcome sunshine, the breeze was quite considerable and Mama had to hold onto her broad-brimmed hat with both hands to prevent it blowing off. As we reached the apartment building quite dishevelled by our ride, Mama gave her purse to Agasha.

"Agasha, you pay the cabman."

"I'll stay with Agasha."

"All right, Moossinka. Koka, you can come along with me."

Agasha never paid people what they asked for in the first place. She bargained with everybody over everything, whether she was buying fruit from a market stall or, as on this occasion, settling with the cabman.

"How much do you want?"

"Sixty copecks."

"That's far too much. I'll give you forty."

"The cost of hay alone…" He did his best but Agasha had got his measure. "Barinya gave me forty copecks."

"Forty five", he wheedled, without result.

"Here's forty copecks."

"O-o-o-oh. All right." The cabman grunted and there was a respectful glint in his eyes as the money changed hands.

Chapter 8

Maundy Thursday 1916

"Is it Thursday yet?" shouted Koka the very instant he woke up.

"Yes, Kokochka, it is. It's Maundy Thursday."

"Hurrah, then it's egg painting day, isn't it? We're going to paint the eggs today, aren't we?"

"That's right. But don't shout so loud. You'll wake Moossia."

"I'm not asleep, Agasha."

"Oh, well, in that case, you'd better get up. Breakfast will be here soon."

"Can we paint the eggs after breakfast?"

"No, Kokochka. We're going to do the painting after lunch."

"But that's ages and ages. Why can't we paint them after breakfast?"

"Because your Mama and Papa are coming to paint them with you."

"Oh… what are we going to have for lunch?"

"Goodness me, you haven't had breakfast yet."

"I was only asking."

"I'm not sure. I think it's chicken."

"Chicken, chicken! We always have chicken."

"Now stop your grumbling, Koka. It's a sin to grumble about your food."

"I know, but just because Moossia gets tummy ache, we always have to have chicken."

"That's enough. No more complaints. Pick up your hobby horse."

It did seem ages and ages to lunchtime, so impatient were we for the once a year delights of egg painting. At long last it came and Koka was pleased because we didn't have chicken but bitki, one of his favourites, and I was pleased because this was followed by kissel which was one of mine. Then we were taken off into the bathroom to be sponged and tidied up and, just as Agasha had put on our aprons in readiness for the serious work of the afternoon, in came Mama with her hands full of transfers and little pieces of cloth, followed by Papa who was carrying the small box which held the all important little bottles of lacquer and the brushes to paint the eggs with. It was all a well-established ritual, even for Koka and me.

"Agasha! Will you spread the oilcloth out over the tablecloth? We don't want to get paint stains on it, do we? And put the napkin rings where the children can reach them, so that they have somewhere to stand the hot eggs when Masha brings them in. Ah, here she is!" Masha set the bowl of cooked eggs in the middle of the table. Papa fished them out gingerly and set them out in the serviette rings so that we could start our painting session.

"I'm going to paint a red one first," I announced to anyone who might be interested.

"Koka! Don't dip your brush so far into the bottle. It's dripping all over the place."

"Don't worry, Lilya. It will all wipe up off the oilcloth."

"Mama, will you paint us one of your nice pretty eggs?"

"All right, Moossinka. You mean the kind with the X and B on one side and the B and the X on the other?"

"Who can tell me what the X and the B mean?" asked Papa.

"I can! I can!"

"Tell me, Moossinka."

"Christos Voskrese, Christ is Risen."

"And the B and the X?"

"Voistinou Voskrese. Christ is truly Risen", chirped Koka before I could open my mouth again.

"What clever children you are!"

Agasha's pleasure at these words of praise for us glowed on her broad face.

"Agasha, you must paint an egg, too", proposed Mama.

"Oh, no, Barinya, no." She looked at her work-worn hands; "I'm much too clumsy. I'll just keep an eye on the children and see that they don't put the brushes in their mouths."

There was a heavy silence as we all concentrated on the important work in hand, broken only slightly by some heavy breathing as Koka painstakingly splashed lacquer on the eggs, not forgetting to bestow a liberal amount on himself. Red eggs, green eggs, yellow eggs, mottled eggs, and some with very strange designs indeed began to refill the large bowl in the middle of the table.

"Agasha, will you ask Masha to bring in about ten raw eggs," asked Mama.

"I'll go and get them myself, Barinya." She was back again in a few moments carrying a little basket. "They came in from the country only this morning, Barinya."

"Now, children, watch carefully. One day you will be able to do it for yourselves."

"Use this transfer of the little rabbit first, Mama," suggested Koka as he picked one out. "This one is for me, isn't it?"

"And this one with the hen and chicks is for me, isn't it, Mama?" I added.

"All right, Moossinka, one at a time, one at a time. Now, watch. You wrap the transfer round the egg like this. Now pass me one of those little pieces of cloth. That's right, Koka. That piece will do very nicely. Now you wrap the cloth right round the egg and the transfer so that you have a little tuft at the top. Then you have something to hold on to when the egg is cooked and you want to take it out of the hot water. Now, Agasha!" Agasha was standing by with a short piece of string at the ready. "Will you tie the string round the little tuft, please? Tightly! Quite tightly! That's right. That's fine. Now that's one done."

"No, Koka, don't poke it like that." Agasha spoke up sharply. "You'll break it!" And she just managed to catch his inquiring finger in time.

With big eyes we watched the many-coloured eggs fill up the bowl in the middle of the table, until most of them were done. Then we suddenly realised that one of us had painted some of the raw eggs, and they had got muddled up with the boiled ones. Since the boiled eggs were now cold, we couldn't tell which was which.

"Oh, dear, Agasha, what shall we do?" I wailed.

"It's all right, Moossinka, don't worry. It's quite easy to tell the difference. The raw ones won't spin, but the hard-boiled ones will spin like spinning-tops – look!" Then she took the eggs one by one and tried to spin them on the oilcloth. Just as she said, some of the eggs did spin and some wobbled and fell over.

"That's a raw one. There's another raw one. Ah! That's a hard-boiled one; you can paint that one."

"Agasha, that was really very clever of you," said Papa. Koka and I looked at each other and smiled. We were very proud of Papa's praise of our Agasha.

"But why do they do that, Agasha?" asked Koka, ever asking questions. "Why do eggs spin when they are cooked and fall over when they are raw?"

Agasha was taken aback for a moment. Then she admitted, "I really don't know, Koka. I've never thought about it. What does it matter? The main thing is we know how to tell one from the other."

"Well, that's the last one," said Mama. "Don't they look lovely?" Mama got up from the table and brushed down her skirt with her hand. "Tell Masha to put them in the pantry. The ones with the transfers can be boiled later."

"Oh, Mama, couldn't we do them now?"

"All right, children. Agasha, could you boil them yourself, then? Ten minutes should be enough, and you'll have to put some vinegar in the water. Bring them back here and we'll open them together. We'll stay with the children."

Koka climbed on Mama's lap and I on Papa's, and we played one of our favourite games while we waited for the eggs. "Granny has sent you a hundred roubles, and you can spend them as you like, but you mustn't buy anything black or white, and you mustn't say yes or no!" The ten minutes passed in fits of helpless giggles as we tried to trip each other up. The questions got sillier and sillier.

Then Agasha came back with the newly boiled eggs. Koka and I tumbled to the floor, and we all gathered round the table as Mama gingerly unwrapped the little hot parcels.

"Here's my hen and chicks!"

"And here's my rabbit!"

"Don't they look pretty?"

"I think they'll look lovely on the table with the tall Easter cake and the Kolich and the Pasha."

Papa was very enthusiastic, and we clapped our hands in delight. Then Mama and he patted us on the head and made to leave the room, leaving Agasha to clear away all the mess. Agasha hastened towards them before they had quite gone through the door.

"Oh, Barinya, could I take Moossinka with me to the Easter midnight service, please? I'll put her to bed early, and wake her up in time to go to church. She could even have a little nap there if she gets tired."

"What do you think, Papasha?"

"I don't see why not. Unless you want to take her yourself."

"No, I don't think so. It's far too late for me. You know how I dislike crowds. It's really quite beyond my strength. All those people, clouds of incense and absolutely no air at all. Remember I nearly fainted last year."

"All right, Lilichka, we'll stay at home, then. You may take Moossinka if you would like to, Agasha."

That evening, after saying our prayers, kneeling at the side of our beds with hands pressed together,

"Dear Jesus, bless us and send our guardian angel to watch over us." We went happily to bed.

There were two pictures on the wall above our beds. One was in a heavy brown frame. It showed a child standing on the edge of a cliff trying to catch a butterfly, with his guardian angel with protective hands preventing the child from falling. The other picture, in a narrow gilt frame, was of a child who might have been a boy or a girl kneeling in prayer, and looking up at the multitude of stars in the sky; underneath there was a line of poetry:

"Pray, child; The Father of uncountable worlds is harkening to you."

This thought always comforted me.

Chapter 9

Easter Saturday 1916

"Wake up, little dove; it's time to go to church."

It must have been about ten o'clock on Saturday evening. Agasha had put me to bed very early as she had promised Papa, and was shaking me gently and whispering close to my ear. "Wake up, little dove!"

I struggled to sit up, shivering and still half asleep. For a moment or two I wondered what it was all about. Everything was done in whispers, quietly, so as not to wake Koka. Agasha lifted me out of my bed and put me on her lap. Even so, I felt very grown-up to be getting up in what seemed to me to be the middle of the night.

"There, put on your bodice. Let me button it up for you. Now your stockings. I'll pull them on, and you can do up the suspenders yourself, can't you?"

"Agasha, can we take the Pashka and the Easter cake and the Koloch to be blessed?"

"No, Moossinka, we aren't going to stay long enough for that. I tell you what. I'll get a red egg to take if you like, and we'll wrap it up in a handkerchief for you to carry yourself. What about that?"

Mama had suggested that we took a cab to the church, because Agasha wanted to go to the Cathedral of St. Nicholas, which was a fair walk away, across the river; but Agasha had gently but firmly refused the offer.

"To the Almighty's House we must walk." She was quite prepared to carry me in her strong arms whenever I got tired.

We both wrapped up warmly against the chilly night air. Agasha wore a kind of woolly cardigan with a kerchief round her head, and I had my winter coat on, with the ribbons of my bonnet tied under my chin.

The streets of St. Petersburg were quite unfamiliar to me at this time of night. The sky was clear but moonless, and pricked with a host of stars, just as it was in the picture above my bed. The avenue was dimly lit, and full of unaccustomed shadows and sounds. The trees I knew so well along the promenade were dark and strange and seemed to hang over us menacingly. I walked next to Agasha as if in a dream, a slightly frightening dream. I held her hand tightly. But she knew what I was feeling, and looked down at me and smiled her usual quiet smile, and I felt better.

The nearer we got to the Cathedral the more people were about. Many were going in our direction. Others were seeking out different churches in the city. People on foot and in carriages were streaming to church. Men and women carried baskets covered with a white cloth containing Easter Cake and Easter Eggs to be blessed by the priest. Children of all ages carried small objects tied in a handkerchief as I did. There was hardly any talking. Everyone was hurrying, like us, trying to get to the churches as early as possible because they were sure to be crowded to overflowing on that night of all nights.

"Is it very much further?"

"No, my little dove, we're almost there."

As we entered the church Agasha bought candles at the door, a red one for me and a white one for herself. We worked our way through the dense crowd of people towards the shrine in front of the altar. Agasha knelt and kissed it.

We went to her favourite ikon of the Mother of God and the little Jesus where we lit our candles. Agasha helped me to fit the candles into the holders and lifted me to kiss the ikon. She kissed it reverently herself. We crossed ourselves and threaded our way to find a place in the crowd right at the back of the church.

This took a little while as the church was already thronged with worshippers. They were of all ages from the very young to the very old and from all stations in life. All the men were bareheaded and all the women had their heads covered; some wore modest scarves on their heads, some women wore fashionable hats and coats. The atmosphere was subdued. Many people stood quite still. Others moved restlessly about trying to find places for themselves to stand through the night. Still more went quietly from ikon to ikon, saying short prayers, crossing themselves and lighting candles. Everyone was careful to keep a path towards the altar quite clear.

"Here's a bench along the wall, Moossia. Let's stop here, then you can rest if the night gets too long for you."

"I feel tired now, Agasha."

"Well, the service hasn't started yet. Sit down on the bench for a while." She lifted me up onto the bench.

Around us the church was dimly lit; the candles flickered in the moving air and the little lamps glowed red in the semi-darkness. The tall golden gates to the Sanctuary were still closed. There was only the sound of people moving gently about and talking in subdued whispers. Somewhere in the crowd a baby cried. A baby? I looked up at Agasha. She smiled down at me.

"Of course. God is glad to hear his voice and to know that he is here, too."

The choir started to sing. At once I was fully awake and got down off the bench. The choir chanted over and over,

"Lord have mercy, Christ have mercy. Lord have mercy."

The shrine was carried into the Sanctuary.

When the priest started to chant from the altar in his vibrant bass voice my arms were covered with goose pimples and shivers ran down my spine in sheer emotion. The smell of incense drifted through the entire congregation. There was only the chanting of the choir, the bass tones of the priest, the clouds of incense. The congregation stood quite still now and silent, listening. I felt drowsier and drowsier and leaned more and more heavily against Agasha. Distantly I felt her lifting me up again onto the bench and her gentle arms were about me pressing me to her firm and comforting body. As I floated away on a wave of music and incense into oblivion an old man's voice nearby was saying, like a benediction,

"Let the little one sleep with God. It's a long night."

There was a pause as I floated on and on.

"Lord have mercy. Christ have mercy. Lord have mercy."

I was fast asleep.

"Christos Voskrese. Christ is Risen." The priest's deep, joyous voice pulsated through the church.

"Voistinoo Voskrese. He is risen indeed."

The watchers burst into life. I woke with a start and slid down off the bench to the floor. It was midnight and I knew you were supposed to stand through the service which was just beginning. The church was alive with a sense of radiant joy. Agasha lifted me right up off the floor.

"Christos Voskrese", she said, happily, and kissed me three times on the cheeks.

"Voistinoo Voskrese," I replied and kissed her in return, three times. The greetings surged though the congregation. Faces alight with gladness turned to each other. Strangers turned to each other, for a moment strangers no longer.

"Christos Voskrese." And strangers replied smiling all over their faces,

"Voistinoo Voskrese."

People I had never seen before bent down to me and kissed me and greeted me.

This wave of joyful emotion was followed by a wave of light! The priest, with the first words of his message, lit the candle of the nearest person to him from the one in his own hand and the flame was multiplied from person to person until the whole church was ablaze with the light from the candles and the happy, smiling faces. Those spellbound moments held the glad tidings of the Resurrection. Then the choir's chanting came to an end and the first part of the service was over. Agasha whispered to me, "Moossinka, hold your candle up straight, my dear. You are dripping wax all over my skirt."

I was beginning to nod off again but managed to pull myself together somewhat and straightened the candle in my hand.

"What about my egg, Agasha? What about my egg?" Panic seized me.

"We'll put it on the table over there and the priest will bless it for us later. Come along. We'll go up to the priest for the Easter greeting."

"But my candle has gone out!"

"Never mind, my little sleepy one. It just got tired of burning, that's all. The wind will blow it out anyhow." We edged our way through the crowd towards the priest standing in front of the altar. He was holding the gold cross usually hanging round his neck on a chain towards us and smiling down like a bearded angel. His deep, soft voice was for us alone.

"Christos Voskrese." We kissed the cross and kissed his other hand and crossed ourselves;

"Voistinoo Voskrese." We made room for those behind us and slowly moved towards the church's main door into the cold, clear fresh air outside. It was like a splash of icy water on our faces.

"Agasha, I do feel ever so tired."

"Of course, you're tired, my little sun. Come along, let me carry you home."

She picked me up and cradled me in her arms and carried me all the way back home through the streets of St. Petersburg just as the sky was slowly beginning to be lightened by the rising moon. Although I was very sleepy I was keenly aware that Agasha and I shared a deep feeling of happiness, of content. Her unhurried but steady swinging step lulled me asleep in her affectionate embrace. As we came into the nursery I woke up and found that my candle had become a shapeless lump of softened wax in my little hot hand. Koka stirred in his bed and so I went over to him.

"Christos Voskrese, Koka. You've been asleep all the time."

He drowsily raised his head from his pillow and had just strength enough to exchange the three kisses,

"Voistinoo Voskrese."

Mama and Papa were there, too, to greet us,

"Christos Voskrese, Agasha." They kissed warmly on her cheeks.

All Easter Day the whole of the city, the whole of Russia, echoed to the precious words,

"Christos Voskrese, Voistinoo Voskrese."

Parents and children, friends and relations, husbands and wives, masters, mistresses and servants exchanged the three kisses. For a while all barriers were down.

Chapter 10

Easter Day 1916

We all went in to breakfast together that Easter Day and found the table already laid as it was to remain through the day. There was cold veal and smoked bacon and the tall Easter cake and the Pashka sweet cake and the multicoloured eggs we had painted three days before and lots of other things to eat and drink. The samovar was humming and tea had already been made.

"Sit down, sit down everybody," said Papa in his most hospitable mood and we all took our places. "Now," he continued, taking one of the painted eggs in his right hand and resting it poised on the table, "who is going to be the first to cock fight with me?"

"I am. I am," shouted Koka, kneeling up on his chair and stretching right across the table to grab another of the eggs.

"Careful, Koka, old chap, you nearly knocked the vodka over!" The two eggs faced each other like two young cockerels in a farmyard.

"Bang, bang, bang!" Koka had the light of battle in his eye. Then there was a crunch and his whole face changed and fell. "Oh, dear," he despaired, "my egg has cracked, Papa." Mama quickly came to the rescue.

"Never mind, Kokochka. Give that one to me. I'll eat that one. Try again with another one." Koka armed himself again for the fray. "But hold it this way." She turned her egg so that the sharp end was uppermost.

"Can I cockfight with you, Mama?" He guessed that victory would somehow be his this time. He grabbed another egg and held it as Mama had told him. "Come on, then," she urged, turning her egg to show the blunt end, knowing pretty well that her egg would be the one to be cracked. Koka was so agog that he didn't notice her manoeuvre.

"Bang, bang, bang, I've won, I've won!" he crowed, showing his uncracked egg round the table. Then he cracked it on the tabletop at once and began to eat it.

"Who would like some Pashka?" asked Mama, "The curds turned out very well this time. It should be lovely."

"May I have some this time, Mama?" I pleaded. But Agasha, ever standing by, intervened.

"I know you like it, Moossia, but her tummy isn't quite right just now, Barinya."

"Very well, Agasha. Perhaps she could have just a tiny piece to taste?"

"She'd better have some lemon tea to go with it, Barinya."

The tea was carefully poured and diluted from the little tap on the samovar. Papa was still in a very jolly mood at the end of the meal.

"Who would like a piece of Koolich?" Mama quailed at the prospect, "Oh, no, no, no, Papachka. I really couldn't manage any just now. What about you, Agasha? Would you like some?"

"Thank you, Barinya, perhaps just a small piece."

Agasha was given a piece of Koolich on a plate and ate it standing up at her usual station just behind Koka and me. Koka's eyes were fixed longingly on the Koolich but he sighed reluctantly, "I can-a-a-an't." I followed his example,

"I'm full right up to here," with my hand held above my head, absurdly. Mama didn't at all approve of my gesture. She was sharp and disapproving.

"Moossinka, that is no way to speak."

After breakfast Koka and I were carefully dressed in our sailor suits with the matching knee socks, all specially for Granny's benefit, and we all set off for the customary Easter visit. We didn't have very far to go at all because the pickle factory which Granny owned and managed was just behind and to one side of our apartment block. You had only to go down the stairs and out of the big main door and walk along the avenue for a few yards and there you were at the entrance gates of the factory grounds. Of course, on Easter day the factory wasn't working. The horses were in their stables and the unharnessed carts were standing about in the yards. We had to pass round the pond to get to Granny's house which was a large low building right at the back of the factory grounds.

We never saw the pond in the summer because we went away to Finland every year for the whole of the summer, but in winter, when it was frozen over, it became a regular meeting place for people of all ages. Agasha always used to muffle us up until we could hardly move to protect us against the cold and we both learned to skate on the pond wearing special "children's skates" with a turned-up edge so that we wouldn't hurt each other when we fell over. Before we learned to skate we were pushed about the pond, which was quite a big one, in a chair sledge. These were great fun for those who were too young or too old or too tired or too lazy to skate. Even Granny would unbend from time to time to be pushed round the pond by a strong, warmly wrapped up maid.

As we ran along the path, well ahead of Mama and Papa who were taking their time, and with Agasha keeping up with us "just in case", Granny was waiting at the window for us, waving and smiling and she bustled into the hall as Dusya, her maid, opened the front door to us.

"Christos Voskrese. Christos Voskrese." Three kisses exchanged and enthusiastic hugs all round.

"Voistinoo Voskrese. Voistinoo Voskrese."

"Here, Granny, see, I've brought you my green egg. I coloured it myself. It's for you, look, Granny, look."

"Thank you, Kokochka, thank you, my dear."

"And here's mine. It's a red one and Agasha and I took it to St. Nicholas's last night and it was blessed by the priest."

"Thank you, Moossinka, very much. If you take their coats off, Agasha, Dusya will hang them up." As we followed Granny into her drawing room I came face to face with myself. It was a framed enlargement of a photograph taken by Aunt Fanya in Finland the year before. I was sitting on a stone like a mermaid. By then Mama and Papa had caught up with us.

"Christos Voskrese, Lilichka." Granny kissed Mama. "Dorothea will be down soon. You know how she feels about our barbaric Russian customs." They both laughed good-naturedly.

"Christos Voskrese, Karloosha"'

"Voistinoo Voskrese, Mamochka. Are Fedya and Fanya coming?"

"Oh, yes, they should be here quite soon. You know Fanya's always late for everything... Walter can't come with her this time, though."

"Oh, dear, that's a pity. Why ever not? Is he ill?"

"No, no. there's been a spot of bother over some German at the hotel. It's the war, you know."

"Ah yes, the war, the war. I'm very sorry. Is she bringing Roonya?"

"Is Roonya coming?" interrupted Koka when he heard his cousin's name mentioned.

"Yes, Kokochka, Roonya is coming. Now, you two, just you come along with me." Granny took us by the hand and led us over to the grand piano in one corner of the room. "I've got some eggs for you, too." She took two small coloured nets from the top of the piano. One was red and one was blue. Each net held ten little coloured wooden eggs and a little wooden slide to roll them down. We were very pleased.

"Oh, thank you, Granny, thank you very much," we chorused. "Can we play with them here?"

"I don't see why not. Play over here on the carpet where I can keep an eye on you." She settled down comfortably on the sofa as we prepared to play a kind of game of marbles with our little wooden Easter eggs.

"Oh, there you are, Dorothea."

Aunt Dorothea came into the room with the Crumb under her arm. She was dressed exactly as always in her prim grey dress with its high collar trimmed with white lace. Holiday time meant little to her.

"Christos Voskrese, dear Aunt." Papa did his best and made to give her the traditional three kisses. She accepted the first kiss and then, independent-minded as always, held him at arms' length and, instead of responding in the Russian way, looked him quizzically in the eye and said, very firmly,

"Thank you, my dear. One kiss is quite enough, thank you." She bowed with a gracious smile to Mama and turned to Granny,

"I'm sorry to be down so late, Emilie."

"It doesn't matter in the least. Come and sit down by me. Here is Kroshka's cushion."

Mama stole quietly out of the room and an atmosphere of family contentment descended on us like a snowfall of eiderdown. The Crumb snuffled disgustingly to himself as he turned this way and that on his cushion and finally settled down with a long snore-like sigh. The little wooden eggs rattled down their little wooden chutes and cracked lightly against each other as Koka and I played with them on the carpet at the grownups' feet. We gave little cries of triumph and despair as our game ebbed to and fro. The grownups looked down at us in smiling indulgence. Mama was playing a record of the new waltz in the dining room and its dreamy strains poured out of the great horn of the wind-up gramophone.

When Koka and I started to squabble over our game there were soft warning words from Agasha who was sitting hear us.

"Children! Children!" This was enough to calm us.

Mama came back into the room still humming the tune of the waltz and half dancing to the tune.

"Did you go to church, Mamoolya?"

"No, Lilichka. Dorothea and I stayed at home. She finds our long services too much for her now. We read the Bible together instead."

The Crumb snuffled on his cushion. The wooden eggs rattled and cracked and then the doorbell rang.

Voices in the hallway were followed by Roonya gusting into the room, followed by his mother, Aunt Fanya. He bounded across the room to Granny.

"Christos Voskrese, Granny!" The greetings swirled round the room as everyone including Agasha rose to their feet and kissed and hugged each other. Aunt Dorothea got up too, but limited her activities as before to a single kiss, given and accepted.

"Roonya! Roonya!" Koka had to shout across to Roonya above the greetings and then he went over and tugged at Roonya's sleeve. "Have you brought an egg for Granny?" Roonya was quite indignant.

"Of course I have. What do you take me for?" He went back to Granny and presented her with the egg, painted by himself, which had been in his hand all the time. In return Granny presented him with a net of wooden eggs just like ours except that his were green. Roonya was two years older than we were and we looked upon him as being practically grown up. Nevertheless he sat down on the carpet with us and joined in our game. The arrival of Aunt Fanya gave rise to a new eddy of gossip.

"What's this I hear about Walter, Fanya? What actually happened?" Aunt Fanya grimaced and threw her hands in the air.

"It was very embarrassing but you know how it is. There was this French businessman and he found himself sharing a table with a German. He made a terrible fuss. The German became aggressive and they almost came to blows!"

"Where was the head waiter all the time?"

"He was quite hopeless, scared out of his wits. Poor Walter had to be called to separate them. He'll tell you all about it when he comes. He's coming on later." She turned to Mama. "Lilya, we simply must enrol for the Nursing Course, absolutely everyone is." I pricked up my ears. Koka and I often played Doctors and Nurses. Mama was doubtful.

"The Nursing Course? Why should we? Where is it?"

"Well, the war, you know. Some of the emergency hospitals seem to need extra help with the wounded coming back from the front."

"You know I can't stand the sight of blood. But I suppose you're right, we ought to. I don't mind lending a hand. Let's talk about it some other time. For heaven's sake, it's Easter. Let's forget all about the war for one day at least."

"The war isn't going to last much longer anyway," Papa intervened.

"No, Lilya's right, Karloosha." Granny ended this conversation. "Today is a holiday. Let's not talk about the war."

Another squabble was brewing among the children on the floor and Papa knelt down by us to try to calm us. My curiosity had been roused by the grownups' talk.

"What is the war, Papa?"

"Oh, it's nothing for you to worry your head about, my little duckling. It's a long way off. It can't hurt us. Now, why don't we all play a different game together?"

"Oh, yes, Uncle. Let's play Fleas. Fleas, Fleas, let's play Fleas."

"Only you must play with us, Papa. If you don't, Roonya keeps on making up new rules."

"All right, Moossinka. Where shall we play, though?"

"Roll the carpet back," suggested Granny, who had been listening. "Then you can play on the parquet."

"But the Fleas hop better when it's soft."

"Well, then, just play where you are!"

"Where are the Fleas?" demanded Roonya.

"I don't know." How could I know? "Agasha?"

"Leave poor Agasha in peace for once," scolded Granny. "Moossinka can go and fetch them herself. They are in the right hand drawer of my dressing table. I put them in there so that they wouldn't get scattered all over the place. Off you go, Moossia, but mind you don't touch anything else."

I skipped up the stairs to Granny's bedroom only too willingly. The errand I had been entrusted with gave me a feeling of great importance. Granny's drawing table was an Aladdin's cave of treasures in itself. The painted china trays, square, oblong, round, heart shaped; the silver-backed brushes, mirrors and combs; the large pots and small pots with their mysterious sweet-smelling potions; the ivory rollers; the china jars with ivory knives and spoons and nail files; the ebony-handled scissors; and then everything seen three times over again in the triple mirrors of the dressing table, filled me with almost breathless delight. I almost fell into a trance at the sight of these many wonders and had to remind myself why I was there. I felt that I had already been in granny's room longer than I should have been and hastily opened the drawer and ran down the stairs with the little round wooden box of fleas as quickly as I could in case someone might think I'd had time to get up to some mischief.

"Here they are! I found them!"

We shared out the red, the blue, the yellow and the brown fleas, to each player a different colour, put the little wooden tub in the middle of us all, and with great concentration and a big flea in each right hand, set about making the little fleas hop into the tub.

"Fanya, isn't Fedya coming today? I haven't seen him all the week. I hope they're all right."

"Of course they're all right. They'll be here before lunch."

"He's probably up to his eyes in his stamp collection. Rosa wouldn't dare to interrupt him." Mama knew her favourite brother only too well.

"Are they going to adopt those two children from the village or aren't they?" Papa's enquiry was quite innocent but it led to a lot of hand waving from Mama and Granny and the laying of forefingers to lips.

"Why, is it a secret?" Very surprised.

"No, it isn't exactly a secret", mysteriously, from Granny.

"It's very sad that they don't have any children of their own." Sympathetically.

"Not in front of the children, please!" From Granny, very firmly. Poor Papa looked somewhat bewildered, but obediently didn't pursue the matter.

"Fedya drinks too much." From Aunt Fanya with great significance, making one of her faces.

"We all know about that!" Papa laughed, but was sobered a little when Granny took him up.

"Now, now, Karloosha. You're not exactly a saint either." But there was no malice in her reproof, and she smiled as she spoke.

Aunt Fanya was fanning herself languidly with a magazine. "Mamooshka, it's so hot in here. I think I've got one of my headaches coming."

The front door bell rang. It must be Uncle Fedya!

"You and your headaches. Fanya. Karloosha, would you open the little window? Children, come over here; I don't want you to be in a draught."

Granny had the welfare of every member of the family close to her heart.

The door from the hall opened and I jumped up and hurled myself into the arms of my favourite uncle, Fedya; a handsome man with a small moustache.

"Careful, Moossinka!" He pretended to stagger. "You nearly knocked me over!"

"Christos Voskrese, Uncle Fedya."

"Good morning, my little duck, and Christos Voskrese and Voistinoo Voskrese." He gathered me in his arms and hugged and kissed me many more than three times.

There was the usual flurry of greetings as everybody got to their feet, and Uncle Fedya's presence spread warmth and delight through the room. Granny looked round.

"Isn't Rose with you?"

"She'll be here directly, Mamooshka. Koka, Christos Voskrese. Roonya, Christos Voskrese. And my favourite sister!" He stood looking a Mama for a moment with his arms outspread. Then he moved to her and embraced her. "Come, Lilichka, Christos Voskrese, my pretty one!"

"There you are, Rosa!" Aunt Fanya crossed the room to great the latest arrival, Aunt Rosa, who was tall and plump and very kind, but, alas, bore no resemblance to a rose at all.

The excitement of Uncle Fedya's and Aunt Rosa's arrivals had only just begun to subside when Granny's maid, Dusya, came into the room to announce that lunch was ready, and we whirled gaily into the dining room, and scrambled round the big table to sit next to our favourites.

"Karloosha," decreed Granny, "you may pour the vodka. You children can have Mors to drink."

"I like kvas!" boldly ventured Roonya. Granny looked down at him with severe disapproval.

"In my house, Roonya, children do not drink kvas. Agasha, will you give Roonya some Mors. Now, help yourselves everybody! To start with there is sakooski, caviar, kilki or salted herring."

"Papa, can I have some bread and kilki, please", asked Koka, "and please will you take the bones out for me?"

"Lilichka, let me pour you some vodka," clowned Uncle Fedya, knowing full well that alcohol never passed Mama's lips. She put her hand over the top of her glass to stop him, and then removed it when Papa poured her a glass of water.

"Fedya, stop your teasing!" he scolded with mock seriousness. Uncle Fedya was not to be put down. The bottle in his hand reached out and hovered over my glass.

"Never mind, if she won't have any, Moossinka will, won't you, my little duck?" As the bottle tilted mischievously, Granny rose to her feet in alarm. She was very cross.

"Fedya! Don't you dare! Don't you dare to give vodka to Moossia!"

Uncle Fedya crowed with delight at the success of his little joke, which we had all seen before. Granny, realising too late that she had been caught out, sat down, relieved but grumbling. "Do stop acting the fool, Fedya!"

Uncle Fedya suddenly managed to look very innocent. "All right, all right, Mamochka, I'll be a good boy. I promise. Cross my heart."

But his eyes were still sparking with mischief as he poured himself a large glass of vodka, and everybody knew he would be up to some other trick before long. True enough, a moment later he swept up the bowl of caviar in one hand, scooped some out with a spoon and made as if to put it on my plate.

"Here, have some caviar instead."

"No, Uncle Fedya, no!" I screamed, "I don't like it. It tastes like that horrid cod-liver-oil!" His hand circled above my plate and his eyes begged me, "Try a little."

In desperation I squealed, "I shall be sick!" His tantalising hand descended to my plate. "Aga-a-a-asha!" I wailed. Uncle Fedya put the caviar on his own plate and simply shouted with good-humoured laughter. Agasha, hovering behind me, came to my rescue.

"Uncle is only playing, Moossinka!" and she put half a hard-boiled egg on my plate.

Easter lunch took most of the afternoon. It was all very leisurely. Uncle Fedya kept the whole table in an uproar with his jokes and games and stories, and got more and more merry as the vodka flowed more freely. The first course was followed by clear soup with little meat pies. Then there was a handsome goose which Papa carved at the table, served with boiled potatoes and carrots in a white sauce, and, to finish up, pashka and stewed fruit. By this time it was nearly four o'clock, and I was yawning my head off. Koka was nodding in his chair.

"Agasha," said Mama, "take the children back home. They're tired out. Let them have a little sleep."

"Shall I take Roonya, too?"

"He can stay here with me," Aunt Fanya replied for him. "We'll come over and see you later, after you've had a rest."

"Say goodbye to Granny, Koka," urged Papa. "Look, the poor boy is practically asleep already. Put on his hat and coat, Agasha. I'll carry him home, and you can look after Moossia."

The excitement of our morning visit to Granny, the games, the delight of the family gathering, and, above all, the enormous meal we had eaten, far more than we were usually accustomed to, had taken its toll of Koka and me. Clutching Agasha's hand very tightly, I almost tottered after Papa and Koka down the garden path, round the pond, across the factory yard, through the big apartment doors and up the stairs to our own front door.

It had been an Easter Day never to be forgotten.

Chapter 11

May 1916 – Off to the Country

It was difficult to settle down to the normal routines of everyday life after the excitements of Easter time. The trees by now were in full leaf and the sun shone higher and higher in the sky as the days passed. We were able to get out of the apartment more and more as the weather improved and Agasha would take us down to the river and into the parks where the spring flowers were in full bloom. Occasionally we would go into the city with Agasha and Mama. But, mostly, it was a period of waiting. In a short while the streets, not long ago deep in snow, began to get very dusty and the high buildings surrounding us as we walked along the avenue began to get more and more like a cage from which we longed to escape. The rooks had come back and we could see them strutting in the parks or wheeling uproariously over our heads. Now that they had come back we felt that the time was getting near when we could fly off to the woods and taste the freedom of the countryside again.

The first signs that this would ever happen were quite small in themselves. Agasha began to get very busy with our clothes. She scurried about the apartment, always with something in her hands, like a sparrow carrying bits of dried grass to its nest, except that she was carrying winter coats and leggings and fur hats and packing them away until the next winter so that all would be in order before we went away. Then Ivan, the bearded yardman, turned up at the front door with the first large skip which he deposited in the hall of the apartment. From that point on more and more cases and boxes and wicker baskets appeared and Agasha, and Mama, and sometimes Masha, became busier and busier packing things for our long summer holiday. The hall became almost impassable. It wasn't just a question of packing a few summer clothes and personal belongings. There was the matter of setting up a whole separate household.

"Now if you will pack the household linen in this basket, Agasha, then Masha can take that box into the kitchen for the other samovar and the jam kettles. We'd better pack some of the Barin's summer suits in my trunk, Agasha."

"Is Papa going to stay with us all the time this year?"

"Why, no, Moossia. He will take us down there on the train but you know he has to be here during the week to help Granny run the factory. He will come down and see us every weekend as he always does and we shall go and meet the train every Friday and Masha and Cook will look after him while we are away."

There were seemingly endless consultations and changes of mind and packing and some repacking, all done at a leisurely pace over many days until, finally, the ropes and the leather straps were tied and buckled round the boxes and the cases, the metal bars were shot home on the skips and the padlocks fastened over the hasps and the labels were written and tied. Ivan took the little mountain of luggage downstairs and off to the station.

After that, absolutely nothing happened. The apartment seemed very empty and there was a dreadful air of anti-climax. We got up in the morning; we played in the nursery; we went for walks with Agasha; we had our meals as usual; we went to bed. For several days all thoughts of going away had apparently been abandoned. Then one morning, when we woke up, we found Agasha busying herself about the place more than usual.

"Come along, children. Get up and get dressed. Your clothes are all ready for you. Moossia, will you help Koka? We're going to the country this morning."

Koka, who was usually a regular little dawdler in the mornings, fairly bounced out of bed, pulled his socks and shoes on and was in the bathroom before I had a chance to lift a hand to help him. During breakfast Agasha was preoccupied with packing the little travelling cases and baskets and Masha came and took them into the hall.

"We're going to the country today, Masha!"

"Yes, Koka, I know. I wonder if I shall recognise you when you come back from Finland? You'll be four whole months older."

"Of course you will, Masha!" I stretched out my hand to say goodbye like a grown up. She solemnly shook hands with me.

"Goodbye, Moossinka, be a good girl." With these words she went off with the last basket to the hall.

"Is everybody ready?" Papa's voice rang through the apartment. "The cabs are outside and Egor has come up for the luggage."

"Masha, where did you put the picnic?"

"It's all in that basket, Barinya," Masha answered, pointing to a largish hamper.

"Good. Now, is everybody dressed and ready to go?" Mama looked round to make sure. "Let's all sit down quietly. We have a journey to make."

We each sat down on the nearest available seat. Koka perched on a small suitcase. Papa and Mama sat down on the settee in the hall. Masha found a stool and Agasha and I shared a chair. We always did this whenever any member of the family went on a journey. In Mama's words, "We go in peace and we do not disturb the peace of the house."

All was still for a moment. My thoughts were racing. What if we missed the train? I looked up at Agasha anxiously. She read my thoughts, smiled, and put her finger to her lips. We were only sitting for a few moments but it seemed like eternity to me. Then we heard Mama's voice say,

"Let us go with God."

In a flash Koka and I were racing down the stairs before Agasha could rein us in, nearly colliding with Egor who had come to get the last of the luggage to load it into the second cab, which followed the one we went to the station in. There was a hurricane of goodbyes, a forest of waving hands to Egor and Masha who had come down to see us off, and then the breathless moment came when the cab started off and we really were on our way to Finland at last.

The Finland Station was a low pink building and quite thronged with people, many going on their long summer holidays like us, with porters going in all directions carrying large piles of luggage. Agasha shepherded us through the doors of the station, across the concourse, on to the platform and up to a saloon coach at the back of the train, a coach with its own little outside platform. This particular train wasn't overcrowded and we had no trouble in sorting ourselves out once we were aboard. Mama had to have a seat by the window and facing the engine otherwise she felt sick. Papa and the porters arrived with the hand luggage which was carefully stowed away.

Moossia

The porters were tipped; the carriage door was shut and Papa subsided cheerfully by Mama. Koka and I settled down on the wooden seats opposite Papa and Mama on either side of Agasha. The smoke from the engine drifted through the open window. There was a deafening hiss as steam escaped from the engine, which made us put our fingers in our ears. It was frightening but we laughed all the same because it made us feel that the train really would leave at any moment. And so it did. There was a whistle from the Guard, an answering hoot from the driver, a shuddering ch-ch-ch-ch and then a sharp jerk which make Koka fall forward right out of his seat. Papa had been keeping a wary eye on him and reached out and caught Koka practically in mid-air. This gave rise to more excited laughter. Agasha got up to shut the window now that the train was moving.

"No, Agasha, leave the window open," said Mama. "It's quite warm." Agasha sat down without a murmur and I got up to look out of the window. We were all restless with the excitement of the journey. Mama wasn't happy,

"Moossia, don't lean out of the window. You may get the sparks from the engine in your eyes." Obediently I sat down and Agasha half rose, looking towards Mama. "Yes, Agasha, I think you're right. You'd better shut it after all." Agasha carefully shut the window and took her place once more.

We looked round us at the other people in the carriage. There was a cheerful atmosphere and it was obvious, from the piles of luggage and the family groups, that we weren't the only ones going into Finland for the summer. No sooner had the train started than hampers and baskets were lifted onto laps and spare seats, food was produced from them, and people began to eat with gusto. They gave Koka ideas.

"I'm hungry."

"I think you should wait a little while, Koka," from Mama.

We were soon out of St. Petersburg and we had a two-hour journey in front of us. Fields and forests, forests and fields flowed past the carriage window. It was mostly forests with a group of houses or a small settlement here and there and an occasional solitary cow in a clearing. Now and then the train would stop at a tiny station with a screech of brakes and much huffing and puffing. The Guard was always impatient to be off again and there would be much shouting and hurrying along and much protesting from the passengers. Then a wave from the Guard's flag, a pip-pip of his whistle, a deafening escape of steam, a toot from the engine which echoed over and over again in the trees, and we would be off again.

"I'm hungry." Koka never gave up hope. Agasha looked to Mama for a decision.

"I think the children might have something now, Agasha."

As usual, Agasha took command and brought out the hamper with the picnic in it. There were cold chicken pies specially made for the journey and lots of fruit very carefully wrapped and packed away by Cook, and soon even Koka couldn't eat any more. Papa got up to stretch his legs and stood by the window drinking in the sight of the forests and meadows and streams which meant so much to him. Perhaps he was daydreaming of the times when he went hunting with his friends for ducks and deer and bears.

"I think I'll go and have a smoke on the platform"; he turned to go.

"Can I come with you?" I entreated, hoping against hope. This time I was lucky.

"Only if you promise to hold my hand tight as tight. It can be dangerous on the platform when the train lurches. You can easily fall off. What do you think, Lilya?" He didn't ask Agasha who was looking as anxious as a hen with chicks.

"Just as you think, Karloosha. Don't stay there too long."

"But, Barin…" Agasha couldn't hold back her misgivings. Papa smiled at her, "Don't worry, Agasha. We'll be back soon."

When we got out on the platform the train was going down a bit of a slope and travelling quite fast. All the sounds seemed magnified many times outside the compartment. The rattle of the hurrying wheels and the rushing of the wind echoed all the time amongst the trees and made conversation almost impossible. It was very exciting and I was really quite frightened and hung on to Papa so tight that he managed to light his cigar only with great difficulty and sleight of hand. Then there was a curve in the line and bits of soot started to engulf the platform. My eyes began to water and I started to cough. Papa saw that I wasn't too happy out on the platform after all and gallantly threw away his cigar, of which he had smoked very little.

"Let's get back to Mama. She will be worried."

We went back into the carriage and worked our way hand over hand from seat to seat down the rocking train and back to our places. Agasha's eyes lit up with relief when she saw that I actually had come back in one piece. She wiped my eyes, patted me on the back and clucked over me until I nestled down on the wooden seat by her side. Koka was asleep on Mama's knee. Papa had closed his eyes. Nearly everyone in the carriage was by now asleep or half asleep. I was just drifting off myself when I had another problem. I tugged at Agasha's sleeve so that she bent down to listen to what I had to whisper.

"Agasha, I want to go on the potty."

"Just a minute, my duckling, Agasha has it right here." She promptly produced the potty from one of her travelling bags.

"Can't I go down there?" I pointed down the carriage to the mysterious little door through which I had seen a procession of grownups disappear and reappear. I was dying to get inside that little door.

"What nonsense, of course not. Here, sit down. Nobody is looking." So I squatted down and then Agasha flipped her apron over the potty and strode off down the carriage and through the little door.

I knew by now that we couldn't have all that far to go and knelt on the seat with my nose pressed to the window looking for familiar landmarks. The ditches by the railway line were smothered in multi-coloured wild flowers. I began to recognise places we would go to later in the summer to pick berries and pick mushrooms. Then a well-remembered black and tan shape leapt the ditch and ran alongside the train for a while, barking furiously. The train tooted loud and long. Round the next bend I could see the little railway halt at Kelomakki. As the brakes of the train began to squeal Papa came to with a start, glanced quickly at his watch and jumped to his feet.

"We're almost there. Wake up, Koka! Wake up, Lilichka!"

He and Agasha began to carry the baskets and cases down the carriage to be near the door.

"Koka, you hold Mama's hand. I'll get off first and give you a hand."

The platform at Kelomakki was very small and the train was pulling up before we got to it, so it was obvious we would have to jump down onto the fine sand at the side of the line. There was a final snort and a lurch from the engine and we stopped. Papa sprang down onto the ground. We wouldn't have much time to get off.

"Careful, Koka. Hold both my hands. Now, one, two, jump! That's right. Now, Moossia, both my hands, one, two, jump! Lilichka!"

"Goodness, it's so high!"

"You're quite safe. I'm here. I won't let you fall." Mama landed safe and sound in Papa's arms. "Now, Agasha, you pass me the luggage. Quick as you can. The train only stops for a minute or two."

Agasha and Papa worked quickly to pass the numerous small cases and baskets we had brought with us on the journey down to the side of the track. The Guard, impatient as always, as ever, raised his flag to start the train. Agasha gave him a piece of her mind and shouted at the top of her voice,

"Can't you see we're not off yet? Goodness me, always in a hurry." She passed the last basket to Papa, steadied herself, and took a flying leap down to the ground, stumbling slightly when she landed but recovering immediately. By the time she had brushed the sand off her skirt and looked round, the Guard had waved his flag, blown his whistle; the driver had let off steam and the train was already disappearing into the distance. We had arrived at Kelomakki.

Chapter 12

Summer 1916

The sound of trotting feet and the rumble of a little two-wheeled cart made us turn and look up the lane leading away from Kelomakki halt.

"Here comes Aino with his cart." Koka ran off excitedly to greet the newcomer.

Aino stopped the horse and got down off the cart. Koka in his smart sailor suit just stood looking up at the old Finnish peasant in his ragged clothes, his face wrinkled like pine bark from the weather and a thousand smiles. The old man stood bending over towards him. They were both equally pleased to see each other.

"Hello, Aino!"

"Hello, young master," adding another layer of wrinkles to the myriad already there. "Master, Mistress," he bowed to Papa and Mama and raised his dilapidated flat cap. Aino didn't always wear this cap. When it was really hot he wore a very ancient straw hat full of holes as a colander, but we never saw him without one or the other. There was quite a sharp line between his weather-beaten face and his comparatively sheltered brow. He made for the pile of luggage by the track without any more ado.

"How are you keeping, Aino?" asked Papa.

"Not too badly, Master, thank you." Aino tested his rheumatism by flexing his fingers.

"That's all there is to go up to the cottage. Has the other luggage arrived?"

"Day before yesterday, Master. I came down to fetch it myself." He was piling the luggage onto his cart and Agasha was helping him.

"You'd better go up on the cart with Aino, Agasha," Mama intervened. "When you get there, sort out the samovar and put it on. I'm sure we shall all want some tea."

We walked off and left them to sort things out.

"Are you sure you're not too tired to walk, Lilichka?"

"No, I feel fine now I'm in the open air. In any case, we can take our time and it isn't all that far."

"Come on, slow coach." I shouted to Koka and we both ran for all we were worth along the path through the woods which gave us a short cut to the cottage. The smell of the pine trees was very strong and the woods were full of familiar but still magical sights and sounds.

"Sh! Sh! Don't move! Look! There's a woodpecker!" We crept towards the sound of hammering and were just in time to catch a flash of green and red slip round to the other side of a tree. There was a clatter of wings on leaves and a cuckoo bubbled above us with its forked tail. Across the plank bridge over the ditch where we could gather truffles in the autumn, over the sandy lane, through the wicket gate into our cottage garden we went. The freedom of the open spaces had gone to our heads at once and we were a little wild.

As we ran up the sandy path across the lawn the cottage garden seemed bigger than ever. We tried to get indoors thorough the verandah door but it wasn't yet unlocked so we went round the side to the kitchen where Agasha had already drawn water from the well, had unpacked the samovar, and was filling it to make the tea. There were cases and boxes and skips all over the place.

"Out you go, children! Out you go! Just you stay out in the garden and play until I call you for tea." We liked nothing better and ran out through the pine trees to have a look at the pond.

"Look at the pond, Moossia! It's ever so much bigger this year!"

"That's because there was so much snow in the winter."

"And look at all the little fishes. Hundreds and hundreds!"

"I'm hungry. Let's go back indoors. The samovar's sure to be boiling by now."

"Look! Papa is unlocking the verandah door. Let's go that way." No sooner indoors were we than our heads went up and our noses wrinkled. "Doesn't it smell funny, Papa?"

"No wonder. The cottage has been locked up all winter. Off you go and wash your hands and we'll all go into the kitchen and have tea."

"Can't we have tea in the garden?"

"Not today. Agasha hasn't unpacked properly yet."

We gobbled our tea perched on one of the unpacked skips in the kitchen, eager to get out into the open again and to look everything over. Just as we were going out Mama caught us.

"Wait a minute, children. Agasha, will you see they change their clothes before they go out into the garden again?"

"Yes, of course, Barinya. Come along you two."

We went back across the kitchen, down the passage, past Agasha's room on the left next to the kitchen and Mama's and Papa's bedroom on the right. Before we reached the dining room and drawing room at the end there was another door into our room which looked out on the orchard and the vegetable garden. There was a bed on either side of the window, a chair by each bed, a chest of drawers on the right and a washstand with a pitcher and basin on the left near the door. All our rooms were on the ground floor of the cottage.

"Can we go and explore upstairs, Agasha?"

"No, Koka, not today. There isn't anybody there now, anyhow. All the rooms are locked up until your Aunt Fanya comes." Agasha got us into the shirts and shorts we both wore in Finland during the summer until it got really warm, when we discarded the shirts and just ran about barefoot in the shorts. We both curled our feet up out of Agasha's reach when we saw her reach for our sandals.

"Oh, no, not sandals, Agasha!"

"Yes, you must have your sandals on for a day or two until your feet harden." As we hurried off into the garden again, Papa's voice called out,

"Don't go too near the pond, children, will you? The water is very deep this year."

Once we were out in the garden again we stopped short. There were so many things to look at we didn't know what to do first.

"Let's go and talk to Aino."

"We saw Aino at the station. Anyhow, he's taken his horse and cart home. Let's go and have a look inside the barn."

The inside of the barn was dim and dusty. There didn't seem to be anything new in it. There was the same assortment of spades and forks and rakes and hoes. There were piles of logs cut by Aino in the winter and put in the dry to burn in the big tiled stoves indoors. There were large baskets to carry logs in and small baskets to pick fruit into. In the corner were some bits of broken furniture thrown out of the house and, overall, there hung the delicious smell of dust and wood and hay and long summer days. With one accord we made for the rickety homemade ladder which led up into the loft. Up here was a treasure trove of discarded bottles. There were green wine bottles with high shoulders and brown wine bottles with low shoulders. There were tall clear bottles and short earthenware bottles with hardly any necks at all and ring-shaped handles. There were heavy bottles with pieces of wire and silver paper still round their mouths. The sun shone through a tiny window in the gable and threw patterns of many-coloured light like a stained glass window onto the sloping roof of the loft. But, most entrancing of all, was the hint of the former contents at the bottom of some of the bottles, inviting and at the same time surely forbidden and so even more inviting. Now that we had renewed out acquaintance with the bottles we gingerly and with our fingertips drew some of them out of the network of spiders' webs which laced them all together and put the mouths of the bottles to our noses, trying, with not much success, to guess what extraordinary potions had been inside them. But the beetles and the spiders which had now made their homes in the bottles stared at us through the glass and blunted our curiosity. So we hastily put the bottles back on the heap and drifted down the ladder and out into the garden again.

Inevitably, and no doubt perversely, just because we had been warned, and just because we were freshly intoxicated by our arrival in Kelomakki, we found ourselves skirting the pond again. On the far side we found a fresh prize, a wooden trough hollowed out of a half a tree trunk, the sort with flattened ends which country people do their washing in. It was half afloat in the water with one end on the bank. We considered its possibilities.

"It's just like a little boat," I said.

"Let's sit in it."

"It's too small, too small for two."

"Do you want to have a ride in it?" Koka egged me on. "Why don't you?"

"All right, then. I'll try. Hold it."

Koka edged his way into the little boat with his arms spread out like a tightrope walker's to keep his balance and then squatted down sideways. This didn't look right to me.

"Turn round and face me." The tree trunk rocked ominously as Koka wriggled his way round.

"Hold on, I'll give it a push."

"No, don't. I don't want you to." He went to get up and out of the little boat but, before he could get back onto dry land, I impulsively gave the log a push with my foot and off it shot into the middle of the pond. Koka instantly settled down on his haunches to keep his balance. A whole rainbow of mixed feelings crossed his face. His initial expression of fear gave way to one of sheer pleasure for a moment or two. This was speedily erased by a look of the utmost terror as he lifted his bottom into the air still clutching the sides of the log.

"There's a big hole in it. The water's coming in. my feet are all wet. I'm sinking." His voice got more and more desperate.

I froze for a second and then ran distractedly between the pond and the cottage, ludicrously beating my thighs with my fists, desperate to get help and finding it impossible to leave Koka and with awful pictures of the appalling possible outcome of my impulse of a moment flashing across my mind as if I were in danger of drowning myself.

"Agasha! Agasha! Aga-a-a-a-sha! Quickly, quickly, quickly. Koka's drowning!" I was shouting even louder than Koka and our cries rang and echoed in all directions.

I heard the kitchen door burst open and Agasha came flying down the path towards me with her hands thrown up in horror. She took the situation in at a glance and, not breaking her stride or pausing to get rid of her shoes, she waded into the pond until the water was halfway up her neck, lifted Koka high into the air out of the rapidly sinking log-boat and carried him back, without pause, to dry land. Koka didn't stop crying and calling for help at the top of his voice even when he was quite safe and he was dripping from top to toe. Agasha ignored the fact that she herself was soaked to the skin and walked briskly back to the cottage with Koka in her arms and with me lamely and ashamedly tagging along behind them.

"How on earth did he get into the pond?"

"He only went for a little ride. It was like a tiny boat."

"Merciful Heavens! We've only just got here, and we're up to our eyes in trouble. Did you push him in, Moossia?"

"Well, yes, I pushed the boat in. Don't be cross, Agasha."

"Don't be cross! Don't be cross! How can I help being cross? Koka might have been drowned. I don't know what your Mama will say when she hears about it," she scolded as we went through the kitchen door.

"What's the matter?" Papa met our dripping procession as we went along the passage.

"Koka's fallen into the pond, Barin. It's all right, though; he'll be all right. I'll just rub him down and wrap him in something warm."

"Moossia pushed me!"

"But I didn't mean to…"

"Never mind all that," intervened Agasha. "You shouldn't have got into the boat in the first place."

"Where's Mama, Papa?"

"She's lying down, so don't make too much noise." Papa gave Koka a hug and a kiss. "I'm surprised at you, Moossia. I always thought you had more sense." Then he left us both to Agasha's care.

My feeling of dejection as I followed Agasha into a room strewn with clothes and toys and half-unpacked suitcases was in total contrast to the mood of exhilaration in which we had arrived at Kelomakki. The accident in the pond put a damper on the first day of our four months in the country, and Agasha wouldn't let us out of her sight until bedtime.

Chapter 13

Summer 1916

Whenever we could, we had our meals out of doors. There was a long wooden table permanently in the garden, surrounded by white-painted cast-iron chairs. If it rained, which wasn't often, the table and the chairs would get wet of course, but they soon dried. A quick wipe over with a cloth, and we could use them again. Breakfast, for us, was very simple – a soft-boiled egg, sour milk with sugar, rye bread and butter, with milk to drink. After that we could run about the garden and play just as we wanted, until Agasha was free from her work in the cottage and could take us further afield into the forest or the open meadows.

A week or two after we had arrived at Kelomakki and had quite settled down, I was sitting quietly with Agasha one Friday afternoon, in the shade of a big lime-tree in the garden. Agasha was wearing a rusty-coloured smock and a white blouse and apron. Her hands were busy as usual, and she was sewing buttons onto our liberty bodices so that they would be ready for us when we went home in the autumn. The lime-tree flowers were open, and the branches above our heads were alive with bees. Their humming was so loud that it shut out every other sound, near or far, except that I could hear Agasha, who was within touching distance, humming a tune as if in sympathy with the song the bees were singing. Sitting in the shade of the lime tree with the bees humming above my head and Agasha by my side humming gently to herself spelled summertime and utter happiness to me.

The verandah door clicked, and there was Mama in her white frilly dress which reached down to her ankles. Koka was standing by her side.

"Moossinka, I'm going to meet Papa off the train, with Koka. Do you want to come with us?"

"Yes, yes, I do want to come. Will you come too, Agasha?"

"No, Moossinka, you go with your Mama and Koka. I must get on with my work." She put her arms about me and kissed me gently.

"Agasha, get the samovar ready. Barin will be sure to want tea when he gets back."

"I'll see to it, Barinya, don't worry. Moossinka, you'd better put your sandals on if you're going to meet the train."

"Must I? My feet aren't cold, and the ground is ever so warm."

"I don't think it really matters, Agasha," Mama intervened. "We aren't going to St. Petersburg, after all. Koka is in his bare feet, too. Come along, children." She swung the parasol lightly over her shoulder, and we strolled along the sandy path to the garden gate. I've never seen Mama tanned by the sun. We were all as brown as berries by the end of the summer, even including Aunt Fanya, who was all the time rushing about with her camera mounted on the tripod, taking pictures of us all.

We were met at the garden gate by a great cloud of dust. The lane we had to go through on the way to meet the train was deeply rutted, and very dusty. A peasant's horse and cart was trotting smartly along it, and we ran back a few steps in haste, and Mama lowered her parasol as a shield to protect herself. When the dust subsided she closed her parasol and used it as a walking-stick; she picked her way across the rutted, dusty road with her tiny feet in their beautiful pointed white shoes, and then, balancing carefully, over the narrow plank bridge spanning the ditch on the edge of the wood.

"Do be careful, Koka." But he had already jumped over the ditch, scorning the plank bridge, and he stood looking at me, silently daring me to jump too. I couldn't resist his challenge, and jumped as hard as I could – but I slipped and landed up in a patch of mud left in the shade after the rain some days ago. I finished up with a pair of black mud-socks.

"Moossinka, just look at your feet!"

"Never mind, Mama. I'll wipe it off." I picked up handfuls of moss from the bank of the ditch, and in a few moments they looked to me as good as new.

Koka stood there laughing happily at my discomfiture, so I chased him through a patch of little Christmas trees and young birch trees. Just as I was about to catch up with him, he cried out and started to hop about on one leg in a very comical way. I held him up and looked at the foot he was gripping, but it was only a pine needle that had stuck in his big toe, and, by the time Mama had reached us, in alarm at his cry, all was well. We got to the station without further incident.

Except that Kelomakki station wasn't really a station at all. It was hardly even what you could call a halt. Perhaps it could be called half a halt. There was just a small one-storey building and a minute platform made of railway sleepers, and never anything like long enough for the trains which stopped there very occasionally with, as far as we could make out, extreme reluctance, because the guard hardly ever gave the passengers enough time to get off the train.

The horse and cart which had raised such a cloud of dust as we came out of our garden was tied up innocently to a hitching post, and the old peasant woman, who was evidently the driver, sat nodding on the bench in front of it. She might have been sleeping there for weeks. Her work-worn hands lay on her coarse dark skirt; her chin rested on a grey cotton blouse fastened with a large metal brooch. We couldn't see her face because her headscarf was pulled so far forward. She must have been aware that we were staring at her because she hesitantly came to life; her face emerged from the headscarf like a tortoise from its shell. She rummaged in the folds of her dusty skirt, and produced a tattered handkerchief which she unknotted, and then, with her lips moving as she did so, laboriously counted out a heap of small change which had been squirreled away for safekeeping.

As we followed Mama, who was treading very carefully to avoid catching her high heels in the cracks between the railway sleepers which made up the platform, we passed a little pale-faced boy, about my age, clutching a butterfly net in which he had obviously caught something. He was arguing fiercely with a beautiful lady dressed in a light blue skirt and blouse, who was talking to him quietly.

"No, no, I won't!" he said crossly. "I've caught it. It's mine!"

The only other people on the platform were a barefoot young peasant woman with a little girl in a dress like a nightshirt clutching her hand. The young woman had two heavy baskets full of mushrooms on the ground in front of her, and she looked hopefully at Mama as we went near.

"Are you selling those mushrooms?" Mama asked her.

"Yes, Barinya. They're straight from the forest. Most of them are white ones." Mama looked the mushrooms over casually.

"Good. I'll have them. Take them to 'Murmela'. It's over that way, on the other side of the wood. Wait for me there. I'll pay you when I come back." She took it for granted that the peasant woman would do exactly as she was told.

"I heard the whistle!" Koka suddenly shouted. We turned to look in the direction from which the train would come, and could just see a trail of smoke in the distance above the trees. As it came round the faraway bend in the track, the train became a black blob which quickly resolved itself into the outlines of the engine. We could see the head of the fireman as he leaned out of the cab, and other heads popping out behind his. The train drew up with many groans and squeaks and wheezes, and finally let fly an enormous cloud of steam which made us jump back in fright. The guard was already down on the ground, eager to be away again before he had properly arrived.

"Kelomakki! Hurry along please. This is only a short stop. Kelomakki!" Nobody took much notice. They all took their time in spite of his repeated shouts.

As the steam quickly cleared we saw Papa jumping down from the train right along the track, quite beyond the tiny platform. We flew along to greet him.

"Papachka! Hello, Papachka!"

"Moossinka!" His arms enfolded me in a bear's hug, and his hat went flying. Koka let go of Mama's hand and ran to pick it up.

"Thank you, my little son." Papa picked Koka up and gave him a bear's hug, too. The train rattled off down the track, and then I saw that there was another man waiting just behind Papa. He was wearing a panama hat, and had taken off his linen jacket in the train, because of the heat, and held it dangling so low in his hand that it almost brushed the ground.

"Lilichka." Papa put Koka down and kissed Mama, first on the hand and then on the cheeks. "May I introduce my friend, Nicolai Nicolaevitch Lomsky. He will be staying with us until I go back to town. He is a manufacturer, too, and a landowner."

Mama held out her hand, murmuring greetings, and the new guest bowed and kissed it.

"I hope it will not inconvenience you."

"Of course it won't. You are most welcome to stay."

"Oh, and may I introduce my daughter," said Papa, turning to me. Mr. Lomsky, with a charming smile, kissed the hand I held out to him. "I am delighted."

Mr. Lomsky's formality, gracious though it was, quite tongue tied me and I could only think to make a bob and to disappear behind Papa, holding on to his hand tightly. I paid no attention to the conversation of the grownups as we all strolled through the woods, until Papa said,

"A young workman came into our carriage, Lilichka, and held forth quite eloquently about the folly of continuing the war. There was a lot in what he said… Dangerous talk, though."

"Whom was he talking to?"

"Anybody who cared to listen."

"Didn't anyone try to stop him?"

"No. That was the interesting part about it," put in Mr. Lomsky. "Half the passengers pretended not to hear. The other half seemed to agree with him." Papa continued,

"We all want peace, Nicolai Nicolaevitch. The war has gone on for far too long. There have been appalling losses on both sides." Mama shivered.

"Karloosha, let's not talk about it. It's such a beautiful day. I'm sure everything will work itself out in time."

"Quite right, Lilichka. Now tell me how you have been keeping yourself busy. What have you been doing?" Mama shrugged her shoulders lazily and elegantly. "Nothing? Busy doing nothing?" Papa was teasing her and laughing all the time. "Going out for walks, no doubt? Lying in the shade with a book!"

Mama took his teasing in good part and joined in his laughter. "Well, I did go to see the Reicherts yesterday."

"And how are the Reicherts?"

"Oh, fine, fine. Mrs. Reichert has servant troubles, of course. Germans always want everything done just so but the servants think it doesn't matter so long as they do it somehow or other. Mr. Reichert goes on and on about the war all the time. He says he'll go to Switzerland if the Kaiser lets him down. It's so silly to talk like that. Why go to Switzerland? It's just as lovely here."

By now we had passed through the wood and had to negotiate the plank bridge over the ditch to cross the road to the cottage garden. Papa was full of attention and helped Mama to walk the plank with affectionate care. She stopped as a thought wandered into her head.

"Oh, Karloosha, a young woman is bringing us some mushrooms. Would you give Agasha some money to pay for them when we get home?"

"Of course, Lilichka, of course." Mama never concerned herself with money matters.

"Papa," piped up Koka, "we've picked a lot of bilberries and we've been out looking for cranberries, too." His close-cropped head caught the sunlight and shimmered golden like the halo in an ikon.

"Yes, and Koka nearly got stuck in the bog where the cranberries grow and Agasha had to pull him out with both hands." I shared Koka's feeling that he and I had been left out of the conversation for far too long.

"Later, children, later," Mama chided, "Papa and Mr. Lomsky must be tired after their long journey. They both need a rest."

As we walked up the path we could see that Agasha had laid the garden table ready for tea. The samovar was already boiling and she was putting out the tea glasses in their little wicker holders. She looked up as she heard us come near, and when she saw Papa her face beamed with pleasure.

"Tea is just ready, Barin."

Chapter 14

Summer 1916

That summer Koka and I were as happy as sandboys. We ran about and played in the garden and the woods surrounding the cottage and every night we would go to bed enjoyably tired and sleep like logs. Koka, who could be a bit of a sleepyhead when we were at home in St. Petersburg, would leap out of bed and tug on his shorts as soon as he was awake. Mostly that was all we ever wore now, just a pair of shorts, because the days were nearly always bright and sunny and we didn't need anything more. We were left to our own devices in the mornings because Agasha was extremely busy about the house, since Cook and Masha had been left behind to look after Papa and, to begin with, there was more than ever for her to do.

The months that had passed since our last stay in Kelomakki had seemed like so many years to us and so everything around us was at the same time familiar and yet fascinatingly new. The most simple things gave us enormous pleasure. We loved to go out into the woods nearby, for example, and just shout to the trees.

"Ahoo! Ahoo!" Koka would cry.

"Where are you? Where are you?" I wanted to know. And the trees would obligingly answer and enquire, "Ahoo! Ahoo! Where are you? Where are you?", over and over again and fainter and fainter so that they seemed to be running away from us.

We would dart behind the trees and pelt each other with pine cones which lay in hundreds about our feet. We could do all sorts of things which were unthinkable in St. Petersburg. It was a special joy, almost to the point of delicious wickedness, though nobody minded in the least, just to take a stick and draw a hopscotch maze in the sand of the path leading from the cottage to the lane, and our first expedition to the sea was a red-letter day indeed.

It was a fairly long walk down to the beach so we had little difficulty in persuading Mama to let us set off before lunch so that we could spend as much time there as possible. Agasha emerged from the kitchen door with a basket packed with lunch over one arm and bathing costumes, towels and a travelling rug over the other. When we reached the little white gate giving on to the lane Mama stopped.

"Agasha, did you bring the thermometer?"

"Yes, Barinya. It's in the basket with the lunch."

We had rummaged about in the barn and found our spades and pails and went skipping off in front of Mama and Agasha through the dappled shade of the tall pine trees.

"Ahoo! Where are you?" Our cries echoed and overlapped the trees' answer all the way to the sand dunes fringing the seashore. We struggled up the dry sliding sand towards the top of the nearest dune and had to dig our spades in from time to time to stop ourselves sliding back to the bottom again. After a bit of a struggle we reached the top fairly out of breath and, lo and behold, the sea was just where we had left it the year before. We could hardly believe it.

"Look, Koka, the sea, the sea! There it is!" We flew down the sandy path and across the foreshore, uttering inarticulate cries of joy and waving our spades and pails in the air, to splash about on the very edge of the tiny waves sent rippling by the gentle breeze over the corrugated sands.

We had the beach almost entirely to ourselves. A small group of people were playing a ball game in the distance and a man in a striped bathing costume was getting out of the water and disappeared into the dunes, and that was all. Mama and Agasha had caught up with us and they found a spot half in and half out of the sunshine under a battered pine tree at the foot of the dunes. There Agasha spread out the travelling rug for Mama. We ran over to join them.

"May we take our shorts off, Mama?" This was absolutely all we had on.

"Are you sure you're not too hot? Come here and let me see." She put the back of her hand to our foreheads. "Agasha, have you got the thermometer?"

"Here it is, Barinya." Agasha's feet were already bare because she rarely wore shoes in the summer. She tucked her skirt up and paddled off into the sea with the thermometer and lowered it into the water. After a minute or two she took it out and ran up with it to Mama for her to inspect. We followed her and watched her every move, panting for a favourable verdict.

"Yes, children, I think it's warm enough." She hardly got the words out before we had sloughed our shorts and were in the water.

I lay back in the bright sunshine and let the waves wash over me while Koka half crawled, half floated about like a four-armed crab. Agasha stood guard at the water's edge, her arms full of dry towels for when we came out. Of course, a splashing match developed between Koka and me and we were leaping about like two little mad things screaming with terror and delight in an all-enveloping cascade of foam and spray. Then our ten minutes were over.

"Come along, children, it's time to get out, your Mama says." Large, sun-warmed towels were wrapped round us and we returned to the pine tree where gentle hands wiped us dry. Our picnic lunch was a simple one of black bread and butter and hard-boiled eggs and lukewarm lemon tea poured from a screw-topped bottle, followed by a slice of cheesecake.

"Just look, my shoes are full of sand." Mama slipped them off and stretched out on the rug. "Children, why don't you build me a nice sand castle? Agasha, I think you'd better put their shorts and shirts on so that they don't get sunburnt." So we spent the whole afternoon making castles and rivers and ponds in the sand and carrying buckets of water hither and thither until it was time to home again.

There was a letter from Papa. Mama got up from her chair on the verandah where she had been reading it and went into the kitchen where Agasha was preparing the evening meal. I followed Mama, wondering what was afoot.

"Agasha, Barin says he's having a lot of trouble with his back again."

"I am sorry, Barinya. We'll all go out into the forest tomorrow so that we're ready when he comes down on Friday. The children will look for some bottles in the loft in the morning, I'm sure."

We had precise instructions from Agasha after breakfast. "Now, remember, they have to be three clear glass bottles, not stone ones or coloured ones. Choose the middle sized ones, not the tall ones or the squat ones. Shake as many of the creepy-crawlies out as you can and bring them to me to wash before we go out into the woods." We went off to the loft and carefully sorted out the three bottles and took them to Agasha. She duly washed them and put them in a basket and, after lunch, we set off for the woods.

"I know where to go," offered Koka. "There are some by that fallen tree where we saw the deer a few days ago, Agasha."

"That's a clever boy, Koka. Now, remember, we want to find nice big ones, big enough to take the bottles."

We tramped deeper into the woods in quite another direction from the ones we took to go to the station or to the sea. When we got near to the fallen tree we scattered in our search. Koka was full of enthusiasm.

"What about this one, Agasha?" We went over to him in answer to his shout. Agasha took one of the bottles and measured it against what Koka had found. "Hm-m-m. No, Kokochka, I don't think this one is deep enough to bury the bottle." Koka turned and pointed, "What about that one, then?"

"Just about right. Now can you find me a nice long stick, as long as you can?" This was quickly done and when she had torn off the side twiglets, she drove it down vertically into the ants' nest which was half as big as a sack of potatoes, and turned the stick round and round to widen the hole. Then she pushed the stick into the mouth of the bottle and forced it right down into the hole so that the mouth of the bottle was just level with the top of the anthill. When she had tidied the displaced soil back towards the top of the bottle the anthill looked just as it had before she had started her work, except that you could just see the mouth of the bottle at the top of it. It didn't take us very long to find another two anthills of the right size and to repeat the operation with the other two bottles.

"There now, we've done our job. We can go home and let the ants get on with theirs."

We had to leave the bottles undisturbed for three days, according to Agasha, who was the expert in this sort of thing.

When we came to examine the first one we were quite disappointed. The bottle was quite empty and lying on its side by the anthill. Koka was dismayed by this unexpected happening.

"Oh, dear, how did that happen?"

Agasha picked up the bottle and examined it with a serious and puzzled face.

"Who can tell? Perhaps the ants did it."

"They can't have. They're too little."

"They're very, very strong, Kokochka. Look at them working away in the nest down there. Some of them are carrying things twice as big as they are."

"But they are so small and the bottle is so big."

"Not as big as the nest they built. There are thousands and thousands of them, aren't there?"

They both stood for a while looking at each other, the bottle and the anthill, quite mystified. But Agasha could read a sermon in every stone.

"Never underestimate even the smallest of God's creatures, children. Come on! Let's see what has happened to the others."

We thought that our luck was out again. We bent over the next nest examining it closely.

"It's gone, Agasha!"

"No, no. It hasn't. It's just sunk down inside the nest. Now, stand back because the ants are going to be very angry. You don't want them to bite you."

She took a stick and cleared the debris from round the neck of the buried bottle. Then she made a quick grab at it and jumped clear of the nest, shaking the bottle from side to side to get rid of as many of the hundreds of ants clinging to its side as she could.

"Look Agasha, you've got ants all over your hand."

"Don't worry, I'll soon settle them." She calmly and systematically flicked the ants away with the forefinger and thumb of her free hand, and brought the bottle over for us to see. There was about half a bottle of clear liquid with hundreds and hundreds of ants floating about in it. Agasha was pleased.

"Not bad, not bad, not at all bad. Nearly half a bottleful." There was great satisfaction in her voice. We found it very hard to share her pleasure.

"It's full of dead ants."

"Ugh, don't they look awful?"

"Just you wait and see." She nodded her head wisely at us.

The remaining bottle was dug out of its anthill in a similar way, and we bore our harvest of dead ants triumphantly back to the cottage. Mama was sitting in the garden reading a book when we crossed towards the kitchen.

"Did you have any luck, Agasha?"

"Oh, yes, Barinya. We did quite well; look!" She picked the two bottles up out of the basket and held them towards Mama, who put up her hands to fend them off, and wrinkled her nose in disgust.

"It's all right, Mama, they won't bite you. They're all dead."

"I know, Moossia. I can see they are. All the same, don't they look horrid?" Her shoulders rose, and she shuddered. "Still, there's quite a bit of liquid there, isn't there, Agasha?"

"Quite a bit, Barinya. We should get a small bottle out of it. I'll do it straight away."

We trooped off to the kitchen and intently watched Agasha as she strained the contents of the bottles through a piece of muslin into a jug. Then she added a quantity of turpentine to the ant liquid from another bottle she got down from a high shelf. As she turned to put the turpentine bottle back onto the shelf, Koka bent over the jug to sniff the contents.

"No, Koka, don't touch it; it's very strong. You know it's for your Papa's back when he comes down to see us tomorrow."

"But doesn't it hurt Papa?"

"No, not really. It makes his back warm, and helps his rheumatism."

Chapter 15

Summer 1916

Aino had set a clutch of eggs under one of his big brown hens a week or so before we came down to Kelomakki, and they were now hatched out and beginning to grow. He had let the hen out of the broody coop in the shelter of the farm, and the chicks were running about with their mother under the trees. She clucked to them all the time, and constantly pecked at the ground, to teach them to fend for themselves. She was a very friendly old hen, and sometimes, especially if we held a few grains of corn in our hands, she would let us stroke her gently, and the chicks would gather round, too.

"Agasha, come and look at the chicks. They've all hatched out now. Aren't they pretty?"

Agasha came over to us with her arms full of washing from the line, and smiled down at the tiny balls of yellow fluff bobbing round us.

"What a proud mother she is. Just you keep an eye on her children for her. They're safe enough when they stay under the trees. It's when they come out into the open, poor little things!"

"But why are they poor little things, Agasha?"

She led us out from under the shade of the pine trees and pointed up into the sky. A kestrel was hovering over the cottage. "Do you see the hawk up there? If he sees the chicks he will drop like a stone out of the sky, and carry one of them off to his own nest."

"I'll tell Papa to shoot him." Koka was indignant.

"Your Papa isn't always here, Koka. I tell you what, if you ever see him going after the chicks, clap your hands, shout, and make a lot of noise. Shoo the hen and her babies back under the trees."

"I'll hit him with my stick!" Agasha stroked his hair gently.

"Hawks have to live, too, Kokochka."

We fully made up our minds to do as Agasha said, and to help the mother hen as much as we could, but of course we weren't in the garden all the time. We did get the impression that there weren't as many chicks as there had been to start with. We tried to count them up a few days later, but we couldn't be sure, because they ran about all the time and you couldn't be certain that you hadn't counted one of them twice, or even three times. So we were horrified when our suspicious were confirmed as we came of the cottage one morning, just in time to see the kestrel swoop down to take one of the chicks in his talons.

We ran towards him, shouting and hallooing as loud as we could, and waving our arms to distract him. We weren't in time to stop him taking the chick, but we did startle him quite a lot, so that he dropped the chick from his claws and wheeled off up into the sky.

We ran over and squatted by the now lifeless little body. To me it was unbearably sad, and tears poured down my cheeks. For once Agasha was not at hand. She had gone down to the village to seek out two young girls who would be willing to come and help in the house when Aunt Fanya and Roonya arrived the following week.

"His eyes are closed, Moossia."

"He's dead, poor little thing."

"Pick him up."

"He's so soft and floppy."

"What shall we do with him?"

"We'll have to give him a proper funeral in our cemetery behind the ice house, with the spiders and the beetles. We'll make him a nice grave."

"He's too big to go with the spiders and the beetles."

"Well, we can't just leave him."

We seemed to have a difficult problem on our hands, and we squatted there side by side, contemplating the chick as I held it in my hand. Luckily, at that moment, Agasha came back from her trip to the village, and she saw us in the garden. Wondering what it was that could claim our attention so intently, she came over to us.

"What's the matter, Moossinka? Why have you been crying?"

Mutely I held out the dead chick for her to see, and burst into tears again. She reached out and stroked my head.

"Don't cry, my little heart. It was the hawk, wasn't it?" I could only nod my head, and gulp. Then I smeared my tears across my face with my free hand, and managed,

"We've got to give him a proper funeral, Agasha."

"Of course we have. Go and get a big leaf from the outside of one of the cabbages in the kitchen garden, and I'll get a trowel from the barn."

We went on our separate errands, and met by unspoken agreement behind the icehouse, on the other side of the pond. Agasha dug a hole in the warm earth beside the graves of the beetles and spiders and butterflies we had laid to rest on previous occasions; the chick was tenderly wrapped in the cabbage leaf, and the little parcel was deposited in the hole. The earth was scraped back and modelled into a little mound.

"He must have a cross, Agasha."

"A cross. Yes, of course. Why not?" She searched about; found a couple of twigs, and bound them round with wisps of grass plucked nearby.

"Should we say a prayer for him, Moossia?" Koka wanted everything just so. But Agasha wasn't prepared to go as far as that.

"No, Koka, I don't think so. We'd better leave the mother hen to do that herself. Let's go indoors."

She took each of us by the hand, and we went back to the cottage, very tear-stained and a little grubby from our grave digging, but feeling ever so much better.

Chapter 16

August 1916

"Fanechka, do at least have some breakfast. Have a glass of tea."

Mama was coaxing Aunt Fanya, who had arrived with Uncle Walter and Roonya the previous week. They usually came down the cottage a week or two after us, and went back sooner. Uncle Walter came down whenever he could, which wasn't all that often, because the hotel was very busy in the summer.

Aunt Fanya was leaning over the table in the garden, her face cupped in her hands, her eyes closed. She was balancing an ice bag, round and lumpy like an old flat cap, on the top of her head. Her face puckered in pain as she feebly waved Mama's suggestion away. She opened her eyes and squinted at the light.

"No, I don't think I will, Lilya. Just forget about me. I would have to get another migraine today. Roonya, finish your egg. Perhaps I'd better go and lie down for a while. I did so want to try out my new camera in the morning light."

"Never mind, Fanya. You'll feel better later on. You can try your camera after lunch."

Koka had been unable to take his eyes off Aunt Fanya ever since she came down with Roonya to join us for breakfast. He could hold it in no longer. "You look just like a mushroom, Aunt Fanya!" he burst out. Mama turned to him crossly.

"Koka, how could you? Don't be so rude. Aunt Fanya feels very poorly."

"It's all right, Lilichka. I think I will go and lie down." She got up and walked slowly into the cottage, holding her head up with the utmost care.

We waited with bated breath, half hoping, half fearing that the ice-bag would fall off; but it just went on wobbling precariously on the top of her head until she went out of sight round the side of the cottage.

That day was a Friday, and we went off into the woods to gather the wild strawberries which were very plentiful at that time. When we came back in the early evening with our baskets full of scented fruit, Aunt Fanya had quite recovered from her migraine. She looked a little pale, but she was full of life and in full cry with her camera. She was lying in wait for us, and had the camera on its tripod pointing in the direction from which we were bound to come. As we crossed the grass she leapt up and dived under the camera's black cloth hood, waving at us with a free hand.

"Stand just there, children. Roonya, go to the other side of Agasha. That's right." She emerged from the hood. "Stand quite still. Smile." She removed the lens cover. "One, two, three." She put the lens cover back. "Koka, you moved! Never mind, I'll do another one. Just a moment while I change the plate." And she dived under the hood again. But she was interrupted.

"Whee-whoo, whee-whoo!" Papa's well-known whistle came loud and clear from the direction of the station. We ignored Aunt Fanya's despairing "Children, children, wait, wait!" and we ran as hard as we could down the sandy path and through the gate to meet Papa just as he was crossing the plank bridge over the ditch on the other side of the road.

Anya and Dasha, the two girls Agasha had gone down the village to engage, were already busy about the table in the garden, dressed in their long white aprons, setting it for the evening meal. Koka and I were allowed to stay up and share supper with all the others. Agasha carried out the bubbling samovar and Aunt Fanya took over the pouring of the tea.

"Do you want jam or sugar in your tea, Kokochka?"

"Jam, please, lots and lots of jam… and bread and butter and cheese and sausage…"

"Greedy guts!" jeered Roonya. Aunt Fanya rounded on him.

"Now stop it, Roonya. Don't use those words. I don't know where you pick up these expressions."

The sun went down late at that time of the year and the evening was a very long one. We took several hours over our supper and Agasha filled up the samovar more than once. The air was very still when dusk began to fall at last, stirred by only the slightest occasional breaths of wind which carried to us all the rich perfumes of high summer, of the roses in the garden nearby, of the pine trees in the woods all around us, with an occasional whiff of newly carried hay from the more distant fields where the peasants were still working to take advantage of the last shreds of daylight. Aino had come round to shut up the hen and her remaining chicks and shield them from all the perils and dangers of the coming night. Two dogs were barking a duet down in the village. The only activity round the table was a hand reaching out leisurely for a glass of tea, or more sharply to slap at one of the mosquitoes which were coming out to begin their nightly prowl. Papa turned to Mama,

"Oh, Lilichka, I almost forgot to tell you. Mamochka says she will be able to get away from the factory for a few days soon. She will come down with me next weekend."

"Will she bring us something?" Koka came to life.

"You know she always does."

"I'll pick her some flowers for her room. I'll pick her lots and lots of buttercups. She likes buttercups. She told me so." I couldn't let this go unchallenged.

"And I'll pick her a whole basket full of strawberries."

Silence gently fell about us as we sat round the table and darkness folded us in its arms. Papa got up with Koka in his arms and took a few steps towards the verandah, calling softly,

"Anya! Da-a-sha!"

"They've gone back to the village. I sent them home an hour ago, Karloosha," commented Aunt Fanya. "It's always so much nicer when we're here just by ourselves."

"Oh, well then, Agasha, perhaps you'd go and get the lamp out of the dining- room. You can hardly see a hand before you out here." But before Agasha could get up Mama intervened,

"Oh, no, Karloosha, no. The lamp will bring every mosquito in the neighbourhood down on us. We shall be eaten alive. The moon will be up soon. You can see it over the trees there. Look!"

Papa took his seat again and we watched the full moon slowly edge its way over the pine trees. Mama started to hum the tune of a waltz under her breath and Papa and Aunt Fanya picked it up. As they hummed their bodies swayed in time with the music of the dance. The tune faded away and silence came over us again. Koka's head had fallen against Papa's shoulder. He was fast asleep. Aunt Fanya leaned over and examined him closely.

"I think someone I know is ready for his bed."

Moossia

The following week saw the start of the serious berry-picking season. The usual routines were quite abandoned, and we all set off into the forest after breakfast as soon as the dew was gone, with our baskets, to bring in the berry harvest for jam making.

Our first target was the strawberries, to be followed by the raspberries. We returned to the cottage with aching backs and laden baskets. We'd all sit round the table in the garden and pick over the fruit to get rid of the bits of leaf and stalk, helping ourselves liberally to the rosy berries; and then Agasha, with her sleeves rolled right up, and with Mama in supervision, would spend all the afternoon stirring the jam with an enormous wooden spoon, in a great copper jam-kettle over the kitchen range.

There was endless fascination for us in the baskets of firm little fruits, the piles of broken sugar and the rows of shining glass jars warming on the rack above the range. We got under everybody's feet, and were being constantly chased out into the garden, only to come back again a few moments later to carry away as our legitimate prizes the saucers of froth skimmed off the top of the boiling jam. We'd cool the steaming froth by blowing on it, and then dip our fingers into the sticky mess and lick them clean, with eyes closed in rapture.

If there were more berries than could be turned into jam on that particular day, they would be made into kissel for our breakfast next morning. Later, we did the same thing with bilberries, and after that we went out to get the red berries which could be turned into a jelly for eating with meat. Then there was the crop of white mushrooms to garner. Aino made me a special flat basket out of birch bark, so that the mushrooms wouldn't pile up and get bruised before we took them home to be threaded like beads on string and hung up over the range to dry for use next winter.

But in strawberry week, before we knew where we were, it was Friday again. Koka came in with arms full of buttercups, which Agasha helped him to arrange in vases all over Granny's room, so that it began to look like a meadow itself. I made a special expedition to get her a basket of strawberries. Then it was time to go down to the station to meet her. She waved to us through the window as her carriage passed where we were standing, and we ran down to the spot where she would get off the train. Her tiny, buxom figure stepped lightly down on to the sandy bit of the platform.

"Babooshka! Babooshka!" Koka was so excited that he jumped in the air over and over again, and he flung his arms round her neck with such enthusiasm when she bent down to kiss us, that Granny staggered slightly, and Agasha and Mama ran forward to support her.

"Careful, careful, children. You'll have Granny over." The old lady straightened up and adjusted her hat. She gave Mama a kiss, and smiled at Agasha.

"Now let me have a good look at you. How well you all look. You too, Lilichka! Now then…" She put her free hand into the handbag slung over her other arm and looked at Agasha, who was quite ready for the little comedy about to be played.

"Good day, Agasha."

"Good day, Barinya." They were both smiling at a secret joke which was a secret to nobody.

"Tell me something, Agasha."

"Yes, Barinya."

"Have the children been good?"

"Oh, yes, Barinya, very good."

"Well, in that case…" Two bars of chocolate appeared out of the handbag and were ceremoniously presented to us. "Koka. Moossia."

"Isn't anybody going to say hello to me?" Papa's voice came a little plaintively from a few steps behind Granny. Koka and I flew to his arms.

"Papachka, Papachka!" In the midst of his embrace I suddenly gave a wild shriek of laughter.

"What is the matter, Moossinka?"

"It's your moustache, Papa. It's ever so tickly." Everybody joined in the laughter, and we all went hand in hand back to the cottage.

That evening, as were sitting round the table in the garden having supper, Papa made an announcement.

"I think we ought to do something special to celebrate Babooshka's visit. I'm sure you will all agree?"

"What do you have in mind, Karloosha?"

"I thought we might all go on a crayfish excursion tomorrow night."

There was great enthusiasm for this idea, and Koka nearly pulled the tablecloth off the table. Everybody else made a quick grab to prevent disaster.

"Now, what about the frogs?" Papa wanted to know. "Are there any frogs in the pond?"

"Oh, yes, Papa, lots and lots. I'll help you to catch them."

"So will I!" "So will I!" There was no shortage of volunteers. Mama wasn't at all happy about this aspect of our intended trip.

"Do you have to catch the crayfish with frogs, Karloosha?"

"We always have, Lilichka."

"It's such a messy business. I hate the idea of you having to skin them all."

"There's no better way to catch crayfish, Lilichka. Don't you worry your head about it. Leave it all to the children and me." He was in high spirits.

After supper, Papa and Koka and Roonya and I went down to the pond with a basket. We caught the frogs and gave them to Papa, who held them by their long hind legs and smacked their heads smartly against a large stone, to kill them. I didn't like that very much, and turned my eyes away when he did it. Then the dead frogs were dropped into the basket to be skinned later on. We were packed off to bed especially early that evening, as we always had to go after the crayfish at night, and it meant that we would be home very late the following night.

When it was time for us to set out, Papa came driving up to the gate with Aino's little cart which he had borrowed for the occasion. We loaded it with travelling rugs to sit on, a basket with soup plates and a loaf of black bread, and the basket with the skinned frogs in it, covered with a cloth out of regard for Mama's feelings. Most important of all, the black cauldron in which the crayfish would be cooked, and the four wicker pots to catch them in.

Koka and I sat in the middle of the cart with our feet tucked under us, and Granny sat up in the front with Papa, and Roonya and Mama sat sideways with their feet dangling down. Aunt Fanya wasn't very well again, and Agasha was staying behind to look after her. I tried to get Papa to bring Agasha too, but he was very firm, and I just had to put up with going without her.

It was quite a long way to the river where the crayfish were, but the distance was totally lost on me. The lighthearted chatter and the magic of the journey along the rough track through woods and fields in the failing light robbed me of all sense of time.

"This is the place." We had reached a little clearing by the edge of the river, and we all tumbled off the cart. The little horse had to be unharnessed and tethered by a long rope to a tree, so that it could nibble at the short grass. The travelling rug was spread out for Mama, and then the serious business of the night began. Papa naturally took command.

"Koka and Moossia. I want you to get all the sticks and pinecones you can find, and make a big heap of them just here. Roonya, you can help me set the pots." Roonya and he took the four pots and the basket of frogs down to the riverbank, and we heard them setting the pots out as we carried sticks and cones to the spot Papa had chosen for the fire.

"I'll put two frogs in each pot to start with, Roonya. Now you hold on to the string and I'll hook the pot onto the end of this stick, and get it well into the stream. That's right. Now we can tie the string to this bit of root here, and then it will be ready for us to pull in when we think there are crayfish in the pots."

When the pots were ready, Papa got a few handfuls of dried moss and started the fire, which was soon blazing away. It didn't take him long to find three sticks and lash them into a tripod, and then to fill the cauldron with water from the stream, and hang it by a bit of chain over the fire.

"Now all we have to do is wait!"

By now it was quite dark, and we gathered round the fire and fed it with more cones and sticks. The flames threw weird shadows onto the trees round the clearing. There were rustling sounds from the movement of small animals in the undergrowth. A bird cried out indignantly as something disturbed it in the branches. A fish jumped in the stream, and fell back with a plopping noise. Granny, on the opposite side of the fire from me, in her dark skirt and blouse, merged into the dusky background and was just a bright face and a pair of hands held out to the warmth of the fire. Mama, on the other hand, in her light-coloured dress and coloured scarf round her shoulders, gleamed like a jewel in the flickering light. Roonya and I were feeding the fire, which sizzled and flared under the cauldron. He was impatient to get back to the stream.

"Do you think the crayfish have found the frogs yet, Uncle?" Papa pulled the watch out of his waistcoat pocket, and turned its face towards the fire.

"I think we ought to wait just a little longer, Roonya."

"Tell us the story about when you got chased by wolves, Papa," begged Koka.

"Oh, Koka, you must all know that story by heart. I've told you so often."

"That doesn't matter. Tell us again."

Papa picked up a stick and poked the fire, looking into the flames as if he could see in them all the adventures of his youthful days. Nobody spoke. Nobody moved.

"Once upon a time, years ago, before any of you children had been born, I was staying with some friends who lived in a big forest in Poland. It was in the very depths of winter, and the snow was very deep. I was driving home in a sleigh from the town late one afternoon, through the forest, which I didn't know very well, and I took the wrong turning. By the time I realised I was on the wrong road, and turned back to pick up the right turning, I was much later than I meant to be, and it was already getting dark. There was a long way still to go, and there were no houses before the one where I was staying, so I just had to keep on going. The winter had been very hard, and there were stories in the neighbourhood of a pack of starving wolves roaming the forest. I suppose I was just over halfway to my destination when my horse suddenly pricked up his ears and, without any prompting from me, started to move faster. I knew that something was wrong, and strained my own ears and eyes to find out what it was. Sure enough, after a few minutes I could hear the howling of wolves some way behind us on the track.

"I didn't have to use the whip on the horse because he was galloping quite quickly of his own accord and I didn't want him to get exhausted as there was still a long way to go, but I kept glancing back to see what was happening behind us. This wasn't easy, as the sleigh was bounding about on the track, and it was getting very dark. Then I could see those grey shapes leaping after us, getting nearer and nearer.

"Now I was really frightened, and took my whip and gave the horse a couple of good smart cuts. It went faster and faster, and soon it was covered in sweat, in spite of the freezing weather. The wolves got slowly closer and closer. I did have my shotgun with me, but when I looked for the cartridges I couldn't find the box. It must have jerked off the sleigh onto the road some way back when we hit a bad rut. I felt about in the bearskin rug over my knees, and managed to find two cartridges which had spilled out of the box before it was lost. I loaded my gun. Then I tied the reins to the front of the sleigh, trusting the horse to continue on its way without my help, and I turned round and lay in the sleigh to take aim at the wolves. When I thought they were near enough I fired my first barrel – but the sleigh jerked just at that moment, and my shot went clean over their heads. I had only one shot left. What could I do? My horse was already very tired and I knew we would never outrun the wolves. So I just waited, and I let the wolves come nearer and nearer. Eventually I could hear the panting of their breath and see the gleam in their eyes. I couldn't leave it any longer; I fired the second barrel of my shotgun, my last cartridge, remember.

"I hit the leading wolf square in the chest, and he rolled over and over in the snow. The other wolves in the pack fell upon him at once, and there was a lot of barking and snarling as we pulled away from them. I untied the reins from the front of the sleigh, and desperately whipped the horse on. I thought I saw a light ahead of us, but I was so tired and scared that I couldn't be sure. The pack of wolves had not stayed behind very long to feast on their leader. They were still chasing behind us, and catching up, too. Then I could see that there really was a light further along the track but as the light came nearer so the wolves came nearer. The horse gave one final effort. People came out with lanterns to meet us. We swept through the stable yard gate – and the wolves fell back. We had reached home."

Granny was looking at Papa with a slightly quizzical smile, but Koka's eyes were round as saucers, and he and Roonya and I had all drawn closer to the fire, and to each other.

"And now," laughed Papa cheerfully, "now Roonya and I will go and have a look at the crayfish pots. No, you two stay by the fire," as we got up to follow, "It's pitch dark down there. You might slip and fall in the river."

We heard them talking in the darkness as they gathered the crayfish and re-baited the pots and set them back in the stream. Then they came back into the firelight with a basket half full of wriggling crayfish.

"Is the water boiling yet? Good. Then here we go!" The crayfish dropped into the boiling water with a hiss and a bubble.

"Get the plates, children; they won't take very long."

Granny took over at this point, and soon she was ladling the reddish-brown cooked crayfish out of the cauldron onto the soup plates. We all sat round the fire, gingerly cracking the crayfish open and sucking out the sweet flesh, without restraint. We mopped up the liquor with pieces of black bread. The shells went straight onto the fire, where they crackled and popped and sizzled. Every so often Papa would go down to the stream and come back with some more crayfish. In the end we could eat no more and Koka, as usual, had fallen asleep. Granny went round us children, mopping up our hands and faces with a cloth brought along specially for that purpose.

"Look, there are still some left in the cauldron."

"Never mind, we'll take them back home. They're very nice cold."

"I don't want to go home yet."

"Moossinka, we must go. Think of Agasha waiting up for us."

Papa harnessed the little horse to the cart, and the wicker pots were recovered, dripping wet, from the stream. At the last moment, when everything had been packed up and we were all on the cart, Papa unhooked the cauldron and tipped the water onto the fire. There was a great hiss and a cloud of steam as the fire went out, and the blackness seemed complete about us. However, the moon was just rising, and there was enough light for Papa to drive us back to the cottage. I sat on the cart with my eyes closed, trying to preserve as long as possible the picture of us all sitting round the fire eating crayfish, with the cauldron bubbling between us.

I felt no end of a pioneer.

Papa started to whistle softly, and Granny joined in quietly, singing

Nightingale, my, nightingale
Sweet singing nightingale,
Where are you flying to?
Where will you sing all night?
Who will be listening to you,
Closing their eyes in tears,
Sorrowful as I am?
Fly, fly away, my nightingale.
Even beyond many worlds,
Beyond blue seas,
To strange shores,
Dwelling in countless lands,
In strange villages and foreign towns,
Never will you find a heart
More sorrowful than mine.

Chapter 17

Autumn 1916

It was a day when nothing much seemed to be happening. We had gathered all the fruits and mushrooms we could and they had all been bottled or dried or turned into jam for us take back to St. Petersburg. The mushrooms had been hung up on strings and turned into little pieces of wrinkled leather.

The three of us were sitting together by the pond whiling away the time and doing nothing in particular. Koka and I were wearing our shirts and socks and sandals because the days were getting colder and the surface of the water in the pond was generously dotted with brown and yellow leaves. We were very still and not talking when, in the silence around us, we became aware of a steady beating, swishing sound. Koka pricked up his ears.

"Feeuw, feeuw, feeuw." The noise went on and on.

"What's that funny noise, Agasha?" he asked.

"It's the storks, the storks, my little one. You can hear the sound of their wings. They're going off to their winter home."

"But where are they? I can't see them." We all searched the sky with our eyes. Agasha, of course, saw them first.

"There! There! Above the trees." She pointed towards the North.

"Yes, yes, I can see them now. One, two, three, four." The little procession passed over our heads flying with the same steady beat of their wings and disappeared into the southern sky. A feeling of sadness came over us.

"Feeuw, feeuw, feeuw, feeuw, feeuw."

Koka was the first to speak.

"Where are they flying to, Agasha?"

"Over the steppes, over the mountains, over the sea, Koka, to the land where the sun is always shining, so they say," she sighed. "When the storks are flying it means that the summer is really over. When the storks are flying it's time for us to go back to St. Petersburg."

"Do we have to? Why can't we just stay here?"

"Merciful heavens! We couldn't possibly stay here all the winter. Your Mama must have warmth and comfort. She would be bored to tears here."

"You're never bored here, Agasha."

"Ah, but Agasha has so much to do, my little dove. I don't have time to think of being bored, do I? Up you jump. The ground is getting damp and it's getting dark, too. Look how black the water in the pond is getting. The night clouds are coming over."

"Feeuw, feeuw, feeuw." Koka flapped his arms slowly, remembering the storks, as we walked slowly back to the cottage. Then he slipped his hand into Agasha's confidingly.

"Agasha, can I sleep with the lamp on tonight? It feels so dark when you go out of the room."

"Your Mama doesn't allow it, Kokochka, you know that. The fumes from the lamp spoil the air you breathe when you're asleep. If you feel frightened, just turn your head and look out of the window. Look up at the sky. God will be watching over you. His eyes are everywhere."

"Yes, I know, but you can't see them. All the trees get in the way."

"I'm not far away."

"Yes, I know, but…"

"I tell you what. I'll put the lamp on a table in the passage and leave the door open. How about that?"

Koka was quite satisfied with this suggestion, let go of Agasha's hand and ran ahead of us to the verandah where Mama was sitting in the warmth left by the sun. She looked up from her embroidery as Agasha closed the door after we had come in.

"We shall have to start thinking of packing, Agasha, shan't we?"

The three of us looked at each other and smiled knowingly. Mama did another stitch and went on,

"Tell Aino to bring the luggage in from the barn tomorrow. He'd better bring it in for the Barin upstairs at the same time."

"He did, yesterday, Barinya"

"O-o-oh, did he? It must have been when I was out for my walk. That's good. They want to leave before us as soon as Uncle Walter comes down from St. Petersburg to fetch them."

The following day we had one of our few really rainy days that summer. It came down quite hard and we couldn't go out. Aino brought in the luggage from the barn during the morning and the verandah was full once more of trunks and skips and suitcases and baskets and the packing began in real earnest. The verandah became our playground and we made endless train journeys and hunted down innumerable bears, much to the hindrance of the busy packers.

"I don't like the rain. It means we have to stay indoors."

Agasha never let a remark like that pass.

"You mustn't talk like that, Moossinka. Rain is a blessing from God. I'm surprised at you."

"Agasha," Mama instructed, "we'd better leave the children's galoshes out. It looks as though we might need them. Just look at the weather. It's simply pelting down."

"It won't last long, Barinya. The clouds are beginning to break up. But I'll do as you say, of course."

"What shall we do with all the jam?"

"We'd better take it with us, Barinya. The jars may get broken if we send them in advance."

"Yes, you're quite right. We must make sure we get it all home safely. Barin says things are getting very scarce in the shops."

At one point Koka disappeared completely for a while and Mama went from room to room calling his name. She was getting quite agitated as she always did whenever there was the slightest hint of any harm coming to him. She finally burst into the verandah with an armful of dresses to be packed, and was in quite a panic.

"Koka! Koka! Where are you? Koka! Koka!"

One of the skips began to shake and heave and up popped Koka like a Jack-in-a-box. "Here I am, Mama!" She was quite cross.

"You naughty boy! Come out of there at once." Koka obediently climbed out of the skip, wondering what all the fuss was about.

"It's all right, Mama. I'm all right. I was only playing hide-and-seek with Moossia."

"Don't do that again, Koka. It's very dangerous."

"Why is it dangerous, Mama?"

"You might have got locked in there. You might have suffocated. Remember the story of the Mistletoe Bough." I did my best to calm things down.

"Come on, Koka. Papa's chess set hasn't been packed yet. Let's go and play Goats and Wolf."

"I don't want to play Goats and Wolf with you. Papa has shown you all the tricks. You always win."

"Moossinka, pass me that long rod for the skip, will you?"

"Let me push it through the loops, will you? Let me!"

"All right. Careful now. Clever. Now Agasha can padlock it and tie the label on. I think Aino could fetch the advance luggage for the afternoon train, Agasha."

Soon after lunch Aino was at the door with his horse and cart. The morning's activities had been too much for Mama. She was lying down in her bedroom with a headache. She suffered a lot with headaches. So Agasha was in charge again as she so often was.

"Agasha, can we ride on the cart to the station?"

"Why not? I have to go down myself to make sure they sign the receipts for the bags." The cart was piled high and there was barely room for us. "Up you get then, Koka. Don't let your legs dangle like that. Tuck them in. You'll catch them in the wheels."

"There isn't any room for you, Agasha."

"Never mind, Moossinka. I'll just walk down with Aino."

We set off slowly, jerking from side to side in the rutted lane. Aino was wearing his old straw hat full of holes and led the way at the horse's head. Agasha walked a little way behind the cart with an eagle eye on the baggage. Every now and then she would leap forward to give a push to a case or a box which showed signs of slipping from the load. Aino called to Agasha in broken Russian from his place at the horse's head.

"When are your lady and gentleman leaving, Agasha?"

"In a day or two."

"It's going to be a hard winter for everyone. Things aren't what they used to be…"

"Things are always changing down here on earth. But they don't change up above in the sky and that's all that matters."

"If you say so." Neither Aino nor his horse were feeling very lively that afternoon and they had almost slowed down to a standstill. Agasha wanted to speed things up.

"Can't you get your horse to go a bit faster, Aino?"

Aino clicked at the horse with his tongue a few times and jerked at the bridle. The horse woke up and the cart gave a lurch and we had to hold on for dear life but within a dozen yards or so that moment of excitement petered out, the horse seemed to doze off again, and once more we were moving in slow motion.

The "station" seemed totally deserted when we got there as it usually was, but we did find an old man half asleep in the sun, which had come out again, slumped in a chair on the other side of the little station building. It took him ages as he laboriously filled out the forms for the luggage to Agasha's satisfaction so that we could all four pile back into the cart and plod slowly back to the cottage.

A day or two later Papa came down from St. Petersburg to take us home. Agasha spread white sheets over all the furniture and we all sat quietly for a few moments, as was our custom, before starting out on the journey. This time, when Mama got up to leave, there was no wild rush on our part to leave. Without speaking a word we said goodbye to the pond, the barn, and the cottage and the garden. We touched the pine trees and the birch trees and even the clumps of heather, so that they would remember us, as we walked through the wood. The wooden planks which made up the minute platform of Kelomakki "station" seemed to give us sympathetic farewell squeaks. Every little thing that happened was a stage of a journey on which there was no turning back. Worst of all was when the train appeared in the distance and, with no regard for our feelings, simply raced into Kelomakki, only too eager to hurry us back to St. Petersburg. Our feet were like lead as we stepped into the train and we craned out of the window to catch a last glimpse as we drew away. Then the silver thread binding us to our magical summer dream seemed to snap. After this had happened things didn't seem quite so bad.

The hard wooden benches were crowded with families like ours, returning from a long summer in the country. The train stopped at every tiny settlement and was immediately besieged by crowds of peasants hawking their wares.

"Whites, whites!" Meaning white mushrooms.

There were old men with long grey beards, young, flaxen-haired boys whose shrill voices could be clearly heard above the general hubbub, and young peasant women carrying heavy baskets of produce and surrounded by barefoot children holding onto their skirts.

The crowded carriages, the frequent stops, people getting in and out of the train, and the many-times repeated fairground atmosphere at every station, gave nobody any chance to settle down and sleep as they had done on our journey out. It had been sad to leave Kelomakki but, all the same, we had a sense of some elation as we got nearer to St. Petersburg.

"Look Mama, look, Koka! Wave! Wave! There are some children over there by the edge of the trees. They are waving at us! Wave! Wave!"

There was another Koka drama. He suddenly pulled back from the window with his hands up to his face, and in tears.

"My eye! My eye! I've got something in my eye! Mama-a."

"Kokochka, let Mama see it. No! Don't rub it. Take your hands away. Merciful Lord, I hope it's not a spark from the engine. Mama told you not to lean out of the window. Agasha, will you close it? It would happen when Barin has gone out for a smoke." Agasha had stayed quite calm and was looking closely at Koka's eye.

"It's all right, Barinya. It's nothing, nothing, really. It's not a spark. It's only a little fly in his eye. There. It's all right. Don't worry. Don't worry, Barinya. Don't worry, Koka." Bad news travels fast and Papa came hurrying down the coach in some alarm.

"What's the matter? What's happened? Someone came out to tell me my little boy has had an accident."

"Everything's all right, Karloosha. Really it is. He just got something in his eye, it was just a fly. Go back and finish your cigar." Another storm in a teacup passed over our heads.

Soon the train began to rattle and sway as it snaked its way over the points outside St. Petersburg. Looking out of the window we could see the Admiralty Spire and the cupola of St. Isaak's Cathedral. Then we drew slowly into the pink and grey Finland station and stopped with a final jerk and clashing of buffers which clanged down the length of the train. The station was crowded and Papa jumped down quickly to get a porter as Agasha ferried luggage to the end of the carriage. A burly man in a green apron tied round his middle with string came up in answer to his cries.

"Here's the luggage. Can you manage it all?" asked Papa.

"Oh, yes, Barin. No trouble." He tucked a case under each arm and then bent his knees first to one side and then to the other to take up another case in each hand. He was just about to spread the fingers of one enormous hand to include Mama's hatbox in his immense grasp when Mama picked it up herself quite quickly.

"No, it's all right. I'll take that one myself. It's very precious."

"We shall need two cabs."

"Yes, Barin. Mind your backs, there. Mind you backs." Like an icebreaker he opened a path for us through the dense crowd hurrying for the exit and we hurried to keep close to him so that the crowd wouldn't close in behind him and cut us off from our belongings.

One old peasant woman had already come to grief at the hands of the uncaring crowd. The knotted shawl which held all her luggage had come undone and everything, boots, spare clothes, onions, potatoes had scattered in all directions. She was desperately trying to get all her possessions together on the shawl. Nobody moved to help her. Indeed her distress was only made worse by two ragged urchins who were kicking her onions and potatoes out of her reach.

We came out of the station and stood waiting for the cabs.

"Papa, look, there's a man on wheels!"

"Shush, Moossinka, don't point," said Papa. "The poor man has lost both legs."

"Give him some money, Agasha." Mama was very upset at the sight of this unfortunate man. Agasha went over and dropped some coins into his outstretched cap.

"From the Barinya over there."

"God bless her and her children," we heard him say.

"Agasha, why hasn't he got any legs?" I whispered.

"Merciful Heavens. Questions, always questions. It's the war, my precious. It's the war."

The two cabs came up and Papa saw all the luggage stowed in the second one, and tipped the porter, who doffed his cap and turned and disappeared into the crowd.

"Now Moossia and Koka will come in the first cab with Mama and me, and Agasha can follow us in the second cab."

The four of us settled into the first cab, sitting so that we were facing the driver's back. I got up and turned round to make sure that Agasha was not being left behind.

"Off you go, driver."

The cabdriver flicked his whip; the little horse trotted off and the cab bumped along the cobbled street.

"I feel cold," said Koka. So Papa unrolled the waterproof cover clipped under the driver's seat and fastened it on either side of the passenger seat so that it made a protective apron practically up to Koka' chin. For a while the horse trotted on and we looked about us contentedly. Then, as we were going down one of the main boulevards we became aware of an enormous crowd of people marching down it towards us. They were singing at the tops of their voices and waving scores of flags.

"Look Mama, red flags. Aren't they pretty? What are they singing?"

The driver gave a shout, jerked sharply on the reins and swung the cab off into a side street. Mama turned anxiously to Papa. "Karloosha, why is he taking us this way?"

The driver must have heard what Mama said. He half turned in his seat, "It's another demonstration, Barinya. Better to give them a wide berth." I was not satisfied.

"But why can't we see them, Mama? There are so many flags and they are so pretty." Mama's face had gone quite white.

"Red ribbons today, red blood tomorrow."

"Aren't you feeling well, Mama?"

"No, Moossinka, not very well. Just sit still for a little while longer."

"Don't worry too much, Lilichka. This sort of thing goes on practically every day. I've got quite used to it by now." He tried to explain to me. "You know, Moossinka, Mama doesn't like crowds." Mama continued to be very agitated.

"Is Agasha's cab behind us?"

"Yes, Mama, I can see it."

"Drive faster, driver; but don't lose the other cab, whatever you do."

When the cab stopped outside our apartment block Papa behaved very oddly. He was quite unlike his usual, leisurely smiling self. He jumped quickly out of the cab, and made for the main door. As he sensed that we were about to get out, too, and follow him, he turned and raised one hand like a policeman stopping the traffic.

"No, don't get out. Stay where you are for a few moments." He rang the bell, waited a short while, and then, since Egor didn't make his customary prompt appearance, fumbled in an inside pocket and unlocked the door with his own key. Then he turned to us and motioned rapidly.

"Come on quickly. Don't waste time."

We scurried across the pavement, and through the door.

"Now go straight up to the apartment."

"But where's Egor?" Mama asked.

"I don't know. Never mind about that now. Get upstairs. Agasha and I will see to the luggage." As we ran upstairs we heard him talking, first to the cabman and then to Agasha, who had obviously arrived just behind us. There was the sound of hurrying feet down below, and the thump, thump of luggage being dropped hastily at the bottom of the stairs. Then the great front door slammed, and by that time Masha was answering our own ring at the door of our apartment. She was wreathed in smiles, and delighted to see us. Koka remembered what she had said to him as we left.

"Do you know me, Masha? Have I grown?" he asked. At the same time Mama questioned her anxiously.

"What has happened to Egor, Masha? Why didn't he answer the door?"

Masha was hard put to it to answer them both.

"Yes, Koka. I don't know Barinya. You've grown ever so much. He hasn't been here all day, Barinya."

Papa and Agasha came through the door laden with the luggage from the second cab, and quite out of breath from the effort of carrying it up all the stairs.

Koka and I flung off our coats and raced off together to the nursery. We hadn't seen most of our toys for four months, and they seemed new and exciting to us.

That evening we were having a bit of a concert, perhaps to celebrate our return home. I was marching up and down banging noisily on the toy side drum hung around my neck, and Koka was blowing full blast on a toy trumpet which Uncle Walter had given him the Christmas before. Agasha was used to the noise, and was quietly putting away the things she had unpacked. Papa came unexpectedly into the room with his finger to his lips.

"Sh-h-h-h, children, please! Please don't make quite so much noise. Mamachka isn't feeling well. She has a migraine and has gone to bed early." Then he patted our heads affectionately and turned to Agasha. "Agasha, I'd like to have a word with you. I'll be in my study." Agasha put down the things in her hands.

"I'll come straight away, Barin." And she followed him out of the room.

We were quite happy to be left alone for a while. There were still lots of toys we hadn't yet got round to saying hello to; but Agasha did seem to be away for a very long time and, eventually, I went to look for her. I was on the point of pushing open the door of Papa's study, which was already slightly ajar, when an unusually serious tone in Papa's voice made me stop.

"You see how difficult things are getting, Agasha."

"Yes, Barin, I do. I understand."

"Barinya isn't very strong, you know. I don't want to upset her."

"I'll keep my mouth shut. I won't say anything to worry her. You can be sure of that, Barin."

"I know I can rely on you, Agasha. But I'm afraid the situation may get even worse."

"We'll be able to manage, you'll see, Barin."

"I hope we can, Agasha, I do hope we can. Remember, if we run short of paraffin or flour, Masha will tell you. Let me know, and for the present, I shall be able to get some through the factory."

"And I can get up extra early and go out in the morning before the children are awake, to do the queuing and the shopping. So don't you worry, Barin. Just you tell me what you want me to do, and I'll do it."

"I know you will, Agasha. Thank you. Remember, if there are any problems, come straight to me. Now you'd better get back to the children. They'll be wondering…"

I flew back to the nursery, asking myself what it was all about.

Chapter 18

October 1916

That autumn was very different from the other autumns we had known in St. Petersburg. Egor reappeared downstairs as mysteriously as he had disappeared in the first place and we were never told what he had been doing while he was away. Mama and Papa were not their usual selves. They clearly had many thoughts we didn't know about. Perhaps it had something to do with the sounds of shouting and singing in the distant streets, which we could sometimes hear in the apartment even behind the double glazing.

Some weeks Mama refused point blank to let us go out for our usual walk with Agasha. Even when we did go, it was never very far, just down the Avenue, perhaps as far as the River Neva but that was all. On the other hand, Agasha did go out as she had promised Papa she would, very early in the morning. She'd take her shopping basket to see what she could buy. Often she came back halfway through the morning and often she was empty-handed.

But she was always very cheerful with us and behaved as if nothing at all was wrong. As we didn't go out much she was very busy keeping us occupied and contented. We started to make our Christmas presents and Christmas decorations particularly early that year.

For several days on end the nursery lost its calm and tidy atmosphere and became an enterprising workshop. Our efforts were beset by weighty problems. I was making a picture for Mama on a piece of cardboard.

"Agasha, I don't know what I'm going to do. My picture won't come right. The house just doesn't look right, and the Christmas tree looks as though it's going to fall over!"

"Don't worry, Moossinka. Some trees in the forest are just like that."

"But it won't do for Mama. Show me your picture, Koka."

"I've wrapped it up. It's been ready for ages."

"I don't believe you, you fibber. You're telling stories. You haven't even started."

We struggled heroically with our different tasks. Koka was cutting out strips of red and green paper, sticking them into loops and making long snakes to hang up in the nursery. He got a lot of the paste on himself and often the strips of paper decided it was easier to stick to Koka than to themselves. He would look to Agasha for help. She would smile and patiently wipe his hands clean so that he could sticky himself up all over again.

"Agasha, what can I do for Uncle Fedya?"

"You've got the poem you've been learning."

"It's too long."

"Do the first bit."

"Mmmmm. Yes, all right. I mean something extra."

"Sing him a little song."

"I'd be too shy. Well, all right. I'll think about it."

Then there was the very complicated business of preparing the walnuts for the Christmas tree.

"I want to paint them this year."

"Better not, Kokochka. Your Papa says the paint is poisonous. The gold and silver, I mean. I'd better do the painting and you can get the matchsticks ready."

"Oh all right. Will you hang the string up on the radiator so that we can put them up to dry?"

"There we are. Now, Koka, you can give me the matchsticks. I'll sharpen them and you can push them into the soft ends of the walnuts. Then Moossia can tie the loops of cotton on to the matchsticks. I'll paint them and hang them over the radiator to dry."

"When we put them on the tree, let's not put them too near the candles. I don't like it when they have wax all over them." Koka was having the last word.

As we got ready for bed the urgent question of what to do for Uncle Fedya was still on my mind.

"Agasha, if I make a sewing picture for Uncle Fedya, will you make the holes for me?"

"Of course I will. We'll talk about it all tomorrow. Come along now, bedtime."

"Goodnight, Agasha, goodnight."

"Sleep with God. May the Almighty protect you."

Moossia

Chapter 19

Christmas 1916

It had been decided by the family that we would go to Uncle Fedya's and Aunt Rosa's this year for the Christmas celebrations, and on Christmas Eve I overheard Mama giving detailed instructions to Agasha about what we should wear.

"It's bitterly cold outside, Agasha, and we shall be coming back very late, so you must see to it that the children are wrapped up as warmly as can be."

"Don't worry, Barinya. I'll see to it."

"If Moossia doesn't want to wear her muff, see that she wears her mittens. Koka, too. They must have their fur hats with the ear flaps, their padded winter coats, the long gaiters and fur-lined bootees."

Agasha knew all this perfectly well. She'd done it all before many times. But she answered patiently,

"Yes, Barinya, of course. And I'll get Koka to gargle with salt water before we leave, just in case."

"I think that would be very wise, Agasha. Barin and I are going with the old Barinya and Aunt Dorothea. They will pick us up on their way. Tell Egor to make arrangements for you and the children to leave at five o'clock."

"Yes, I'll do that, Barinya."

We were fully dressed in our party clothes just before five o'clock when Egor came up to tell us that there was a sledge waiting for us at the door. We ran down eagerly in front of Agasha who was carrying a basket with all the Christmas presents we had made. To our delight Egor had managed to get a "Vanka" for us. As we burst out of the main door on to the pavement we must have startled the horse because it jerked its head and started to move forward.

"Tr-r-r-r-r," said the driver, who had been standing by the sledge stamping his feet and swinging his arms across his body to keep himself warm. He was so muffled up that you could hardly see his eyes, which squinted out between his fur hat and the scarf wrapped tightly round his neck. He made a grab for the reins which had been lying loosely across the driving seat.

"Tr-r-r-r," he went, and the horse stood quite still.

"Vankas" were very small and were really intended for two passengers but there was room for the three of us as Egor had known there would be. When Agasha sat in the middle with her arms round us there was plenty of space. The driver bent over kindly to wrap the bearskin rug round our legs but Agasha, who took such pride in the care she showered on us, seized it before he could lay his hands on it.

"That's all right, driver, that's all right. I'll do it. Now tuck your hands under the rug. I'll just put the basket down here between my feet. Are you warm enough, Koka?"

"Yes thank you, Agasha."

"And you, Moossia?"

"Yes thank you. Are you warm enough, Agasha?"

"Yes thank you my poppet. See – Agasha's got her padded jacket on and her lovely wool headscarf with the big roses. She's as snug as a bug in a rug."

Egor, who had been standing on the pavement nearby, ready to help us if necessary, now shuffled back to the doorway, with his shoulders high and his old man's steps and stood there ready to give us a last wave before burrowing back into the warmth of the building. The driver of the "Vanka" climbed back into his seat, flicked the reins on the horse's back and gave a click with his tongue. The ground was very icy just at that spot. The horse plunged to get a foothold and sent the sledge rocking all over the place. Koka and I would certainly have shot off the back of the sledge and landed in two little crumpled heaps on the roadway if Agasha hadn't been holding us tight. There was no back rest to the sledge and you had to hold on as well as you could. Agasha immediately went into action.

"Careful, driver, careful. You nearly had us on to the road. And just mind how you go round the corners, too." The driver took her reproaches very calmly.

"All right, love, all right. Don't get worked up. You'll be all right. It was a bit icy just there. Very hard frost tonight, you know."

Travelling to Uncle Fedya's was like a journey to the Snow Queen's Palace. The sky was very clear and there were thousands and thousands of the brightest stars I had ever seen. Everything, everywhere, was covered in frosty whiteness and the ice on the branches of the trees lining our way reflected the lights of the street lamps over and over again like a series of crystal chandeliers. We were in Fairyland. We looked about us, almost breathless with the wonder of it.

I couldn't contain myself.

"Look, Agasha, look!"

But Agasha was a lot more matter of fact.

"Don't talk, Moossinka dear. Keep your mouth tight shut. The cold air could be bad for your chest. You can tell me later."

Our enchanted journey didn't last long. We were soon turning into Bif Avenue to pull up outside Uncle Fedya's house. Someone must have been looking out for arriving guests because the front door opened just before we got to it. In a moment we were out of the bitter cold and safely cocooned in the bright warm interior. Koka and I were so busy looking about ourselves and trying to peer into the drawing room that our outdoor clothes were removed by unseen hands as if by magic. Aunt Rosa wafted into the hallway to greet us, closely followed by Uncle Fedya.

"Moossinka, my little one!" She bent down to embrace me before I could do anything to defend myself. She clasped me to her bosom with great feeling. It was like being swallowed by a deliciously scented affectionate eiderdown. I struggled for breath. She smelled of flowers and custard powder.

No sooner had she released me, gasping for air, trying to gulp in as much breath as I could, than I was swooped up into the air, high above his head, by Uncle Fedya. It was like going up in a very fast lift.

"Moossinka, my little duck, my Moossutka." He lowered me to the level of his face and pressed his prickly moustache first against one cheek then the other.

He didn't smell of flowers and custard powder. He smelled of cigars and vodka. His party had been going on for some time. When he had swooped me down to the ground he turned to give the same enthusiastic treatment to Koka, just released by Aunt Rosa.

"Hello, Kokochka, have you got a kiss for your Uncle Fedya too?"

Koka had seen what had happened to me and was very wary.

"No, no!" he squeaked in alarm. "I don't want to!" He slipped out of Uncle Fedya's grasp like an eel and hid behind Agasha, then peeked out from behind her skirt.

Uncle Fedya roared with laughter and, not to be frustrated, kissed Agasha instead.

"Never mind Koka. Hello, Agasha. Now tell me, have the children been good?"

Agasha couldn't help joining in the general laughter at Koka's reaction to Uncle Fedya's behaviour. Now she straightened her face and put on a very serious expression to answer solemnly.

"Yes, they have, Barin. They have both been very good."

Uncle Fedya picked up her tone of voice.

"I'm very glad to hear it because Father Frost will be paying us a visit later on in the evening."

When we were swept into the drawing room we stopped on the threshold, quite overwhelmed by the sight. It was a much bigger crowd than the one we had at Easter. The whole room was dripping with intricately cut paper decorations. Every picture carried its spray of holly. Every light was lit and, at the far end of the room, stood a most handsome Christmas tree reaching right up to the ceiling, covered in lighted candles, different coloured shining glass balls and nuts and little parcels. Every face was animated and the chatter was almost deafening. Cousin Roonya burst through the crowd, seized one of us in each hand and hurried us off to the Christmas tree.

"Come on you two. Come and look at the presents. No, Koka, you mustn't touch!" as Koka made to turn over one of the parcels at the foot of the tree to find out whose name was on it.

Lusya, Dosya and Bobya were already bending down, standing on tiptoes and craning their necks to read the names on the parcels. They were our other cousins, children of Mama's sister, Olia. They were older than we were and therefore very superior. Aunt Olia was small, wiry, and very very bossy. Her husband, Arthur, was just the opposite, a nice, gentle man, very tall in comparison, "as long as a day without bread", I heard someone say. When Aunt Olia saw that she had upset Uncle Arthur with her bossiness, which happened very often, it could be very funny really because, if Uncle Arthur wanted to show her that she couldn't get round him as easily as all that, all he had to do was to straighten his back and leave Aunt Olia floundering.

We ran up to Granny to give her a warm kiss. I always loved to do this because Granny always smelled of violets. Aunt Dorothea was sitting by Granny and she didn't smell of anything at all. Koka was trying to get information out of Granny.

"Papa told me that Father Frost might bring me a new drum, Babooshka."

"You never know, Koka, you never know," she smiled. "Agasha, go and talk to everyone. I'll take care of Moossia and Koka."

"Thank you, Barinya. I won't go far in case you need me."

"Let's go and ask Uncle Fedya for some crackers off the tree. Then we can pull them and get the paper hats," said Roonya. But before we could find Uncle Fedya I saw someone I didn't recognise.

"Roonya," I caught him by the arm, "who's that lady over there in the black dress talking to Uncle Walter?"

"Which one?"

"The one over there by the long mirror on the wall. The one doing something to her hair, the one with the fan hanging on her arm?"

"Don't be silly, that's Aunt Theresa."

"I don't believe you."

"Ask Borya or Goolya." Borya and Goolya were Aunt Theresa's sons, one year and three years older than I was.

"Look, there they are, with Uncle Rupert."

"But she looks quite different."

"That's because she's wearing a wig."

"A wi-i-ig?"

"Mama says."

"What's a wig? Where is it?"

"You are a chump, Moossia. On her head, of course."

"But she's got hair on her head, brown hair."

"That's not hers. It's somebody else's."

"You're having me on."

"Go and ask Goolya then."

"I don't like to."

"It's up to you. I don't care."

"But how does it gro-o-ow?"

"It doesn't grow. You are an idiot. It just stays the way it is. It's another lot of hair on top of her own hair."

"I don't believe you."

"See if I care."

"You're pulling my leg."

"Go and ask her."

"All right then, I will."

I was so annoyed with him for having me on like this that I was crossing the room to ask Aunt Theresa all about this wig. Luckily I was prevented.

The dining room door was flung open.

"Ladies and Gentlemen." It was Uncle Fedya at his most formal but with a twinkle in his eye all the same.

"Dinner is served."

Conversation stopped but nobody made a move. He walked in a very courtly manner over to Granny, bowed deeply and offered her his arm. Granny inclined her head to him graciously and smiled with great delight. She rose in a courtly manner and Uncle Fedya led her into the dining room and seated her at the head of the table. They were just like the Tsar and the Tsarina for a few moments.

Everybody began chatting again and filed into the dining room after them. There was the usual scramble for places by the children. I wanted Borya to sit next to me but Goolya took the seat and announced that he was going to sit there. It took all Agasha's diplomacy and skill to prise Goolya out of the place and get Borya into it. Goolya went off in a bit of a huff to sit next to Roonya. I finished up between Borya and Aunt Dorothea with the 'Crumb' on her lap.

The incidents weren't confined to the children. Aunt Fanya didn't approve of the 'Crumb' being allowed at the table. She was sitting opposite us and leaned over the table towards Aunt Dorothea.

"Aunt Dorothea," she suggested, "let Agasha put the dog on the settee while we eat."

"Oh, no!" replied Aunt Dorothea, and she covered the 'Crumb' with her napkin so that he couldn't be seen, and stroked him through the napkin.

Uncle Arthur fixed his pince nez more firmly on his eagle's beak and peered mildly round the table.

"Where would you like me to sit, Fedya?"

"Sit by Mamochka, Arthur, and tell her all about your visit to Odessa."

"Yes, Granny joined in. "Come and sit by me, Arthur."

Aunt Olia liked ordering Uncle Arthur about and started to interfere.

"Mama, I particularly wanted Arthur to sit..." but she had met more than her match in Granny.

"I know, Olia, I know. But you must remember you have your husband by your side every day of the week. Let Arthur have a bit of peace for once! There's a seat for you over there between Lucie and Dosya." And Granny pointed firmly to the other end of the table near Uncle Fedya, as far away from herself and Uncle Arthur as possible. Aunt Olia made no more ado and did as she was told. Granny's wish was law.

Papa was still without a seat. He hadn't joined in the general scramble. Uncle Fedya saw this and jovially called to him.

"Come and sit by me, Karloosha. I'm quite surrounded by beautiful ladies. It's too much for me! Come and help me out!"

He made a little bow to Mama, his favourite sister, whom he adored. Out of politeness he had to include Aunt Olia who was by now sitting on the other side of him. Her sharp face didn't fit Uncle Fedya's description at all but she couldn't resist his overwhelming charm. She smiled warmly up at him and then she turned and smiled at Papa. Uncle Fedya beamed round the table.

"Now has everybody found a seat? Good, then we can start."

Although food had been difficult to get sometimes in the autumn, Uncle Fedya and Aunt Rosa had made a great effort to have their table as lavish as it always had been. Perhaps Granny and Papa and some of the other members of the family had contributed to it discreetly. We started off with the customary hors d'oeuvres of caviar, salted herring, and little open sandwiches with sausages and kilki, the little Baltic sprats. And then we had a clear soup with tiny pieces of meat floating in it.

Aunt Rosa hardly sat down at all through the meal. She was so busy looking after her guests. She was continually on the move, carrying plates of raw ham cut at the table by Uncle Fedya. Papa also joined in and helped with the carving. He had charge of a leg of lamb, and one of the maids took the plates from him as he cut it. There were masses of salads and cheese and home-made pickles. To finish we had fruit compote and fresh fruit from the laden dishes down the middle of the table.

Early in the meal I found myself with a difficult problem. The table we were sitting at was a very long one but there were a great many guests and I was sitting awkwardly close to Aunt Dorothea.

The 'Crumb' was sitting quietly under the napkin but his tail was sticking out so that it lay in my lap. Now and then as I bent forward to take a sip of soup from my spoon, the 'Crumb's tail flicked upwards towards my face. This made me jump and I nearly upset a spoonful of soup all over myself. I didn't want to spend the rest of the evening with a great soup stain down my front so, after two or three tries, I decided not have any more soup in case of disaster. Agasha was spending her time between Koka and myself, making sure we were all right, and she noticed I wasn't making any headway.

"Moossia, drink up your soup, my dove. It will get cold."

"I can't, Agasha. Kroshka Crumb's tail keeps flapping in my face. I'm afraid I shall spill it!" I was whispering desperately, trying to make myself heard by Agasha, without informing everyone else in the room. This was difficult, with all the animated chatter, the laughter and the chink of cutlery and glasses. Agasha shifted her position so that she was on my side away from Aunt Dorothea.

"You must ask Aunt Dorothea if she would…"

"I couldn't. She wouldn't for Aunt Fanya. Agasha, you ask her!"

"Moossinka, I can't my angel. It's not my place."

This conversation was all in a frantic stage whisper. Of course, we spoke in Russian, which Aunt Dorothea could barely understand, so that there wasn't much chance that she would know what we were talking about. Granny could speak Danish so Aunt Dorothea hadn't taken much trouble to learn Russian. It seemed that there was no answer to my problem. The answer was, in fact, a very simple one, and it took Agasha only a few seconds to work it out. She turned to my cousin, Borya, who was sitting next to me.

"Borya, would you mind changing places with Moossinka. Please. Be a good boy."

Borya looked at us as if were slightly wrong in the head but obligingly did as he was asked. His empty soup plate was exchanged for my nearly full one and I finally managed to finish my soup. Neither Agasha nor I tried to explain to him why we wanted him to change places, but he didn't seem to have any difficulties with Kroshka Crumb's tail, so no harm had been done to him.

Fragments of gossip floated over my head. I overheard Granny telling a lady I didn't know about our cook and her complexion.

"Do you know how she does it? She washes her face in the washing up water. I suppose it's all the grease that does the trick. I can't say I could ever bring myself to do it. Not even if it turned me into the Queen of Sheba!"

Papa was leaning over Aunt Olia and chatting to Uncle Fedya.

"I'm going over to Paris and London in the Spring, Fedya. If there are any stamps you would like me to get for your collection, perhaps you'd let me know."

"Thank you, Karloosha. I will. If you could go to the big dealer in London…"

Then he looked round the table and, seeing that the meal was coming to its end, he got up from his seat with his glass of vodka and tapped one of the glasses in front of him with a spoon. A comparative silence fell on the gathering.

"Please fill your glasses, my friends." Hands reached out all along the table to comply with his request. The children's glasses were filled with Mors.

"First of all I want to tell you how delighted we are to see you all here. We wish you all a happy holiday." He chinked glasses with Aunt Rosa who had come to his side, and they both drank to their guests. Uncle Fedya drained his glass at one gulp and held it out for one of the maids to fill, which she did, to the brim. Then Uncle Walter got up and proposed a toast to Uncle Fedya and Aunt Rosa and we all stood up and drank our vodka or our wine or our Mors to them.

When everybody but the two hosts and the maids and Agasha had sat down again Uncle Fedya walked the length of the table to where Granny was sitting at the head of it. There was a different note in his voice.

Perhaps he was rather drunk by now but he spoke with great feeling.

"Mamoolya, your health, Mamoolya."

We all rose to our feet again and drank to Granny's health.

Uncle Fedya followed up the toast by giving Granny a smacking kiss on the cheek. A sigh of affection for them both ran round the table. This turned to a note of comical alarm as Uncle Fedya, going to stand up straight, staggered back and might have fallen backwards. Several hands stretched out to catch him although they were out of reach. Luckily he had flung one arm out automatically towards one of the maids who was standing near ready to fill his glass again and she was able to catch him and steady him. There was another sigh, this was one of relief from the guests, followed by a t-t-t-t-t-t of severe disapproval from Aunt Olia, the prim.

Aunt Rosa was quickly at Uncle Fedya's side.

"Fedya, go easy. Don't you think you've had enough?" she warned, in a soft voice, and she kept her eye on him until he had weaved his way back to the end of the table and sat down again.

"You'll see, he'll get the stick from Father Frost." Roonya leaned across the table towards me and whispered hoarsely.

Borya, now sitting on my right side, giggled so violently at this pleasurable prospect that he started to cough and Agasha had to come over and slap him on the back to get him to stop.

A growing feeling of complete disaster descended on me like a sudden thunder shower and I began to go hot and cold. Agasha divined that there was something very wrong with me.

"What on earth's the matter, Moossinka?"

I couldn't tell her there and then and have myself overheard by everyone in the room, so I said the first thing that came into my head.

"I feel sick."

Aunt Rosa overheard me.

"Take her into my bedroom, Agasha." But Agasha, just to be on the safe side, hurried me off to the bathroom. Once there, I burst into tears.

"Now, now, my chicken," she soothed, sitting on the edge of the bath with me on her knee, "tell me, tell Agasha what the matter really is."

"I can't remember the words. I can't remember the words of my song, my song for Uncle Fedya!"

Agasha was so surprised that this was the cause of my upset that, for the moment, she didn't know whether to laugh or cry, but she knew exactly what to say, as always.

"Moossinka, don't cry, don't cry, my little one. Agasha remembers, I remember." She cradled me in her arms and rocked me. "You'll remember too as soon as you begin. There's my clever girl. Calm down. Calm down. Just look how crumpled your pretty dress is getting. Now, how does it begin? Try singing it after me. Tell us first what you're going to sing. Now, what's it called… "There was a gypsy…"

Then it all came back. I scrambled off her knees, went to stand with my back to the bathroom door, and sang very softly so that nobody else could hear.

There was a gypsy
Who had a long nose,
She was asking how
To shorten her nose.
She was advised
To buy some Vaseline,
Put it on her nose

And then

Cut it off with an axe!"

Agasha cooled my face, hot and flushed with tears, by gentle application of a flannel wrung out in ice-cold water, patted it with a towel, rearranged my hair ribbon, tidied my dress all round and we went back hand in hand to the dining room. But the dining room was empty by now and we ran into the drawing room from which the snapping of crackers and happy shrieks of laughter could be heard. All the lights in the room had been turned off and the candles on the tree were ablaze. Because of all the multicoloured glass balls hanging on the branches there seemed to be hundreds and hundreds of candles and I ran towards the tree as if drawn by a magnet. Agasha cried out in some alarm.

"Don't go too near the tree, Moossinka, your hair, your dress might catch fire."

"I'll be careful, Agasha."

Uncle Fedya was handing out crackers from the tree and he gave me one too. Borya helped me to pull it and there was a pink paper hat inside it and a round, glass-covered little box with three little silver balls and a picture of a clown with his eyes popping and his mouth open. I took it over to Roonya for him to explain it to me. He was standing with Aunt Fanya by one of the tall windows looking out on the snow-covered street. I forgot all about the little box and joined them looking out. There was virtually no sound at all from the street because of the double glazing and the thick blanket of snow over everything. You could just hear the faint tinkling of the bells over the horses' heads as they distantly clip-clopped by. Uncle Fedya's yardman was trying hard to keep the pavement clear but every time he made a stroke with his broom the wind caught the snow he was brushing and whirled it into the air so that every stroke he made caused another miniature snow storm.

"Look, Roonya, look! The yardman looks just like a Baba Yaga witch riding her broom!"

The street outside was brighter than usual because the snow reflected the light of the gas lamps but it was very dark in comparison with the blaze of light in the drawing room. It must have been very cold for the coachmen waiting outside. They were all heavily muffled up but they never stopped stamping up and down the pavement and beating their arms across their bodies in a vain effort to keep themselves warm. They weren't the only sufferers either.

"Look, Roonya, look!" I pointed down the street. "That poor horse hasn't got a blanket, poor thing!"

There was a loud knocking at the hall door. The maids ran forward and opened it and there stood Father Frost himself. There were flecks of snow on his long red coat and his boots and even on the long white beard reaching nearly to his waist. On his back he carried a bulging sack. He stamped his feet and brushed his coat and his beard with his free hand to remove some of the snow. All the chatter in the room faded to nothing in a twinkling. Everyone was still as still.

Uncle Fedya stepped forward and bowed elaborately to Father Frost who inclined his head majestically in return. Then Uncle Fedya turned to us all and said to us in a solemn voice,

"Ladies and Gentlemen, Father Frost has come."

Father Frost moved a few steps into the room.

"Good evening to you all," a deep voice echoed round the room. "I'm very glad to be in a nice warm room. It's very cold in the forest tonight!"

At the sound of his deep, booming voice, Koka gave another little squeak and dodged behind the chaise longue on which Mama was sitting. I was covered in goose pimples with excitement. Father Frost swung the bulging sack, on which all the children's eyes were riveted, from his shoulder and let it fall with a bump on to the floor.

"Have all the children been good since I came last year?"

"Oh, yes, Father Frost, they have, they have, we have."

"Now who would like to be first to get a present?" To our surprise it was Uncle Fedya who stepped forward.

"Please, I would like to be the first."

"And what is your name?" the deep voice boomed. Uncle Fedya hung his head shyly, twisted his hands together, and shuffled his feet.

"Fedya."

"Fedya? So you're Fedya; have you been good?"

"Oh yes, I've been very, very, very good. Haven't I?" He looked round the room and appealed to us but nobody spoke up for him and a chuckle ran round the guests.

"Good, I'm very glad to hear that. Now," stroking his beard, "let me see. Can you recite a poem for me?"

Uncle Fedya scratched his head, looked up in the air, put a finger to his forehead and twisted it to and fro and even pawed the ground with one foot, but finally shook his head in despair. We could see quite clearly that he couldn't remember a thing. I was very sorry for him because I knew just how he felt. Father Frost tapped one foot on the floor and rubbed his hands together.

"Well, Fedya, I'm waiting."

Nobody said a word on Uncle Fedya's behalf. I was bursting with pity for him. Roonya and Borya were standing near the tree and their eyes were shining with joy at the prospect of what was to come. On the other hand, for a reason I couldn't make out, all the grownups were heartlessly chuckling to themselves. At length Uncle Fedya blurted out, shamefaced,

"I'm sorry, Father Frost. I've forgotten to learn a poem for you."

"Forgotten? What do you mean, forgotten?" Father Frost's voice boomed out louder than ever.

"I'm sorry, Father Frost."

"Sorry? Sorry? It's too late to say you're sorry. Bend over."

Uncle Fedya bent over and parted the skirt of his coat. Father Frost delved into his sack and produced a long cane. He gave Uncle Fedya what appeared to be three very hard whacks on his bottom. Poor Uncle Fedya howled loud and long at each blow and finally ran to Aunt Rosa for comfort, rubbing the seat of his trousers in pain. She was laughing so much that tears ran down her face and she put her arms round him as if he had been a little boy, but the boys, Roonya and Borya were white-faced because Father Frost had laid the blows on with such apparent vigour and they were wondering who might be next. Koka had completely disappeared under the chaise longue by now and I was clinging to Agasha and burying my head in the folds of her sarafan.

"I want to go home. I want to go home." I sobbed over and over again.

"So do I. So do I." A little voice piped from under the chaise longue. The booming voice went on, only making matters worse.

"What's the matter, little girl? Don't you want to come and get your present?"

"I don't want a present. Agasha, take me home!"

"Me too. Me too." Koka was crawling out from under the chaise longue. Granny and Papa and Aunt Rosa and Uncle Fedya were gathered round us in a little knot.

"It's all right, Moossinka, really it is. It's only Uncle Fedya being silly, really it is," soothed Mama.

"Why is she so upset, Lilichka?" Papa asked.

"She thought Fedya was really being hurt, Karloosha."

"I think they're both overtired, Barinya. Perhaps I'd better take them home." Agasha came to the rescue.

"I'm all right, I promise you, Moossutka." Uncle Fedya sweetly bent down to kiss me better, but I was too upset and closed my eyes and turned my head away. He turned to Mama.

"I'm sorry, Lilichka. I didn't mean to frighten her."

"It's nothing to worry about, Fedya. Agasha is right. They're both overtired. She'll take them back home. There's nothing to worry about, Rosa. You know how soft-hearted Moossia is."

"I'll go and get a cab for them." Uncle Fedya went off.

We left the party without saying proper goodbyes to everybody and, as we got into the cab, we could hear the distant booming voice of Father Frost and the laughter of the guests as the party picked up again. It was a very bumpy ride because this time we were in a wheeled cab and not a sleigh. Now we were alone with Agasha and away from the crowd.

"Driver," instructed Agasha, "don't go so fast. The air is sharp enough as it is."

"Agasha," Koka croaked.

"Shush, Koka, don't talk. The night air is very cold."

"I feel ever so hot, Agasha."

"We shall soon be home."

"I want a drink. My throat hurts."

"Just a little while, my dove. Agasha will make us all some tea when we get back."

When we did reach home we went straight to our room and straight to bed. Agasha brought us both glasses of tea and they had big spoonful of blackcurrant jam in them to ward off any chills we might have caught on the way. I only just managed to finish mine before my head hit the pillow.

Chapter 20

February 1917 – Agasha

"Past the woods and mountains steep,
Past the rolling waters deep,
You will find a hamlet pleasant
Where once dwelt an ancient peasant.
Of his sons, and he had three,
The eldest sharp was as could be:
The second was neither dull nor bright
But the third a fool all right.
Now, these brothers planted wheat,
Brought it to the royal seat.
By which token you shall know
That they hadn't far to go."

Moossia gave a huge yawn. She had been learning lines from The Little Hump-Backed Horse, a favourite of all of us. The idea was that she was to recite some of it to Uncle Fedya at the next family party. She loved the story almost as much as she loved Uncle Fedya and had worked hard. But that was enough for one night and I clapped my hands.

"Someone is getting very sleepy. Time for bed. Come along, you two, time for bed."

I tucked them both in, had a good look round the kitchen to make sure that everything was ready for the morning, said goodnight to the Barin and the Barinya and went to bed myself. I was just drifting off to sleep when there was a huge explosion right above the apartment. Without being aware of what I was doing I found myself at the door of the children's room. Koka was screaming and Moossia had buried herself under the bedclothes. I thought, for the moment, that terrorists had let off a bomb nearby but the rumblings in the sky made me realise that we were in the middle of one the biggest thunderstorms I had ever heard. I picked Koka up in my arms and went to sit on Moossia's bed to comfort them. Moossia emerged from the bedclothes and snuggled up beside me.

"It's all right, my darlings. It's just a thunderstorm. It'll go away soon."

Koka's lip quivered.

"Tell it to go away now." To calm him down I flipped one of my hands towards the window.

"Go away, nasty storm!"

The Barin had heard Koka's screams and came into the room in his nightshirt.

"Is everything all right, Agasha?"

"Yes thank you, Barin. They were just frightened by the thunder."

"I'm not surprised. It frightened the life out of me." He went over to the window, parted the curtains, and looked out over the city.

I was embarrassed because I was still in my nightgown.

"It looks as though someone has been struck by lighting. I can see a huge fire up in the north of the city." He closed the curtains. "Well, if you're all right, Agasha, I think I'll go back to bed. Busy day tomorrow. We've got the auditors coming in. Sure you're all right?"

"Quite sure, thank you Barin."

He came over and ruffled the children's hair.

"Goodnight, little chickens. Don't be afraid. Agasha will take care of you." He bowed comically to each of us in turn.

"Goodnight, Madame. Goodnight, Madame, goodnight Sir."

The children scrambled to their feet and joined in the fun. They imitated the Barin and bowed to him in unison, "Goodnight, Sir," like waiters in a restaurant. And so a drama had been turned into a comedy.

I tucked the children up in their beds again, kissed them goodnight and made up a bed from cushions on the floor. They had really been frightened by the storm and I thought they would be happier if I stayed close to them.

Before we went to sleep again there was a rattle of hailstones on the windowpanes. They must have been very big hailstones. The noise was quite deafening. The foul weather lasted three whole days. The thunderstorm came and went. There wasn't much snow but the violent wind tore branches off the trees and swept them down towards the Neva. On the fourth day the wind dropped; the storm was over and we woke up to sunshine and a clear blue sky. I hadn't been able to take the children out for their daily walk down to the Neva, of course, so when the Barin had gone round to his office in the factory, I suggested to the Barinya that it was time to take the children out again. She was glad to get them off her hands for a while and Moossia and Koka were in a state of high excitement. They hated being cooped up in the apartment as much as I did and started to put their outdoor clothes on as quickly as they could. Moossia could dress herself by now but Koka had always lost something.

"Agasha," he would wail, "I can't find my scarf, my gloves, my fur hat," and so on. I would have to help him put on his valenki and fasten the buttons down the front of his coat and tie the flaps of his hat under his chin. Moossia showed off by dressing in double quick time and, standing with exaggerated patience, would tap her toe on the floor, sigh and look up at the ceiling. We were just going out of the door onto the landing when the Barinya's voice sounded behind us.

"Children! Haven't you forgotten something?"

Moossia and Koka trotted back to her, a question written on their faces. She held out her two closed hands. They understood, and Koka tapped her right hand. She opened it to reveal a twenty-kopeck piece. Koka pulled off his glove and scooped up the coin and ran back to me to put his glove on again. Moossia gathered her twenty-kopeck piece and the pair of them scampered down the stairs towards the outside door. The Barinya was anxious.

"Not so fast, not so fast, you'll fall over! How many times do I have to tell you?" Then she turned to me.

"Tell him I hope he's going to Church every Sunday. Poor man, he must be very hungry. He must be starving. He simply has to be there today." By now the children had reached the door. They were confronted by Egor the doorkeeper ready for the game he always played with them.

"And where do you think you're going this fine day, my little friends?" He stood with his back to the door and spread his arms as if to stop them going out. Moossia became very coquettish, stamped on the ground and stood, arms akimbo, pretending to be cross.

"Oh, Egor, you know very well! Don't be silly! We're going for our walk like we always do!"

Egor was a very impressive man. He was very dignified and unusually tall. Although he must have been well into his sixties he stood ramrod straight like the Guardsman he had been for many years. He was a good looking man and had a rugged face and a well-trimmed beard. He obviously looked after himself. I think he must have been a regular ladies' man when he was younger. I often wondered just what he got up to in his spare time.

He swung the door open, stepped aside and drew himself up to his full height.

"To be sure! To be sure!" and he gave us his best military salute, clicking his heels and with his fingers quivering. As I passed him he gave me a roguish wink. I didn't know what to make of that. Egor had hidden depths.

When we were walking hand in hand and in high spirits down the middle path of the boulevard towards the Neva I got Moossia to go on with the poem for Uncle Fedya. She readily did and we took no notice of the amused glances of passers-by.

"But, upon an evil day
Dire misfortune came their way.
Someone, twixt the dark and dawn
Took to trampling down their corn;
Never had such grief before
Come to visit at their door."

We had come to the end of the boulevard and there, at his usual post, in rags, stood the old tramp the Barinya had been talking about. His weather-beaten face was framed by a long, grey, untended beard which had bits of his last meal clinging to it. Nobody knew his name. He never said a word but made his meaning clear by holding out his hand for alms. The children went up to him shyly and put the twenty-kopeck pieces in his hand. They didn't say anything either when the old tramp just nodded his head in thanks. His eyes puckered. That was a smile. Then the children pattered back to me, looking up for approval. When we looked back at the old man he was lost in his dreams.

We waited at the crossing for a handsome sleigh to pass. Clearly it belonged to somebody with a lot of money. The horse was a spirited chestnut and shook his head and dilated his nostrils as he passed us. The decorations were all the same maroon colour, the yoke, the saddlecloth and the padding in the sleigh itself. The brass ornaments were highly polished and tinkled merrily. The young man driving wore clothes in the latest fashion and his cheeks glowed with the cold.

As we walked along the path by the Neva the children looked longingly at the men cutting blocks of ice from the river and at the skaters whizzing about the ice. Someone had made a Father Frost out on the ice. To amuse the children I scooped snow from the edges of the path and made snowballs which I threw at the Father Frost. But I wasn't strong enough and the snowballs fell hopelessly short of the mark. The children laughed at my feeble effort. Then Koka said,

"I want to do it." So I made another snowball, put it in his hands, and lifted him up so that he could throw it over the railings. But his effort was worse than mine. I consoled him.

"Never mind, Koka, when you grow up…" He interrupted me.

"When I'm big and strong I'll throw one right over to the other bank."

We laughed at him, he was so funny. Then I bent down to pick up some more snow. As I got up a surprising sight met my eyes. A young soldier was coming towards me along the path. His uniform was one I recognised at once. He was tall and my head would just reach the level of his shoulders. He was fair and had a fully-grown fair curly moustache. After all these years! Why hadn't he got in touch with me? He passed me with a cursory glance. Then I couldn't contain myself and ran after him along the path, calling to him.

"Oleg! Oleg! Don't you recognise me? It's Agasha! Don't you know me?"

The young man turned round and came towards me, smiling. He must have thought I was trying to pick him up. I had a shock. Of course, it wasn't Oleg. How could I have been so stupid? Oleg was in Georgia and would always be there. I backed away and held the palms of my hands out in front of me.

"I'm sorry, I'm sorry. Please forgive me. I thought you were someone else."

He shrugged his shoulders, disappointed, and turned away, and silent tears poured down my face. The children were puzzled by my behaviour and ran after me. Moossia was the first to speak.

"Agasha, what's the matter, why are you crying?"

"I'm not crying, my darling, I've just got something in my eye," I lied. "Come along my dears. Let's go for a good long walk and get some fresh air in our lungs. Moossia, why don't you go on with your recitation? You want to do your best for Uncle Fedya, don't you?" Moossia did as I asked. They took my hands and we went, swinging our clasped hands, along the pavement.

"Day and night they sat and thought
How the villain could be caught.
Till, at last, it dawned upon them
That the way to solve their problem
And save their crops from harm
Was, each night, to guard the farm..."

But I couldn't hear what she was saying. I was still shaking and crying inside myself.

Chapter 21

March 1917

I was trying to trudge through a rocky mountain pass. It was very difficult because my feet were caught up in some kind of marsh and I kept sinking into it right up to the knees. Not only were my legs impeded but the thick fog all around me seemed like treacle and held my arms pinioned to my side as I tried to wade forward. Giant shadows were thrown up by a dim light somewhere in front of me onto the walls of fog and the mountainsides which I could glimpse through the fog from time to time. There were frightening creatures muttering all round me but I couldn't see them, only their shadows which I couldn't make out properly. The shadows got bigger and bigger. The voices got clearer. I struggled forward more and more desperately, trying to free my legs and my hands. I didn't dare make a sound for fear that the owners of the voices would find out where I was and come chasing after me. Then I managed to pull one hand free from the clutching treacle fog and then the other. The fog started to clear very quickly. I saw that the mountainsides were really walls, the walls of our room. The huge shadows were those of Mama and Agasha.

They were bending over Koka's bed and Mama held a lamp in her hand. I was sitting up in bed with the bedclothes heaped up all about me by my restless sleeping. Papa opened the door softly and crept over to join Mama and Agasha.

"How do you think he is now?"

"He's very feverish, Barin."

"Doctor Pepkin should be here soon."

"I'll just put another cold flannel on his head, Barinya."

I could see that Mama and Papa were in their dressing gowns but Agasha was still in the clothes she had worn at the party. She had obviously not been to bed. They were all three talking very quietly and I could no longer make out what they said. For a moment I drifted back into my nightmare again but was able to shake myself free of it. But when I came to, the atmosphere in the room was just as frightening as the atmosphere of the dream. I couldn't bear it any longer.

"Agasha, what's the matter? Is Koka ill?"

She came over to me, straightened my bedclothes and held them for me to snuggle down again.

"Yes, my dove, Koka isn't well. Don't you worry yourself. Agasha will look after him. Now close your eyes. Lie down and try to go to sleep." I did exactly as she asked but had no hope of going to sleep. There was a short discreet tinkle of the doorbell, the sound of Masha's voice, very subdued. Papa left our room. The front door opening; voices; the front door clicking to; voices again. The door of our room opened and Papa ushered in Doctor Pepkin, tall, thin-faced, with a pince-nez lopsided on his nose. He put down his bag, unbuttoned his frock coat, took out a handkerchief which he used to wipe the snow from his moustache.

"I shall have to examine him. Could you get him to sit up?" Mama put her arms behind Koka and got him into a sitting position but his head lolled to one side. He was just like an India rubber doll and when Mama took her arms away he flopped back to his pillow. In the end Mama had just to sit on the bed and support him all the time Doctor Pepkin was examining him. He was coughing a bit and I could hear his breathing from the other side of the room.

"When did you last take his temperature?" He turned to Mama, who looked at Agasha.

"Just before you came, Doctor. It was 38.9."

"Hm-m-m." He tapped Koka on the chest and on his back and then took out his stethoscope. "Now, Koka, I just want to listen to your chest. Yes, yes, that's good, that's good. Now, may I have a spoon, please? Open your mouth, Koka. Wide. That's a good boy. Will you bring the lamp a little nearer, please. That's it. Yes, I see. I shall have to paint his throat." He went over to his bag and came back from it with a little bottle of dark liquid and a stick with a lump of cotton wool on the end of it. "Open your mouth again, Koka." He dipped the stick into the bottle and popped the end in and out of

Koka's mouth before Koka knew what was happening. Koka coughed and spluttered but, by that time, it was all over. Doctor Pepkin held the little stick up in the air, not knowing what to do with it and Agasha took it out of his hand and out of the room. Mama tucked Koka in as he slid rubberily back into the bedclothes.

"Are his lungs affected?" she asked anxiously.

"Mm-m-m, yes, I'm afraid so. There is a certain amount of congestion. You'll have to give him hot compresses on his back and his chest. I'll be back in the morning to see how he's getting on." He touched Mama lightly on the elbow, looking in my direction. "Can I have a word with you outside?" And they both left the room.

Because it was all happening in the middle of the night, because I had just woken up from a frightening nightmare and because of the waves of anxiety which were coming from the four grownups, every detail of what was happening to Koka, my little brother from whom I was hardly ever parted for more than a few moments, every detail seemed charged with a fateful significance, the more so because I didn't really understand what was going on. I was sitting up in bed again, very frightened indeed. Papa came over to soothe me.

"Try to lie down again and go to sleep, Moossinka."

I obediently lay back on my pillow but, if anything, felt worse because Papa's face lacked its usual smile, and was furrowed with care.

"Is Koka really very ill?"

"Let's hope he's not too ill. Be a good girl. Don't worry Agasha. She must be very tired. Go to sleep, my duck; goodnight, my little snow-white." He went over to Agasha, who had come back into the room and was sitting by Koka again, putting a fresh cloth on his forehead.

"Goodnight, Agasha."

"Goodnight, Barin."

"Do try to get some sleep, Agasha, once Koka has been seen to." He met Mama in the doorway, her hands full of all the things for the compress. "Do you want me to lend a hand, Lilichka?"

"No, it's all right, Karloosha. You go back to bed. Agasha and I will do it."

Poor Koka was raised again into a sitting position. Agasha gingerly fished the towels from the steaming hot water in the bowl Mama was carrying, and wrung out as much of the water as she could, holding the towels in her fingertips and passing them from one hand to another because they were so hot.

Koka complained weakly when they were put on his back and then on his chest, but he submitted to the further layers of cotton wool and waterproof cloth laid over the hot towels. In a few minutes he had been swathed in bandages, secured by the inevitable English safety pin, and warmly tucked up in bed. Mama sighed, and said to Agasha quietly, "We've done all we can, Agasha; now we can only pray."

"The Almighty is merciful, Barinya; he will watch over Koka." She sat down in the chair by Koka's bed, ready to spend the rest of the night there.

"I will come and take over from you in the morning, Agasha. All we can do now is just wait. Call me if you need me. Goodnight, Agasha."

"Goodnight, Barinya. The night is always darker than the morning." Mama crept away, and a strange peace descended on the room, dimly lit by the heavily shaded lamp. Agasha sat absolutely still. I just repeated over and over again in my mind,

"Please don't let Koka die, please, God, don't let Koka die," until I fell asleep.

It seemed to me that Koka was ill for a very long time. My bed was moved out into my parents' room, where they made me another tiny room surrounded by ruffled silk screens, so that Koka wouldn't be disturbed. I hardly saw either Agasha or Mama, because they never left Koka's side, and I felt deserted and unloved. Granny came round to our apartment to be with me as much as she could, but it wasn't the same. She was very kind, and played Ludo and draughts and card games with me, and read me stories to keep me occupied. Sometimes she took me for short walks along the avenue, but, although I loved Granny very much, the loss of Agasha at my side was an unending heartache.

New Year's Day was usually a time for celebration on a scale like that at Easter, but this year, owing to Koka's illness, the party was much smaller. I was put to bed in the afternoon, so that I could stay awake at night.

Mama managed to steal away from Koka's bedside for a few hours, and she and Papa took me round to Granny's, where the party would be held. Agasha couldn't come this year because she had to stay behind and look after Koka. Aunt Fanya and Roonya were there, but not Uncle Fedya. Aunt Dorothea came down and joined us too, although she thoroughly disapproved of all our special Russian customs for this time of the year. She looked upon them as being completely barbaric, and didn't hesitate to let us know what she thought, although it didn't make any difference. We used the walnut and the lead pouring to foresee what Fate held in store for us, all the same.

After the usual cold buffet and the drinks of vodka and wine and Mors, and, in Mama's case, the tea, a large sheet of oilcloth was spread on the drawing room carpet in front of the tall stove. On the oilcloth was placed a big bucket of water.

"Did you bring your lead with you, from last year?"

"No, I couldn't find it. I looked everywhere."

"It doesn't matter. We'll give you some. We've got some to spare."

"I told them to put all the logs they could onto the stove," said Granny, "so that there would be plenty of red hot coals. Karloosha, would you open the stove and see how it's getting on?"

"There's still too much flame, I'm afraid. We shall have to wait a bit."

"Can we do the walnut first then, Granny?"

"I don't see why not. Dorothea, would you tell Dusya to bring us that large flat bowl, about three quarters full of water? She'll know what it's for."

The bowl was brought in and placed on the oilcloth. Papa stuck little slips of paper, on which he had written the different predictions, at intervals round the rim of the bowl. As they had been cut from a large sticky label, they just stuck there with the moisture already on the bowl. Then he got out of his pocket half a walnut shell and a tiny candle, which he lit, and stuck with some of its own melted wax into the shell. He placed this gently on the surface of the water, and then he stirred the water with his finger, so that the little boat went whirling round the bowl. Then he waited for a few moments until it came to rest by one of the slips of paper on the rim.

As Roonya was older than me he had the first turn. The walnut shell stopped at the words: "You will fall off a tree." This made everybody laugh, because Roonya hated climbing. Then it was my turn. Papa stirred, and the walnut set off again.

"You will kiss a monkey." Now it was Roonya's turn to lead the laughter at my expense; but it was so silly that I didn't mind, and laughed as loud as anybody.

"Let's do one for Koka." This time the words were a bit unkind. "You will wet your pants." Roonya and I laughed a lot, but the grownups only chuckled sympathetically, because Koka sometimes did wet his pants when he got too excited. Papa suggested,

"Please don't tell him. He might be upset."

"No, all right, I won't Papa. I promise."

Then some of the others joined in, and there was lots of laughter because Papa had written some very silly fortunes, and they seemed to go to the wrong people all the time. Aunt Fanya would be a millionaire. Granny would have twenty children. Mama was going to the moon for her summer holiday.

Papa got up and opened the front of the stove, which was red and glowing.

"I think the fire is just right now. We can start. Babooshka, you go first."

Granny gave him the small piece of lead she had in her hand. He put it in an old ladle which was specially kept for the purpose, and placed the bowl of the ladle on the red-hot coals. It didn't take long for the lead to start to melt, and soon it was a little silvery pool in the ladle. Granny took a thick old mitten and reached out for the ladle, keeping her face away from the heat of the stove, which was baking hot. She poured the melted lead, her arm still at full length, into the water in the bowl. There was a fierce hiss, and everybody jumped. Then Granny pulled up one sleeve, dipped her hand into the bowl, and brought out a curiously twisted shape of lead, with many holes in it. This she put on a spread-out towel to dry.

After that she was followed by Aunt Fanya and Mama and Papa and Roonya. Aunt Dorothea refused point blank to take any part.

"Foolish superstition, that's all it is. Barbaric Russian custom."

Nobody minded in the least. We were all used to Aunt Dorothea's opinions.

My lead, which Papa had put in the ladle and over the fire for me, was just about ready to pour.

"Put your hand on mine, Moossinka," he said, "and turn your face away from the water." He picked up the ladle and moved it over to the bowl, but, in my excitement, I jogged his hand, and not only the lead but the ladle itself went right into the water, and there was a tremendous hiss, and a cloud of steam rose up. I shrieked and pulled my hand away from his, but no harm had been done. When the fright had evaporated, I put my hand into the water, fished out my lead shape, and placed it on the towel to dry.

Now came the interesting part. A large candle was lit. All the other lights were put out and the stove closed up so that the light from the red-hot coals wouldn't spill out into the drawing room. Then everyone took it in turn to pick up their own lead shape and hold it up so that its shadow was thrown by the candle's light onto the wall. Then you had to study the shadow, and decide what interesting shape it resembled.

If it had the shape of a mountain you would be successful. A round garland meant that you were going to die. If the shadow was like a boat, you would travel during the year to come. Aunt Dorothea swore that she could never see anything but the shape of a lump of lead. Mama and Granny were quite expert at pointing out resemblances to all kinds of objects. But Agasha was the best of all. The year before she had seen the Devil.

"Merciful Heaven, the Evil One!" and she crossed herself vigorously.

"No, no, Agasha, it looks more like a goat to me," Papa laughed, but Agasha had her own ideas, and for days Koka and I were made to be extra careful about everything we did, so that the Evil One wouldn't have a chance to do us any harm.

A week or so after the New Year party, I woke up when my parents were making ready for bed. I could see Mama's shadow through the ruffled silk screen round my bed, as she sat at her dressing table brushing her hair. Papa's shadow, too, crossed the screen from time to time.

"This will have to change all our plans for the summer, Lilichka. As soon as he is well enough to travel, you had better take him and Moossia and Agasha down to the cottage. The forest air will be much better for him than staying in St. Petersburg."

"Yes, my dear, I'm sure you're right. God has spared him. We must do everything in our power, too."

"We shall have to talk to the doctor, or course, but it would be early in February at the soonest."

"Doctor Pepkin says he should be able to leave his room and walk about the apartment soon."

"Well then, I shall go down there as soon as I can, and see that they start to get the cottage ready. We must make absolutely sure that it's really warm for you when you get there."

"I'll tell Agasha to start preparing straight away. We shall need so many more things for such a long stay, and in the cold weather as well."

"Just take what you need for the next month or two, and Masha and will pack all the rest and send it down in due course."

"When are we going, Mama?" I couldn't hold myself in any longer.

"There, Lilichka, we've woken her up."

"Oh, no, Papa, I've been awake for ages. Is Koka really better?"

"Yes, my little duck. Thank God, he's really better."

"Then how soon are we going?"

"Not tonight, that's certain," he laughed softly. His shadow crossed the screen. He came round it and bent over my bed and kissed me goodnight. "So close your eyes and go to sleep. We'll talk about it tomorrow. All is well. The bad times have passed."

So in the first days of February we went down to the cottage in Finland. Papa arrived just in time to see us off at the station, and when we were settled in our seats he put his hand in the roomy pocket of his overcoat, and pulled out a little wriggling black bundle, and placed it in Agasha's arms.

"Goodness, a puppy!" she said, rocking it like a baby.

"His name is Pikko. He's a Doberman. His job will be to protect us all when he grows up." The guard's whistle blew, and there were hasty hugs and kisses all round, and Papa got out of the carriage as the train began to move. He kept pace with us for a few steps to say,

"I'll be down to see you all at the end of the week."

We took turns to cradle the puppy all the way down to Kelomakki. Wrapped in all our winter clothes, we looked contentedly out at the snow-covered forests and fields. The showers of sparks from the engine showed very clearly against the snow, an endless rain of falling stars.

Chapter 22

March 1917

The cottage at Kelomakki had always been just a summer holiday place. All our winters were spent in St. Petersburg. Everything seemed strange for a while and took some ge tting used to. Most of the familiar landmarks were smudged by the overall covering of snow and some were quite blotted out where the snow had drifted under the force of the biting wind which whipped through the pine trees. In the summer we were used to run about with the absolute minimum of clothes and with no shoes at all. Now we could only go out occasionally when the weather allowed, and were carefully swaddled in fur hats, long padded coats, mittens and valenki or felt boots. Aino was kept very busy cutting logs in the woods and bringing them in on his sledge to stoke the tall tiled stoves which were kept burning night and day. It was too cold for us to use the verandah and all the cracks in the doors and windows giving onto it were stuffed with grey moss to keep the draughts out. Even the space between the two layers of glass in the double-glazing was lined with grey moss. Only one small area was left clear and Agasha was able to open this window for a short while each morning to let a little fresh air into the stuffy rooms. She would stand looking out at the snow and the silent landscapes and the canopied trees, peering through the fringe of icicles hanging down from the cottage roof.

"How beautiful it all is. It makes my heart ache," she would murmur.

The snow in the garden would be crisscrossed with the fresh tracks of birds and animals which had travelled through it during the night and early morning. Papa had taught us how to tell one track from another during the summer from the imprints on patches of soft ground when it had been raining. They were even easier to recognise in the fresh snow.

"Look, Koka, there's a hare's tracks, and there's a fox's. See how it twists and turns!" We followed the almost single-file marks of the fox's paws about the garden and found the traces of an early morning hunt, scratchings in the snow, a few loose feathers and a frozen pink stain. We looked at each other knowingly and followed the fox's tracks to a gap in the fence. Koka was just about to go through the gap, bent double and bottom first, in pursuit of the fox when there was the sound of the kitchen door opening and Agasha's voice rang out loud across the snow in some alarm,

"No, Koka, no! You must stay in the garden! Moossia, Koka, you must stay in the garden." She was ever watchful.

There weren't so many things to do outside in the winter as there were in the summer, but there were some. In the summer the icehouse, just on the far side of the pond, was just a hump of soil covered in a tangle of tall grasses and wild flowers. Then we had little use for it and only went there from time to time with Agasha to get something stored on the blocks of ice cut from the pond in the winter. But now when Aino poured water down one side of it and it froze solid it made a quite thrilling slope for our toboggan. We would help Aino clear the path with our little square plywood shovels, and then there were snowmen and snow houses to build.

We were just putting the finishing touches to a rather handsome snow house one day when Koka suddenly let out a most dramatic cry,

"Look, Moossia, look! Over there! By the hole in the fence. Boys, it's boys, coming through!"

We rarely saw any other children as there weren't any living close to us. So I looked up not really believing what he said.

But sure enough there were three strange boys squeezing through the hole in the fence through which the fox's tracks had led. They were about the same age as me and dressed much as we were. They stood for a few moments just inside the fence and we watched each other with curiosity. I had no idea what they wanted. Then they began to scrape up handfuls of snow and advanced towards us threateningly, shouting words we couldn't make out.

"Run, Moossia, run. Look, they've got snowballs." Koka dodged behind the snow house. But I was rather annoyed by the trespassers.

"I'm not going to run. It's our garden. I'll show them. Come on, Koka, let's fight them. Take your gloves off. The snow sticks better."

The three small boys stalked us across the garden. They let fly with their missiles. We made a tactical retreat. The battle raged at a distance. There was an enraged squawk from Koka,

"Moossia, he hit me right down my neck!"

"Never mind. Aim at their faces. There! Got him!" I was getting quite bloodthirsty. One of the boys, taller than the other two, now reached our snow house and kicked it in with his feet, shouting loudly,

"Revolution, revolution!" For the first time we understood their words. The tall boy must have thought he had gone too far because, at the height of the victory, he turned round and made for the gap in the fence followed by his two companions. Koka became recklessly brave and chased them all the way to the fence, shouting at the top of his voice, "Hit them! Hit them! I'll get you!"

But the boys had scrambled through the hole and were safe from Koka's revenge and out of sight. We could only hear their cries, ever fainter as they ran off through the woods,

"Revolution! Revolution! Revolution!"

"Koka, look! They've knocked our snow house down, the pigs!"

Koka had crossed his arms and tucked his hands into his armpits. "O-o-o-oh. My hands are freezing! No, they're not!" He shook his hands in the air and danced about, first on one foot and then on the other, "They're burning!"

"Never mind. They'll be all right again soon."

"I got one right in his mouth," Koka triumphed.

"I got one right down the back of my neck," I moaned. "Can you see if you can get some of it out?" I knelt down in the snow and Koka put his hand down my back. "I'm soaking."

"I can't find any. It must have all melted. My valenki are full of snow. Agasha is going to be ever so cross."

"She'll just put them on the stove and they'll be dry by tomorrow. Oh, dear, I think I've lost one of my mittens. It must be under the snow somewhere."

Agasha saw us coming through the kitchen window and ran to open the door. She threw up her hands at the sight of us.

"Just look at you! what a sight you are! No, don't come into the kitchen until you've got some of that snow off. Whatever will you be up to next?"

"Agasha, we had a fight." Koka stated with some pride.

"A fight? Merciful Heavens. Who with?"

"With some boys from the village. They got through the hole in the fence where the fox went."

"Hole in the fence?" Agasha was already at the kitchen door. "Where are they? Show me!"

"They've gone now, Agasha. It's all right."

Agasha's eyes were burning with anger as she helped us off with our dripping clothes and boots.

"We pelted them with snowballs and they ran away," I boasted, and then added with all the scorn I could muster, "The pigs!" Agasha nearly dropped my valenki which she was holding in her hands. She spoke to me sharply.

"Moossia, never let me hear you talk of pigs like that again. We depend upon pigs for food." She spoke like a true peasant and a true believer. I was brought up abruptly by her tone of voice and apologised humbly.

"All right, Agasha, I won't. I'm sorry." But Agasha was really cross about the whole incident and didn't let us off the hook lightly. She continued to scold us as she took off our wet clothes and rubbed us dry in front of the hot kitchen range.

"You are not to get into fights, Moossia! Just look at your dress! You're soaked to the skin. I ought to stand you both in the corner for coming back in such a state."

"Revolution! Revolution! Revolution!" I rehearsed the words I had heard in the garden. Agasha's manner changed in an instant. She froze and went pale, looking at me with startled eyes.

"What did you say, Moossia?"

"It's what the boys were shouting in the garden," I answered innocently. "Revol…" I got no further because she silenced me with a gesture, "Don't, Moossinka, don't. Never let me hear you say that word again!" She became very silent as she continued to set our wet clothes round the fire and dressed us in warm dry things. By the time she had done all this she was back in her usual sunny humour again. She patted us on the head and sent us off to the dining room where Mama was sitting near the stove reading a book. She had heard nothing of the drama which had passed in the garden nor of its aftermath in the kitchen. She looked up at us in smiling approval.

"What lovely rosy cheeks you have, my little ones."

Koka went to the bookcase, pulled out a well-known, well-worn book and took it to Mama. He laid it on her knees and leafed through it until he found the story he wanted and then looked up at her appealingly without saying anything. She chuckled, laid aside her own book and began to read the story of The Little Hump-backed Horse as Koka settled down on a stool at her feet.

"Beyond the mountains, beyond the forests, beyond the wide seas, opposite the sky, yet on earth, there lived an old man in his village. He had three sons. The youngest was called Ivan…"

I was listening dreamily to the story leaning with my back to the warm stove. Agasha had entered the room. She came over to me and whispered in my ear,

"Don't lean against the hot stove, Moossinka. Your bones will dry up."

Chapter 23

Spring 1917

Framed by the blue-whiteness of the water-laden snow, patches of dark earth began to appear round the roots of the birch trees in the garden and groups of snowdrops started to push up through the sodden earth. Koka and I would get out into the garden whenever we could to see how they were getting on and to encourage them by gently easing off the casing of ice which the coldness of the night had formed about them. We hoped that they would grow and blossom all the more quickly for our care. But we never thought of picking them.

"The snowdrops are ringing the Spring in," Agasha would say, "how could we think of stopping them?" So, of course, we couldn't.

We hadn't seen Pikko for several weeks. He had been a very affectionate little puppy-companion, with his floppy ears and curly tail endlessly wagging, and was into everything. However, after a few days we found that he was very fond of chewing things and making messes all over the kitchen which had been decided upon as his home. Agasha put her foot down and insisted that Pikko be put in Aino's care during the winter. When Aino turned up with him on a lead we had almost forgotten him and hardly recognised him, so much had he changed. He was many times bigger than when we had last seen him and no longer a bouncy puppy but a sedate, well behaved grown up dog. Not only that but he now had a tiny tail and trimmed, pointed ears. His bright brown eyes were alert as ever, though, and he seemed pleased to see us because his little stump of a tail wagged non-stop.

"No, Aino, don't bring him into the kitchen," said Agasha firmly, "Look at all the mud on his feet."

"No, all right then. But I've made him a kennel. He can stay outside in that, only I don't know where the Barin will want me to put it." Just then we heard Mama calling us and we ran off and left Pikko to his fate.

Mama was talking to a tall gaunt lady in the dining room. The tall gaunt lady turned round and looked at us in her tall gaunt way.

"This is Frau Tremer, children," smiled Mama. We hesitated, fearing the worst.

"Say how do you do." We dutifully stretched our hands to be shaken by this ominous stranger. I remembered a little late to give her a quick bob. Then the blow fell.

"Frau Tremer has kindly agreed to come here every morning to teach you to speak German." We looked at each other fearfully.

"German, Mama?"

"Yes, Moossia. I want you to be good children and learn this important language with Frau Tremer." We were too stunned to say anything and fled from the room at the earliest opportunity to find Agasha and complain to her. Agasha seemed quite heartless about the whole business.

"You aren't babies any more, my little ones. It's your Mama's and Papa's wish."

"But, Agasha, she looks like a horse!" Agasha was shocked.

"Never forget, Moossia, a horse can be man's best friend."

So Frau Tremer walked with us in the garden every morning when it was fine, or else sat indoors showing us pictures, talking all the time in German. Koka did his best to wriggle out of the lessons and took a leaf out of Mama's book.

"I've got a headache," he would say at regular intervals during the first few days. But I was rather heartless because I had no idea of suffering all by myself so every time he said he had a headache, I said quickly,

"No you haven't Koka. You know you haven't." So that, after a few more attempts, he gave up this little ploy.

We were used to hearing a number of different languages spoken. When our parents didn't want us to understand what they were saying they spoke in German. Granny and Aunt Dorothea and Mama often spoke in Danish. Mama and Granny spoke French together and when Cousin Kathe and Papa's sister Aunt Olga came on a visit from the Baltic States they would speak together in Estonian.

Our favourite phrase to start with was no doubt, "Auf wiedersehen, Frau

Tremer." "Auf wiedersehen, Kinder," she would invariably reply as we said goodbye to her at the garden gate. As we walked back up the path together on the third day I confided to Koka,

"Agasha says that her house is full of cats."

"Yes, I know. I heard Mama talking about them. I wish she would stay at home with her cats."

"Mama says she's really an artist. She draws pictures."

"Look out, she's coming back. Hide! Hide!"

"Don't be silly, Koka." I held him firmly by the arm. "Don't run away! She's seen us." But Frau Tremer hadn't come back to start our lessons all over again. It was a false alarm. She had only left her purse in the dining room.

So the mornings passed with Frau Tremer pointing to this and that and making us repeat things after her, talking all the time in German. Soon she started to play games with us and drawing pictures and even playing card games like Black Jack. She had no difficulty in getting on the right side of Koka. On the day she had the inspiration to paint a picture of a train coming in to Kelomakki station he changed his mind about her completely.

"You know," he said, nodding his head like a little wise man, "Frau Tremer isn't too bad."

We soon got used to her ways and began to chatter away in German in no time. Mama was visibly pleased but Agasha, curiously, made no comment at all. Our days fell into a regular pattern and the only thing that changed for a while was that Mama became rather less well than usual and retired more often and for longer spells to her room. Agasha began to be away from the cottage for hours at a time, often leaving quite early in the morning. We didn't give this much thought at the time and weren't encouraged to ask questions. Now that the snow had gone there was plenty to occupy us in the garden. Aino often left his garden tools about and I took it into my head that I might start a little garden of my own somewhere. I was practising wheeling the wheelbarrow about one Wednesday afternoon when a familiar sound caught my ears.

"Wheee whoo, wheee whoo."

"Listen, Koka! That was Papa's whistle."

"I didn't hear anything."

"Listen, there it is again. Come on, let's go and meet him."

"It isn't Friday, is it?" Koka shouted as we ran down the garden path, through the gate, across the lane, over the plank bridge and full-tilt into Papa who was sauntering along through the trees swinging his favourite silver-mounted walking stick and whistling softly to himself as he often did.

"Papa, Papa," we shouted excitedly. He bent down, gathered us both in his arms, and kissed us both. His eyes were glistening as he stroked our hair.

"How good it is to be back with you all."

"Nobody said you were coming today."

"Nobody knew, Moossia. It's a sort of surprise."

Koka was just happy to have Papa with us and seized the walking stick and swung off along the path framing his lips unsuccessfully to produce an imitation of Papa's whistle. But there was still something I didn't understand.

"Papa, you didn't tell us when you left that you were coming back on Wednesday."

"I didn't know myself, darling. Mind! Look where you're going. You nearly walked into that tree."

"How long are you going to stay this time, Papa?"

"For ever. I'm going to stay with you always. I'm not going back to St. Petersburg." I looked up at his face, overjoyed at such good news, but there was no answering happiness in him. His brow was puckered and he seemed to be thinking of other things.

"I'll go and tell Mama." I let go of his hand and started to run on ahead. He stopped me quickly.

"No, Moossia, no. I want to tell her myself." I was totally mystified but stayed obediently at his side as we went through the garden gate. Mama seemed to have been aware of his arrival in some odd way. Perhaps she had heard his whistle, although this seemed very unlikely. She was standing expectantly at the door of the verandah and came running down the path, half laughing, half crying, and fell into Papa's arms. They stood for a few moments in a close embrace without saying a word. Mama managed to get out,

"Karloosha, it's so unexpected. But I'm so relieved to see you, my dear." He put his arm round her waist and they moved towards the cottage. I was walking by their side but they seemed quite unaware that I was there.

"I managed to get the last train out of town."

"You look so tired, my dear."

"I don't think anybody got much sleep in St. Petersburg last night."

"But what about Mamochka and Aunt Dorothea?" Mama was trembling with anxiety. Papa continued, not answering her directly.

"Egor sent me word to the office not to go back to the apartment so I stayed in the office all night. I went to the station as soon as it was light. I must have caught the last train to leave St. Petersburg for Finland. It's all over, Lilya, it's all over."

"But Mamochka? What about Mamochka?" Papa pulled himself together.

"She refused to leave, point blank. I managed to get through to her on the phone. She refused. So did Aunt Dorothea."

"Was she at home?"

"Oh, no, my dear. She didn't stay at home."

"I'll tell Aino to go down to the station to get your things."

"No, don't bother him, Lilichka. There isn't anything to get. I didn't bring anything. I couldn't. Only my silver-mounted walking stick. Koka has gone off with that." I tugged at his jacket to draw his attention. Something was very clearly very wrong.

"Papa, why didn't Granny want to come? Why?" I asked anxiously. He put his arms round my shoulders and spoke very gently.

"It's nothing for you to worry your little head about, Moossinka." Then he brightened up with an effort. "Go and find Koka, will you, my dear, and rescue my walking stick for me?"

"But, Papa..."

"Granny wanted to be with us but she couldn't come just now."

"Will she come soon, Papa?" My question made Mama burst into tears and rush indoors. Papa made as if to follow her, changed his mind and turned back to me.

"Later. Granny will come later. Very likely." He squared his shoulders and became very practical. "Where is Agasha?"

"She went down to the village. She goes down to the village all the time."

"Well then, we'll go into the kitchen ourselves and put the samovar on and make some tea for Mama."

As we were getting the tea things together Koka reappeared through the kitchen door. Papa turned to him and held out his hand.

"Koka, old chap, I wonder if I could have my walking stick now?" His manner was strange and unusual and Koka handed over the walking stick without saying a word. Papa handled the walking stick lovingly and stood it carefully in a corner. He seemed to think his behaviour needed explanation.

"It means a great deal to me now, you know. I wouldn't like to lose it." We hadn't the slightest idea of what he meant.

"Go into the garden, my dears. I'll call you when the tea is ready." We followed each other outside still totally mystified.

"What does Papa mean about the walking stick, Moossia? He's got lots more at home."

"No idea." Nothing that had been said since Papa's arrival made any real sense to me. "We can ask Agasha when she comes back."

There was a rattling sound beyond the wood.

"Listen, what's that?"

"It must be a train. It comes from down near the station."

"It doesn't sound like a train. It's different somehow."

There was another burst of rattling. Ra-ta-ta-ta-ta.

"I know what it is. It's guns shooting."

"Guns…? Shooting…? Don't be silly."

There was a long hissing sound followed by a bang on the other side of the village. Agasha came tearing through the garden gate and up the garden path. She was carrying an empty shopping bag. Without pausing she spread her arms and almost pushed us through the kitchen door with all the haste she could muster.

"Quick, quick, indoors, indoors, quick." As she banged the door to, Papa spoke.

"What was that, Agasha?"

Agasha was startled at the sound of an unexpected man's voice in the kitchen and nearly jumped out of her skin. When she saw who it was she put a hand to her heart in relief. Her face glowed with happiness.

"Barin, Barin… you've come home."

"Yes, Agasha… I've come home."

"Praise the Lord. Now we are all together."

"I've made the tea, but I can't find the sugar, Agasha."

"There isn't any more, Barin, we've run out."

"Never mind. Just take this glass to Barinya. You'd better take her valerian as well." He gave us some tea and poured out some for himself and perched on the edge of the table.

"Sit down, children. I want to talk to you." We squatted on the low stools by the kitchen range. "Did you hear that bang just now?" We nodded vehemently.

"Yes, we did. It was over on the other side of the village. It was ever so noisy."

"That was a gun." Koka nearly tumbled off his stool in excitement. His eyes popped.

"A gu-un?"

"Why was it shooting, Papa?"

"Why, Moossinka, why?" He passed a hand wearily over his forehead. "It isn't at all easy to answer that question my dear. The main thing is that you must stay indoors for a while."

"Can't we even go out into the garden?"

"No, not for a while. Not until I give you permission. Do you hear me? On no account." Papa looked so serious that we would have promised him anything at that moment.

"We won't Papa, we won't."

He patted us on the head and went into the bedroom to see Mama, leaving two very puzzled children behind him in the kitchen.

Chapter 24

March 1917

"Aga-a-a-sha! Moo-oo-oossia! Ko-o-o-ka!" Papa was standing at the door of his and Mama's bedroom. "I want you all to come and help me."

"Did you call me, Barin?" Agasha came out of the kitchen drying her hands on a cloth. Koka and I rattled down the stairs from the upstairs rooms which were still silent and empty.

"What's the matter, Karloosha?" Mama appeared from the dining room.

"I want you all to come into the bedroom and help me to move the furniture." We looked at each other in great surprise but followed him into the room. Mama protested,

"Karloosha, leave it to Agasha and me to help you. The children really aren't strong enough."

"No, Lilichka," replied Papa very firmly, "I think it's very important for them to lend a hand. It will help them to understand just how serious our position is. Now we'll start with the big wardrobe. I want to put it right across the window."

They edged the heavy wardrobe little by little to where Papa had pointed. He and Agasha did most of the work but Koka and I did our best to help without getting under their feet too much. Soon the bedroom window was completely blocked and the room had become very dark indeed. Mama stood watching it all in the doorway. Her face looked very pinched and sad.

"How gloomy and depressing it is, Karloosha."

"Yes, yes, it is, Lilichka. But it's a lot safer, too."

"I don't like it in here now," Koka muttered, and slid out of the room.

Papa had opened the wardrobe door and was turning all the clothes hanging there sideways. He called Koka back and explained to us,

"Now, children, try to understand. You know that the soldiers have been shooting."

We nodded solemnly.

"Well, the wardrobe will help to protect us from flying bullets. The clothes will help a little bit, too.

"But the bullets will make holes in the clothes!"

"Clothes aren't very important at the moment, Moossia."

"They'll make holes in Mama's pretty dresses."

"Perhaps they would. That would be a great pity, but at least they would be helping to protect us." He sat down wearily on the bed. "What times we do live in, to be sure." Then he shook himself into life again and had a fresh burst of energy. "Come on, everybody, let's go and have a look at the other rooms and see what we can do."

Chapter 25

May 1917

Agasha came back from one of her long absences in the village with a shopping bag which appeared to be quite empty. Mama met her anxiously.

"Did you have any luck this time, Agasha?"

Agasha fished inside the shopping bag and produced, like a conjuror bringing a rabbit out of a top hat, a small floury cloth bag. Cheerfully she held it up for Mama to see.

"Yes, I did, Barinya. I had to wait a long time and I was almost the last in the queue. I got some flour." It was quite a small bag and Mama's face dropped in disappointment.

"Never mind, Barinya. I know it's not much but I'll try again tomorrow. Perhaps I'll be luckier then."

"What can you do with such a small amount, though?"

"I know what. I think I'll make some pancakes, some little ones. Then I can share them out and make it go round."

I pricked up my ears.

"With jam or sugar, Agasha?" She looked at me in an odd, comical way with her head cocked on one side. It was a silly question to ask and didn't deserve an answer. The jam had been finished weeks ago and we had almost forgotten what sugar looked like.

Later on I went to look for Agasha but found that the kitchen was empty. She had made the pancakes and they were arranged on a plate on top of the kitchen range to keep warm and ready to be taken in for lunch. There weren't very many, especially as Frau Tremer, who seemed to be getting gaunter and gaunter all the time, had been invited to share with us whatever we might have that day. As I stood contemplating the meagre feast a wave of irresistible temptation swept over me. There was a little devil in my tummy which rumbled to egg me on. I prayed that someone would come into the kitchen and prevent my evil deed.

The plate of pancakes drew me like a magnet towards it. I prayed and prayed but nobody came. Then my hand went out of its own accord, picked up one of the pancakes and stuffed it into my greedy mouth. Scarcely pausing to chew the precious morsel I bolted it down like a dog swallowing a hunk of meat and ran out of the kitchen pursued by heaven knows what demons of remorse.

The sun was shining brightly and its warm rays caressed and hugged me but I felt cold and shivery with inner shame, and fled across the garden to the barn, climbed the ladder, and squashed myself up into a tiny ball in a corner of the loft amongst all the bottles. I sat there with my arms clasped round my legs and my head pressed down onto my knees, quite horrified by what I had done. The garden was deserted and still. Even the birds had stopped singing. All I could hear was the thud, thud, thud of my heart pounding away. I sat there for several eternities, feeling smaller and smaller and hoping that I might, with a bit of luck, disappear altogether.

"Koka, Moossia, where are you?" Agasha's voice came from a million miles away. I slowly swam upwards towards it out of my nightmarish daydream.

"Moossia, where are you?"

"Here I am. I'm coming." I unfolded myself and crawled down the ladder. Feeling like a bedraggled wet fly I made my way across the garden to the cottage. Then I braced myself with the thought that no-one was going to miss one tiny little pancake, and went indoors more or less boldly and joined the rest of the family and Frau Tremer who were already sitting at the dining table. Papa got up and prepared to say grace and we lowered our eyes and folded our hands in our laps. Papa never missed saying grace nowadays. The less food we received, the more thankful had we become for what we did receive.

"Lord, for our food we thank you." With these words my own crisis seemed to have passed and I breathed an inward sigh of relief. Agasha came in with the dish of pancakes but, instead of setting them in front of him so that he could serve them onto the plates and pass them round to us, she leaned close to him and whispered something in his ear. Papa looked puzzled and looked at Agasha questioningly. She leaned towards him again and repeated what she had whispered. Now he looked terribly shocked.

"Repeat aloud what you have just told me, Agasha!" Papa's brows were drawn together and he looked unbelievingly round the table at all of us. I went quite cold. Agasha was on the verge of tears and said in a trembling voice, "There is one pancake missing off the plate, Barin." Her hands were shaking so much that the pancakes started to slide towards the edge of the plate and Papa had to take it from her.

"How many pancakes are there now, Agasha?"

"Seven, Barin."

Papa carefully counted the little pancakes and said, as if to himself, "Two each for the children, one each for us, and, as Frau Tremer is with us, this should make eight... You're quite right, Agasha... and there are..." he counted them afresh, "only seven."

Mama sat up quite straight and gripped the edge of the table. Frau Tremer didn't say a word and I was as if turned to stone. Only Koka didn't seem to realise the extreme seriousness of the situation and was more entertained by the drama than anything. Papa's voice continued carefully,

"I know for certain that Mama hasn't taken it, nor has Frau Tremer. I haven't taken it and Agasha certainly hasn't. So it must be one of you." His eyes travelled between Koka and me. "You, Koka, or you, Moossia."

Everybody looked at everybody else. Agasha stood with her brimming eyes lowered. Mama swayed towards the table and was clearly near to fainting. Koka's eyes got larger and larger.

"I repeat," Papa's voice was very cold but he looked so sad, "it must be either you, Koka, or you, Moossia. Did you take it, Koka?" Koka's reply was hardly audible,

"No, Papa, I didn't, I didn't." He began to cry out of sheer fright and Mama got up to go and comfort him. Papa stopped her sternly, "No, Lilichka, no." He looked at me and spoke very slowly as if it was painful for him to form the words. "Then it must be you, Moossia." By now I was quite hysterical and shrieked,

"No, no! It wasn't!" I pushed my chair back and ran out of the room. As I crossed the kitchen I tripped and fell. At that moment I heard Papa say, "Then it must be you, Koka." I lay on the wooden floor unable to move.

"No, Papa, I didn't take it, really I didn't." Koka burst into tears.

"What are you crying for, then?"

"I don't know. I don't know. I'm hungry." Koka began to mumble and sob so that I couldn't make out any more what he was saying. Papa silenced him. "I've heard quite enough, Koka. Come with me."

"Oh, Barin, let it be." Agasha's voice was unrecognisably hoarse; "Take mine. I'm not really hungry."

"That isn't the point, Agasha."

"Karloosha, please…"

"No, Lilichka." The door of the bid bedroom was firmly closed and I faintly heard the words, "Bend over, Koka."

I jumped up from the kitchen floor, pressed my hands to my ears and fled out of the cottage to my hiding place in the loft. In normal times one little pancake more or less wouldn't have mattered in the least but times were far from normal now. What's more, I had told a deliberate lie. I expected the world to tumble about my ears at any moment. The birds sang accusingly in the garden. A butterfly was trying to free itself from a spider's web. Fingers of sunlight probed through cracks in loft walls and roof, seeking me out. After a while I heard Agasha speaking quietly to Koka who was snuffling and giving little choking sobs.

"Let's go for a little walk, Kokochka. Dry your tears. Don't cry any more. You know how much your Papa really loves you."

Koka mumbled something indignantly.

"Of course I believe you didn't take it." She took a lighter tone. "Perhaps it was Booka the Evil One who took it. Here… let Agasha dry your little face for you." Koka's gasps and snuffles subsided. There was a brief silence. Then his sense of injured innocence reasserted itself.

"Papa would only give me one pancake for my lunch."

"Never mind. I wasn't very hungry. Look! I kept half of mine for you. Here! Eat it up!" Another short silence. Koka burst out again.

"It was Moossia! I know it was Moossia! You ask her, Agasha."

"If it was Moossia, think how unhappy she must be. Remember, Koka, God will make her heart ache long after your botty feels better."

I moved slightly to look up at the sky through one of the cracks, half expecting to see God looking down at me angrily. The fingers of sunlight fell across me and clutched at my heart. Uncontrollable terror drove me out of the loft screaming Agasha's name. As I stumbled out of the barn she was running towards me and I ran straight into her, sobbing my heart out. She knelt down and held me very tight, murmuring over and over again,

"It's all right, Moossinka. Agasha's got you. Don't cry, my little one. I know. I know. Agasha understands. Agasha understands. Oh, merciful God, help us all." She dried my tears, too, and went on, never stopping, "We'll all go back to the kitchen. I've kept your pancake for you. Your Papa and Mama don't want you to starve, you know. Let's all go back to the kitchen." As she got up to her feet and released me from her embrace I could see Koka standing just outside the barn looking at us mistrustfully.

"Ask her, Agasha. Ask her about it."

"Nobody is going to ask anybody about anything." She took us both by the hand and we started back to the cottage. "We have found Moossia again. It's all over and done with. I don't want to hear any more about it."

"Where is Papa?" I asked anxiously.

"He's gone down to see Aino about something or other. Your Mama is lying down so we mustn't make a noise."

We crept into the kitchen and spoke very little and then in whispers. Agasha miraculously produced a whole pancake for each of us and the whole painful episode was allowed to be forgotten.

Chapter 26

April 1917

"Porridge, porridge. Nothing but porridge. No milk and no sugar! I hate porridge!" Koka threw his spoon to the floor with all the strength he could muster. There was a deathly silence round the lunch table. Mama went pale and tears appeared in her eyes. Papa jumped to his feet and reached right across the table to smack Koka's hand. But Agasha spoke up before he could do so, and his hand stayed in mid-air.

"How dare you, Koka! How dare you say that! I stood in that queue for five hours to get you that porridge. Pick up your spoon and eat it and thank God for it!"

Such an outburst from Agasha in the presence of Mama and Papa was unheard of but it brought us all to our senses. Papa sat quietly down again and Koka picked up his spoon and wiped it on his napkin. There was complete silence. Papa and Mama didn't look at each other. I sat scooping up the hateful porridge and Koka did the same. When the porridge was finished lunch was over because there wasn't anything else to eat. I fled to Agasha's room, threw myself on her bed and sobbed my heart out not knowing why. After a few minutes Agasha's soft warm arms closed round me. She lifted me up and hugged me close.

"What's the matter, Moossinka, my little pigeon? What's the matter?"

"Oh, Agasha!" I sobbed, "everything is so different now. It's all so horrid. Even Papa isn't the way he used to be."

"Hush, hush, my precious. Your Papa has a lot of things on his mind. We must thank God we are all together. We must thank God for what we have."

She rocked me to and fro in her arms without saying anything more. Her presence soon calmed me down and my sobs faded away.

"Come along, my chicken." She gently let me fall back on her pillow. "Lie down on Agasha's bed and have a little sleep." She covered me over with her woolly jacket and I fell fast asleep though it was right in the middle of the day.

At this time there were frequent bursts of gunfire, near or far, longer or shorter, and for a week or more we were kept strictly inside the cottage. We lived in a twilight world even though the late spring sun was shining brightly in the garden. Our only excursions were into the rooms upstairs which remained cold and empty although the time had gone by when our aunt and cousin might be expected to arrive.

"Agasha, when are Aunt Fanya and Roonya coming to stay?"

"They aren't coming this year, Moossinka. They won't be coming, the Lord protect them."

Koka and I were kneeling in a patch of bright sunshine which had wheedled its way past the obstructions in the dining room window. We looked out longingly at the outside world into which we hadn't been allowed to stray for so many long days. Papa came into the room and saw us kneeling on the floor and looking out into the garden. He read our thoughts instantly and sat down in a chair nearby.

"Children, listen to me. I know how much you would like to be able to go outside and play in the garden. I might let you do that. But only if you will promise faithfully that you will behave exactly as I tell you."

"We will, Papa. We will." This would be the best thing that had happened to us for weeks.

"Then listen very carefully. I can't make you stay indoors the whole summer, that's certain. There's still a fair amount of shooting going on. You've heard it yourselves, haven't you? The ra-ta-ta-ta you hear comes from machine guns. Machine guns fire a lot of bullets very quickly and it only takes one bullet to kill you. So when you go out into the garden I want you to stay at the back of the cottage away from the railway line, and when you hear the ra-ta-ta-ta or the whistling sound which comes from the bigger guns, throw yourselves down flat on the ground and lie still, absolutely still, until it's over. The shooting never seems last very long. The armoured trains don't go very fast but it only takes them a few minutes to pass through Kelomakki."

"What are they shooting about, Papa? Why are they doing it?"

Papa leaned forward and stroked Koka's hair. He seemed very sad.

"It's the war, old chap. People are quarrelling with each other, you know."

"Wouldn't it be safer for them to say indoors, Karloosha?" We hadn't noticed Mama standing in the doorway listening to what Papa had been saying to us. He shook his head in a perplexed way.

"You're quite right, Lilichka. It would be safer. But we can't keep them locked up inside the cottage all the time. Look how pale they're getting. They must have some fresh air."

"Perhaps they'll make it up soon and be friends."

"Perhaps, Koka, perhaps."

Chapter 27

May 1917

"Five petals are lucky. Seven petals are very lucky. If you find a bloom with ten petals then you will be very lucky indeed."

"But here's one with only three petals, Frau Tremer."

"Ach, unlucky, unlucky! Put it on the ground. Here, give it to me and I'll show you." Frau Tremer took the three-petalled blossom from me and put it on the ground and, raising her skirt ever so slightly so that she could see quite clearly what she was at, she stamped the blossom firmly into the ground with the heel of her black-buttoned boot.

It was something totally new to us when the lilac trees were in full bloom, and Frau Tremer took us down to them and taught us how to tell our fortunes by seeking out blossoms with the right number of petals. We gathered handfuls of the luckiest blossoms we could find and shared them into the open palms of any willing grownup we could find. Reactions differed. When we told her that you had to swallow the blossoms to make the charm work, Agasha hesitated. Because the idea came from the foreign Frau Tremer she suspected that there might be something a bit sinister about it and that it probably wouldn't work in any case. On the other hand, she had to admit that the lilac trees were the Almighty's creation so that there might be something in it after all. So she swallowed the lilac blossoms just to be on the safe side, and to please us. Papa cheerfully swallowed all the blossoms we gave to him.

"Thank you, Moossia. Thank you, Koka." He was very polite indeed. "We can do with all the good luck we can get, can't we?" But Mama's response fell between Agasha's and Papa's.

"No thank you, Moossia. I don't think I'll have any more. I think I've swallowed enough good luck for one day. Let's only hope it works. Go and tell Agasha that I want her to help me go through my furs." So we had to swallow an extra helping of good luck blossoms ourselves. If you chewed them they were rather bitter but if you just swallowed them they tasted rather nice.

Mama's furs were kept in a large trunk in the darkened big bedroom. Agasha brought in one of the oil lamps from the dining room and the two of them took the furs out one by one and examined them in the lamplight. They exchanged a very few words and seemed rather nervous.

"What do you think, Agasha?" Mama would ask, and Agasha would nod or shake her head. When she shook her head the fur would be bundled back rather carelessly back into the trunk. This surprised me rather as Mama had always been very particular and careful with her furs. Just to see what would happen, I asked if I could try some of the furs on and was even more surprised when Mama agreed without a murmur. It took only a few moments for me to hang a sable muff round my neck, pop an ermine hat on my head and swathe my shoulders in a most beautiful silver fox cape. This one was my favourite of all Mama's furs and I almost looked upon it as a sort of family pet.

Koka didn't like the silver fox because of its big glass eyes. He always imagined that they were staring him out. I was parading up and down, trying to see myself, not very successfully because the lamp was in the wrong place, feeling no end of a fine lady, when Koka came into the room and finished face to face with the silver fox. He was quite startled and began to growl and bark like a little dog, scratching about in the air with his hands as if they were paws. When I turned my back on him he got hold of the fox's tail and pulled it this way and that, growling and barking all the time.

"Don't, Koka," I cried out, "You'll pull the tail off. Agasha!" She came over to us laughing and clapping her hands at Koka and shooing him off. He dodged her and ran out of the room chanting, quite idiotically,

"Silly old fu-urs. Silly old Moossia. Silly old fu-urs."

"All right, Moossia, that's enough. I'll take them now." Mama removed my borrowed finery and laid the furs with the bundle at the end of the bed. "Agasha, go and look. See if he's coming."

"Yes, Barinya. Come along, Moossia, come with me." We went into the dining room and Agasha positioned herself so that she could see through the verandah and up and down the lane.

"Who is it, Agasha? Who are you waiting for?"

"The devil himself, Moossinka." She saw that this remark had frightened me, and bent down to give me a hug. "Nobody is coming, my dove, God forgive me, nobody is coming." She was oddly flustered. She returned to her post at the window, only to leave it at once to go to the door of the big bedroom.

"He's coming, Barinya. I can see him coming down the lane. I'll bring the furs." The atmosphere was nervous and rather furtive and I tagged along after Agasha to see her pop briefly out of the kitchen door and beckon to someone who must have been coming in through the garden gate. When she came in again and saw me ready to eavesdrop she took me by the shoulders and ran me back into her room. She picked me up and sat me on her bed.

"No, Moossia, no! You are to stay here, do you hear? You are not to come out." She hurriedly left the room and pulled the door to. But Agasha's door never shut properly so I just sat and listened to what was going on. It was very, very strange.

I heard Agasha move about the kitchen which was next to her room. The kitchen door clicked open, creaked to and fro, and clicked shut again. The sound of a man's deep voice was followed by that of Agasha's. Mama's high heels tapped along the passage as she joined the two of them. The deep voice was silent and there were movements I couldn't understand. A succession of hurried whispers followed. Agasha sounded angry about something. The man's deep voice uttered only single words in an emphatic, rather brutal way. Mama spoke out with unusual clarity and firmness.

"All right, then. The fox fur and this one."

My curiosity completely overcame me and I opened Agasha's door to tiptoe down the passage and peep inside the kitchen. Agasha had her back to me and was facing a tall, thin man with a swarthy face and quick dark eyes who had Mama's silver fox in his hands. Mama was holding out towards him her brown fur cape and was near to tears as the dark man stuffed the silver fox roughly into a sack. I was horrified by the atmosphere and crept closer behind Agasha to peek round her and see what was going on. She sensed my presence and swept me right behind her with one arm and kept me there, pinned close to her, so that the swarthy man couldn't see me and I couldn't see him.

"What about the rice?" Agasha raised her voice and put out her arm to grab the brown fur cape before it could disappear into the sack. "What about the rice?"

"You've got the oats! You've got the oats!" The man spoke harshly and said other things I couldn't understand because of his strange accent.

"No, no, no!" Agasha replied to him in the same harsh tone, and her whole body trembled. This was another Agasha I had never even caught a glimpse of before. Under her attack the man calmed down and produced a cloth bag about as big as Papa's pointed fur hat from one of the many folds in his clothes.

Agasha took the bag and released the cape, which disappeared into the sack. The man disappeared through the kitchen door. None of us moved for a few moments. I was quite unable to move because Agasha still held me close to her. She let go of me and went over to Mama.

"Here, Barinya, sit down on this chair." Mama was rooted to the spot and couldn't move until Agasha touched her gently on the elbow and she subsided into the chair.

"It's all right, Barinya. He's gone. Let me take the bag of oats from you. There."

"Agasha, give me a glass of water." Mama was on the point of fainting. She caught sight of me for the first time as I stood in the doorway when Agasha moved to get her the glass of water. She gasped and looked extremely alarmed.

"Moossia, what are you doing here?" I was made speechless by her vehemence, but Agasha stepped in calmingly.

"Don't worry, Barinya. I'll talk to her. There's nothing to worry about."

"We shall have to hurry in case the searchers come!"

"We will, Barinya, we will." She took both of my hands in hers and looked very seriously into my eyes. "Moossinka, you must forget this man. You must forget you have ever seen him. God will forgive you." She made the sign of the cross on my forehead. "Almighty, forgive me, a sinner, but, Moossia, if anybody asks you about him, say nothing. Do not lie. Say nothing. This man can only bring us trouble. And say nothing to Koka either. He is only a little boy and you are a big girl. Do you understand?" I didn't understand a thing but I realised she was asking something special of me so I promised.

"Yes, Agasha, I understand. I'll forget him. I won't say anything."

"That's a good girl." She let go of my hands and looked at Mama, who was clearly greatly relieved.

"Where are the little bags we made the other night, Agasha?"

"I hid them under my mattress, Barinya. I'll go and get them. Moossinka, I think you'd better go and play."

"Please let me stay. I promise I won't get in the way."

So Agasha came back from her room with a bundle of small calico bags about the size of playing cards. We all went into the dining room where she set a large tray on the table and she and Mama began to fill the bags, some with rice and some with oats.

"What are you going to do with them?"

"All in good time." The little bags were tied very tight with bits of string and I started to count them. There weren't very many. When I had got up to twelve Agasha scooped up the small amount of rice left into an empty bowl.

"Well, it isn't much, Barinya. But it's better than nothing."

"Yes, Agasha, it is. We can eat what's left over for lunch today. Now then…"

"I've got the needle and cotton, Barinya."

They then started to play a kind of version of hunt the slipper except that, instead of hiding one slipper, they had to hide the twelve little calico bags. Every imaginable hiding place was brought into use. One little bag went behind some books in the bookcase. One was put in the bottom of a Japanese vase. One went into the bottom of the box where the rest of the furs were stored, but the most ingenious of all the hiding places was the reverse side of the curtains where the wardrobe had been dragged in front of the bedroom window. That was where the needle and cotton came in. Agasha climbed up on a chair and sewed one bag to the inside of the top of one curtain and Mama sewed another to the inside of the bottom of another. As the curtains couldn't be drawn because of the wardrobe, the little bags were most unlikely to be disturbed.

"Why are you hiding them all over the place like that, Agasha?"

"So that we are the only ones who can find them again, my sunshine. Just remember what I told you. You mustn't talk about this to anyone. It's a secret." But I was hard to satisfy.

"Why is it a secret?" Agasha stopped sewing and bent down to me from her perch on the chair. She spoke very quietly.

"Because it all comes from the black market, my dove, and the black market is a bad thing. If it weren't for the black market we would starve but, all the same, it's a bad thing."

This totally convinced me. I had taken a strong dislike to the swarthy man who had taken Mama's furs and bundled them into a dirty old sack. His tall black hat and dark complexion and disagreeable manner made him an out and out black character in my book. Any market he was involved in was bound to be black, a thoroughly bad thing, and not to be talked about.

Chapter 28

June 1917

"Where did she say we would have to go, Karloosha?"

"To Byeloostrov, Lilichka."

"Shall we be able to get there?"

"I'm not sure. I think there are still some trains going that far."

"They've given us so little time."

We were all sitting in the lamplight round the dining room table after our meagre supper one evening, drinking glasses of very weak tea. Koka and I were trying to put off the time when we would have to go to bed. Mama reached out her hand and Papa handed her the letter which had been lying on the table in front of him together with the envelope it had come in. I recognised the writing on the envelope.

"Is Aunt Fanya coming?"

"Sh, Moossinka. Don't interrupt, my dear." Mama had started to reread the letter in a choking voice. "'They have decided to deport us all because Walter is a Swiss national. It breaks my heart to have to leave like this. We haven't seen Mama lately but we know she is all right. They will allow us to come as far as Byeloostrov on the frontier on the fourteenth to say goodbye to you. Please try to come if you possibly can...' Dear God, Karloosha. We must try! We must try!"

"Can we come and see Aunt Fanya, too? Will Roonya be there?"

"No, Kokochka, no, my dear." Mama could hardly speak through her tears

A few days later when we got up we found that Mama and Papa had already left the cottage to go to Byeloostrov. It was already dark and we had been put to bed by the time they got back that night. We both jumped out of bed and put our heads round the bedroom door when we heard the sound of their voices.

They were both very tired and travel-stained and clearly most upset, Mama in particular. Her face was flushed and her eyes were pink with crying. She kissed us both goodnight, hardly said a word, and went straight off to bed. We heard Papa walking up and down restlessly in the dining room a little later and ran in our nightclothes to see him. He hugged us and kissed us.

"I thought you two had gone back to bed," Agasha chided amusedly when she came in from the kitchen with a small bowl of soup and a slice of black bread for Papa's supper.

"Barin, you must eat something. You must be tired out."

"Sit down, Agasha. I'll tell you all about it."

"I'll just bring the samovar in, Barin. I won't be a moment." She bustled off and Koka and I settled on either side of Papa at the dining room table. He stirred the thick mushroom soup about in the bowl, took a spoonful or two, and then let the spoon fall back in the bowl.

"It's no good, Agasha. I can't eat. I just can't." His usually jolly face was clouded over. Agasha gently tried to encourage him to eat.

"The soup is quite thick today, Barin. Just you try it!" Papa stirred the soup in the bowl with the spoon but just couldn't bring himself to raise it to his lips. He saw that our eyes were riveted on the soup.

"Why don't you two finish it off for me? No, don't bother to go and get another plate, Agasha. Here, Koka, Moossia." He took two teaspoons out of the tea glasses and we set to, drinking up the soup on either side of him. Papa was lost in thought for a while then he roused himself. "Agasha, pour me out a glass of tea, will you? And take one to the Barinya. If she's asleep, don't wake her." He leaned back heavily in his chair and shook his head wearily to and fro several times.

When Agasha came back into the room with the untouched glass of tea still in her hand, he looked up at her.

"You know they wouldn't allow us anywhere near them."

"Not at all, Barin?"

"To start with, we thought we were never going to get to Byeloostrov. The train was an hour late at Kelomakki. It kept stopping all along the line for no apparent reason. Soldiers and inspectors got on and off at every station to examine everybody's papers. Several times we thought they were going to turn us back. We didn't get to Byeloostrov until nearly midday.

When we got there the military directed us along a long muddy road. There wasn't any transport at all and so we had to walk for what seemed hours. When we got to the frontier post it was on a river and there was a bridge leading over to the Russian side. There were Finnish soldiers on our side with rifles and fixed bayonets and Russian soldiers on the other side with rifles and fixed bayonets. Neither the Finnish soldiers nor the Russian soldiers would allow anybody to pass over the bridge. We couldn't see Fanya and Walter and Roonya on the other side and we began to think we might have missed them as we had been delayed so long by our train."

He paused for a few moments and sipped at his tea, reliving in his mind every moment which had passed that day. We had long finished the mushroom soup and were listening spellbound to Papa's words. There was no mistaking the tragedy behind them. Then he started to talk again.

"It would have been silly just to turn back and come home again when it had taken us so long to get there. We decided to wait as long as we dared. We had no idea when the return train might leave Byeloostrov because the trains weren't keeping to the timetable. We waited all the same. At about three o'clock in the afternoon we saw Fanya and Walter and Roonya trudging down the road on the other side of the bridge. It must have been even more difficult for them than it was for us. We waved to each other and they got into conversation with the guards on their side of the bridge and we explained everything to the guards on our side. We told them that Fanya and Walter and Roonya were going abroad that Barinya was Fanya's sister and that they might never see each other again. It didn't make any difference. We pleaded with them to let us go and meet each other halfway across the bridge and, obviously, Walter was doing the same. When Walter started to walk across in spite of them the guards threatened him with their bayonets. It looked very dangerous indeed for a few moments until Walter turned on his heel and walked back to Fanya and Roonya."

"So what did you do, Barin?"

"What did we do, Agasha? What could we do? We just stood there at either end of the bridge and shouted across to each other. We were at least fifty metres apart and the wind was blowing so that it was difficult to hear each other. We managed somehow."

"And Barinya?" Papa put his hands to his face and couldn't speak for a few moments.

"It was quite heart-rending. I shall never forget it. She stood there with her arms stretched out towards Fanya, shouting… and crying as if her heart would break."

"Barinya was fast asleep just now, Barin." Agasha had been holding the full glass of tea all this while. Now she put it down on the table.

"Good, good. She's quite exhausted. It will help her to sleep."

"Could you hear what they were shouting, Barin?"

"Sometimes yes. Sometimes no. the wind made it difficult." He swayed to and fro in his chair, distractedly. "I don't suppose we'll ever see them again. Walter had lived half his life over here. He was practically one of us. What will they do in Switzerland without any money? It was awful, Agasha! Awful!" We sat in a stunned silence for a while and then Agasha picked up the soup bowl.

"You must have something to eat, Barin. You've had nothing."

"Tomorrow, Agasha, tomorrow. I don't have any appetite. None at all. Just pour me another glass of tea. That will do." He suddenly became aware of Koka and me. "Isn't it time that you two were in bed? Goodnight, my little ones."

"Papa, why wouldn't the soldiers…?"

"Not now, Moossia, I'll tell you another day. Off you go with Agasha… It's the war, you know. How will it all end?"

That night we were very restless and wouldn't let Agasha leave us. She sat on the edge of my bed telling us endless stories to get us off to sleep. Stories of the Grey Wolf which always helped to rescue the Prince, of the Magic Pike which granted all your wishes.

"All of them, Agasha?"

"All of them, my precious."

"Even if I wished for a hundred roubles?"

"Sh, it's late. Look, Koka's asleep."

Chapter 29

June 1917

"I really don't know what we're going to do, Lilichka."

"Isn't it worth anything at all?"

"It's not worth the paper it's printed on."

"What are we going to do for money then?"

"I don't know. I don't know. We just can't pay our way. I suppose we can try to barter things to keep ourselves alive."

"Couldn't we try to get out?"

"Without new papers? Not a hope."

"What are we going to do then?"

"There's nothing we can do. We shall just have to stay put here."

"What shall we do about Agasha?"

"Agasha's no problem, thank goodness. I've already had a word with her. She says she'll stay with us no matter what happens... you know she'll never leave Moossia."

As they moved out of the verandah and their voices died away, I felt a sharp pain in my hands. I looked down and found that I had been digging my fingernails into my palms without knowing. There was a series of deep red marks in each hand. I had been sitting by the window in the dining room overhearing this snatch of conversation between my parents. The grownups did their best to conceal from us the extreme seriousness of the general situation and tried to present their best reassuring smiling faces; all the same it was impossible for me not to realise in moments such as these that they were very worried indeed about the future. My own anxieties led me into becoming somewhat of a skilled eavesdropper so that I learned a great deal more about what was going on than the grownups thought I did. The thought that Agasha might be leaving us filled me with instant horror and despair and all I could feel at this point was that this was never going to happen, come what may.

"Wake up, Moossia, wake up! Look what I've got!"

Koka came hurtling into the dining room waving handfuls of coloured paper. I came to out of my reverie with a start to see him strutting up and down waving his arms in the air.

"Look at me! Look at me! I'm rich. I'm ever so rich."

"What are you talking about, Koka? What is it?"

"Look at all this money Papa has given me!"

"Fibber! I don't believe you. Let me see."

Koka was so surprised and excited by his new riches that he couldn't stay still. He threw his arms up in the air in such a paroxysm of delight and sheets of coloured paper came showering down all about us.

"Roubles and roubles and roubles and roubles," he chortled over and over again. I went down on my knees to have a proper look at all the banknotes and to help Koka who was scrambling about on all fours grabbing the money in handfuls.

"Let me see them. Why did Papa give them all away?"

"I don't know. I expect he's got too much. Come on. Let's go down to the barn and play shops."

"Half each! Half each!"

"Oh, all right then. There!" He thrust an extra handful or two at me in an extravagantly generous gesture. I had a sudden misgiving.

"Let's show it to Agasha first."

"What for?" He clutched the notes to his chest defensively. "Papa gave them to me."

"All the same. Let's show it to her." We ran off to the kitchen, where Agasha was usually to be found these days, and waved the money triumphantly before her eyes.

"Look, Agasha, look what we've got."

"Good Heavens! What are you doing with all that money?"

"It's ours, Agasha! It's all ours; Papa gave it to Koka."

"Come along with me, both of you. We must get to the bottom of this." She took us both firmly by the wrist and made to lead us off to find Papa. But he had overheard our exchange and met us before we had gone more than a few steps.

"It's all right, Agasha. Moossia's telling the truth. I did give it all to Koka. It isn't worth anything now. They may as well get some fun out of it. Did you get anything down in the village this morning?"

"No, Barin, no. I shall have to go even earlier tomorrow. I've never seen such a queue. There wasn't anything left for us at the end of it."

"We shall have to have a talk about what we're going to use instead of money, Agasha."

"Yes, Barin."

We had no idea what they were talking about and were just delighted that our newly gained riches were not going to be snatched away from us. We jumped up and pulled Papa down by the lapels so that we could kiss him.

"Thank you, Papa. Thank you ever so much for the money. Will you be coming down to our shop?" He smiled wanly.

"I might, children, I just might. Later."

We ran off to the barn to play shops with real money for the first time in a state of high excitement.

"Moossia, I wonder why Papa really gave it to us? How can it be worth nothing?" I thought for a moment or two and considered the beautifully printed pieces of coloured paper. I couldn't come up with the key to mystery however.

"I don't know," I said slowly, "I don't know, I'm sure. They're only pieces of paper after all. But just look at the eagles. They're ever so pretty."

Chapter 30

July 1917

We had all become so used to the sounds of machine gun fire and shelling that often, at night, except when it was very close, we would sleep right through it. When I woke up in the small hours one night it wasn't because of the sound of gunfire but because of strange noises overhead. I raised myself on one elbow and listened to the unaccustomed footsteps upstairs and the murmur of voices that I couldn't place. The thought struck me that Aunt Fanya and Roonya might have come after all but the voices didn't sound like theirs and I grew tired of listening and turned over and went to sleep again.

Everything seemed quite normal when I woke up quite early the following morning. I began to think that I had just dreamed of the footsteps and the voices. When I pattered out into the kitchen in my nightgown Agasha was at the kitchen range simmering some berries we had picked in the woods the previous day in a large flat pan. Mama followed hard on my heels. She looked very tired. Her long white dress looked all crumpled and she was wearing her soft white shawl round her shoulders, the one which was so fine you could thread it through a wedding ring.

"Have you been upstairs, Agasha?"

"No, Barinya, not yet. I haven't heard a sound up there. They must be very tired. I expect they're still asleep." I pricked up my ears. Obviously I hadn't been dreaming.

"Who are they, Mama?"

"They're a Polish family, Moossia. Don't make a noise, will you? Is there any tea, Agasha?"

"Yes, Barinya. I made it just now." Mama helped herself to a glass of tea and went out of the kitchen before I could ask her anything else.

"What kind of Polish family are they, Agasha?"

"I don't know, Moossinka. I only saw them for a few minutes. They went straight to bed. They were dead tired with the journey. They'd been travelling for a fortnight."

"Are there any children?"

"Yes, my dove, two. There's a boy and a girl."

"Hurrah! Then we can play Whites and Reds with them."

"Don't say such horrible things, Moossia. It isn't hurrah at all. More trouble, I shouldn't wonder. I don't know where I'm going to get food for them all."

Oddly enough Frau Tremer chose that morning not to arrive to give us our German lessons. Not that we complained, but she had been coming very regularly every day except Sunday for weeks now, and was always with us on the dot. So everything that day was unusual.

We spent the free time gathering some muhamoor mushrooms for Agasha from the edge of the forest. The shooting had died down for a few days so we were allowed to go a little further afield than before. We gathered these mushrooms as often as we could, and took the speckled red caps with their creamy white collars to Agasha to combat the plague of flies which had invaded the kitchen. She chopped them up into little pieces in a saucer and the flies would come along and sip the liquid which oozed from them. Then we just waited to go round and count the dead flies.

Afterwards we busied ourselves in the barn trying to get a polish on some shell cases we had picked up on one of our walks. We came across them first with Frau Tremer but she wouldn't let us touch them although they were quite empty and harmless. We thought they would be nice to use as vases for wild flowers and spent a lot of time polishing them to make them shine. Mama didn't approve at all and shuddered when she saw them.

A boy came out of the cottage towards us. He had thick black curly hair and was rather taller than I was. We dropped the shell cases and ran across to meet him, full of curiosity and questions.

"What's your name?" I opened the enquiries.

"Heneck. What's yours?"

"Moossia."

"Is this your brother?"

"Yes, this is Koka. Have you got a sister?"

"Yes, she's called Janechka. She's only four. Here she is now."

"Was it you coming in last night?"

"Yes. We got here at two o'clock in the night."

"Agasha says it took you a fortnight to get here."

"Fifteen days."

"Where did you come from?"

"St. Petersburg."

"It doesn't take fifteen days to get from St. Petersburg."

"We had to walk."

"All the way?"

"Yes, all the way."

"Oh… Do you want to play?"

"All right. What at?"

"What does your sister want to play?"

"What I tell her to."

"Are you a Pole?"

"Yes I am. What about it? Can you speak Polish?"

"No. But we can speak German."

"German? Whatever for?"

"Because Frau Tremer teaches us."

"Who's Frau Tremer?"

"She comes every day to teach us German."

"Is she coming today?"

"Well, she usually comes in the morning. Agasha says that she'll probably come this afternoon."

"How boring. Nobody teaches me anything, thank goodness."

"Who's that coming down the path?"

"That's my father."

"He's as tall as ours."

"He's a judge. He can hang people." Koka gasped and his eyes were like saucers.

"Don't take any notice of him, Koka. He's telling stories."

The tall man in the long dark jacket came up to us.

"Hello, children. You must be Moossia and Koka."

I had been right. Heneck had been telling stories. His father looked much too kind to hang people. He took Janechka's hand.

177

"Heneck, your Mama is looking for you. Time for your reading lesson." Heneck looked at me sheepishly and ran off into the cottage with a toss of his curly head. His father bent down to little Janechka; "Shall we ask Moossia and Koka to show us their garden?" Janechka still didn't say a word but she did manage to nod with some enthusiasm.

We showed them all round the barn, although they wouldn't go up the ladder to see the loft; we introduced them to Pikko and took them to see the pond and the icehouse. When we got back to the cottage the nice tall man took Janechka upstairs. Frau Tremer still hadn't come.

"I wonder where she is?" mused Koka.

"Why worry?" was my reply, but we went off to ask Mama all the same.

She was sitting on the verandah with her sewing. The wicker chair creaked as she turned to look at us in surprise.

"Shouldn't you be with Frau Tremer?"

"She hasn't come yet."

"How strange. She's usually so punctual."

"Perhaps she's ill."

"Perhaps one of her cats is ill."

"How many cats has she got, Mama?"

"I really don't know, Kokochka."

"When we ask her, all she says is viele, viele, viele, many, many." Mama got up out of her chair looking puzzled and worried.

"I'd better go and see if she's all right. Just in case."

"Can we come, too? Then we can see her cats."

"No. You'd better stay here. She might have had another call to make before coming to us. Don't run away now."

We were playing 'fleas' in the dining room later when we heard Mama running up the garden path and crying out in a distracted way, "Agasha! Karloosha! Agasha! Karloosha!". We ran into the kitchen just as Mama came in through the outside door. She was out of breath and her cheeks were very red. She leaned against the doorpost. Agasha had heard her cries and was there ahead of us.

"Agasha, where is Barin?" She faltered a few steps. Agasha took her by the arm and guided her to a chair.

"Barin's not here, Barinya. He went out some time ago. Whatever is the matter?"

"She's dead, Agasha, dead!"

"Who's dead, Mama?" She looked at me without seeing me.

"She's dead, with all her cats." Agasha sprang into action. She took us by the arms and almost pushed us into the dining room. "This is no place for you just now, children. Off you go. Your Mama must have quiet." But although we were in the dining room we could still hear what was said in the kitchen.

"We shall have to tell the children anyway, Agasha."

"Later, Barinya, later."

"There she lay on the floor, Agasha, with her cats all over the place. They were all round her, on top of her, even in her hair. And they all looked famished to death. It was awful, Agasha, awful."

"May she rest in peace! Don't go back there, Barinya! The authorities will deal with it all."

"What authorities are you talking about, Agasha?" Papa had just come in. "What on earth is the matter, Lilichka? You look as white as a sheet." We could hold back no longer and burst into the kitchen with the dreadful news.

"Papa, Papa, Frau Tremer is dead. Mama found her in her house and all her cats were sitting on her."

Papa crossed to Mama in great concern and put his arm round her. "Come and lie down for a while, my dear. It's been a terrible shock. Agasha, make some tea and find the valerian. It will help to tranquillise her." It was only then that it was brought home to us how severely upset Mama had been. We watched dumbly as Agasha restarted the samovar and Papa led Mama away. We only found our tongues again when he came back some minutes later.

"Shan't we have any more German lessons, Papa?"

"Well, no, I suppose not, Moossinka. What an unfortunate end."

"Hurrah!" shouted Koka inappropriately, and threw his arms into the air.

"Merciful Heavens! May you be forgiven, children!"

"Sh! Children! Don't make so much noise. Mama has had a very bad shock."

We ran out into the garden unfeelingly.

"Who will feed her cats, Moossia?"

"I don't know. They'll have to catch mice and birds or the foxes will get them." I felt a belated pang for poor Frau Tremer. "We ought to be sad about Frau Tremer. All the same, I can't help feeling glad in a way. No more 'Wiederhole, wiederhole, repeat again, repeat again.'"

Moossia

Was it the oddity of Frau Tremer as a person, our resistance to her as a teacher, the bizarre nature of her passing, or the fact that we were half-starved ourselves at the time, or a combination of all these things, which led us to deal in such an apparently heartless way with the demise of our poor, unfortunate German teacher?

Chapter 31

August 1917

The last tiny little bit of the last candle sputtered and sparked in the candlestick. Koka and I sat up in bed waiting for total darkness to engulf us. I didn't mind all that much but Koka had his hands over his eyes and was making little whimpering noises. Every so often he took his hands away to see if the worst had happened. Blackness descended on us at the very moment when the wind set up a particularly eerie howl outside in the garden, and this was too much for Koka. He wailed loudly and called for Agasha who rustled in softly from the dining room.

"What's the matter, Koka?"

"The candle went out. It's dark. I don't like it."

"Could we have another candle, Agasha?" I asked practically. She looked at me worriedly.

"There aren't any more, my dove. That was the very last one." Her face brightened. "I tell you what. I'll prop this door and the door of the dining room open and then you'll both be able to see the light of the lamp. What about that?"

Koka grudgingly agreed and Agasha went back into the dining room for a short while. There was a nighttime murmur of voices, Agasha's and Papa's and Mama's. The oil lamp was moved onto the table so that a little more light shone down into the passage. Agasha came back and sat on the edge of Koka's bed, murmuring to him in a soothing way and stroking his head. Koka nestled down in the bedclothes and, after a while, Agasha came over to me, pulled the bedclothes up round my neck, tucked me in, kissed me goodnight and stole back into the dining room. I settled down to sleep.

But sleep wouldn't come to me. The wind howled relentlessly round the walls of the cottage. The dry leaves scurried to and fro outside like the rustlings of a thousand busy little animals, a thousand mice perhaps. Inside there was an intense silence broken only occasionally by a whispered remark. I grew more and more wakeful. Perhaps I did sleep for a short while. As I opened my eyes again a large shadow loomed on the passage wall. It was only Papa moving across the dining room in front of the lamp but it filled me with unreasoning alarm. I slid out of my bed and padded barefoot to the door of the room where I would find the grownups.

They were all seated round the table straining at various angles towards the very inadequate light from the lamp, turned low to economise the lamp oil which was in very short supply. Mama was holding her book out beyond the lamp; Papa was hunched forward, a pen in his hand, working through some official-looking papers. Agasha, who had her back to me, was turned a little away from the table to throw the light onto a piece from her never-ending pile of sewing. She was the first to be aware of my presence as I stood on the threshold, hesitating. She put her sewing down onto the table in surprise and came over to me.

"What's the matter, Moossinka?" She must have read the alarm in my face.

"I can't go to sleep." I was on the edge of tears because I thought I would be scolded for being out of my bed at that time of night, but Agasha was completely understanding.

"Of course you can't, my pigeon. I don't wonder at it. Just listen to that old wind. Listen to the noise it's making in the chimney. I'll just go and get a blanket for you and you can lie down on the sofa for a while." She went off towards our bedroom. Papa looked up from his papers absently over his spectacles. He didn't seem to have seen me up till then.

"It's very late for you to be out of your bed, isn't it, Moossia?"

I wrongly thought he was being cross with me.

"I tried to go to sleep, Papa, really I did."

He held out a hand to me and drew me close.

"It's all right, Moossinka, it's all right. Agasha will tuck you up in here."

Soon I was lying under the blanket on the sofa, drowsily listening to the quiet voices of Mama and Agasha, and to the rustling of Papa's papers. The howling of the wind in the chimney and the sinister dark corners of the dining room beyond the range of the feeble lamplight didn't worry me any more. I had a feeling of complete safety. I could see Agasha between Mama and Papa from my position on the sofa. Every so often she would look over towards me to see if I was all right. When our eyes met her face would crease slowly into one of her most beautiful smiles and it would positively glow in the yellow light.

At one point Papa sighed, took off his spectacles, laid them on the table and stretched his arms.

"It's really too difficult in this light. I can hardly see what I'm doing. I'll finish them off in the morning."

There was complete silence inside the cottage except for the ticking of the clock. Papa had a thought, pushed his chair back and went out of the room into the passage, only to return a few moments later putting his overcoat on. Agasha stopped in mid-stitch and Mama put her book down and rose to her feet in some alarm.

"What are you doing, Karloosha? Surely you're not going out at this time of night?"

"I've had an idea." He buttoned up his overcoat, smiling mysteriously.

"But it's pitch black outside. You can't see a hand before you!"

"Aha! That's just the way I want it to be." He put a forefinger up and tapped the side of his nose. Moving close to Mama and Agasha, he lowered his voice. "I think, I just think, I know of a place where I might, just might, be able to get us some milk."

"At this time of night?"

"Well, it wouldn't be any good going in daylight, would it?"

"Do you want me to come with you, Barin?"

"No, Agasha, you stay and look after everything here. You never know." He went over to Mama and gave her a kiss. She held onto his lapels.

"But where on earth are you going, Karloosha?"

He put a finger to his lips. For a moment he looked just like Koka.

"Never you mind. I shouldn't be too long. But don't wait up for me." He went to free his lapels and Mama let him go reluctantly.

Agasha followed him into the kitchen and there was a jingling sound as they sorted out the milk cans.

"Take Pikko with you, Barin."

"Mm-m-m... no... no. Better not. He might start to bark and then the fat would be in the fire. I'll be better off on my own. It's all right, Agasha. I can find my way there blindfold."

We listened as Agasha let him out of the kitchen door and his footsteps faded. Agasha came back into the dining room and found me sitting up on the sofa. She lifted my legs up off the ground and settled the blanket round me once more.

"Close your eyes, Moossinka. It will soon be morning. It will soon be light again."

A moment or two later someone was shaking me violently and shouting in my ear,

"Moossia, get up, get up. Get your clothes on."

I sat up quickly and found that I was back in my own bed. There was Koka jumping up and down and already fully dressed.

"What's the matter? Don't shout so loud."

"Papa's got a surprise for us."

I was out of bed in a moment and shrugging my clothes on.

"What sort of surprise?"

"Come and see!" Koka shot out of the room into the kitchen.

"How do you know about it?" I was frantically doing up the buttons of my liberty bodice. Koka came back and poked his head round the door.

"I heard Papa talking to Agasha. Come on." He disappeared again like a jack-in-a-box. I dragged my dress over my head and ran after him into the kitchen where the grownups were waiting for me to arrive.

"I was lucky," I heard Papa say. "Ah, there you are, Moossinka. Good morning."

"Good morning, Papa, Mama, Agasha." There were morning kisses all round. Whatever the surprise was it would have to wait for a little while. Papa was laughing at our impatience.

"What have you got for us, Papa?" He went all mysterious, just as he had the night before, led us towards the back door and opened it with a bit of a flourish. We crowded over towards him. There in the corner by the step were three small, lidded cans. Agasha helped him to carry them carefully to the kitchen table. The lids were propped open slightly with little twigs.

"But what is it, Papa?" demanded Koka impatiently.

Papa folded his arms importantly and looked down on the two of us from his full height.

"It's milk, my little ones. Milk! I've managed to find you some milk."

We danced up and down in great delight. It had been weeks and weeks since we had set eyes on any milk.

"Yes," said Mama, "isn't it marvellous? Three cans filled with milk." Her face beamed with joy. I was already greedily looking forward to an even more infrequent treat.

"I bag the first saucepan to scrape when Agasha boils the milk."

"Ah, well," Papa looked round us all importantly, "Agasha is only going to boil a little of the milk. So we'll have to see about that. What we are going to do," he paused to make the suspense even more agonisingly delightful, "what we are going to do... is to make... some... BUTTER!"

The word exploded like a bombshell. Our eyes popped. Our mouths watered. We were rooted to the spot. We nearly fainted with this unheard of promise of pleasure still to come.

"BUTTER, Papa, BUTTER?"

"BUTTER, my little ones, BUTTER! Real BUTTER!"

"But how, Papa?"

His mysterious air vanished in the blink of an eye. He became very businesslike and practical.

"Now, listen carefully. Go up into the loft and get me six wine bottles. Just a moment! Listen! Not the earthenware ones. They must be clear glass ones." We were already on our way across the garden. Agasha called after us warningly,

"Don't break your necks, children. You're not the fire brigade."

We rummaged recklessly through the stock of bottles and took no notice of the cobwebs and the creepy-crawlies which we just wiped off hastily with our hands and shook out onto the floor. Agasha washed them carefully in the kitchen sink, scrubbed them out with a bottlebrush, and put them on the kitchen range upside down to drain and dry for a bit.

Mama and Papa came back to see how we were getting on. We proudly showed him the clean, shining bottles.

"They're just the very thing," he said approvingly.

"How much do the cans hold, Karloosha?"

"About a litre each, Lilichka. Now, give me one of the bottles. We'll put about half a litre into each bottle and then..." He broke off as he lifted the lid of the first can and his face, so cheerful and business like and full of anticipation a moment before, fell a mile and he groaned in disappointment.

"Oh, no! Oh, dear! I left them outside on the step so that the milk wouldn't go sour in the heat of the kitchen. Now look what's happened!"

185

"What's the matter? What has happened? What? What?" we chorused.

Without saying another word, he sadly put two fingers into the milk and fished out the limp body of a dear little field mouse by the tail. All our excitement and enthusiasm disappeared at once. Mama shuddered, turned away from the table, and started to look out of the window. Ever practical, Agasha asked Papa as he shook the drops of milk off the mouse back into the can and handed the little creature to her by the tail,

"Is that the only one, Barin?"

Papa got a fork and gingerly fished about in the other two cans and produced a drowned little body from each one. He handed them to Agasha who stood there holding a bunch of field mice by the tail and, in her frugal way, also shaking the drops of milk from the mice and back into the cans.

"Are they dead, Papa?"

"Yes, Moossia, I'm afraid so. They've drowned themselves in our milk."

"Poor little things!" I prodded them with a forefinger to make absolutely sure. To my surprise this upset Agasha somewhat. She raised the bunch of mice high out of my reach and rounded on me.

"Don't, Moossia! Don't do that! Don't be cruel! They've suffered enough!" She then, inconsistently to my way of thinking at the time, proceeded to the kitchen range, lifted the cover and dropped the little bodies into the glowing fire. Mama came away from the window and said, mournfully,

"Well, that's that! So much for our milk! What a pity!"

Papa and Agasha looked at each other with the same question on their faces. Papa squared his shoulders and visibly steeled himself.

"Have you got a bit of muslin, Agasha?"

"Yes, Barin, here's a piece." Reading his mind, she also handed him a large jug and spread the muslin over the top of it and held it in position with her hands while Papa poured the mousy milk through. They did this in an awed silence from the rest of us and half-filled the bottles as the jug filled up. When the six bottles had been prepared Agasha pushed some corks halfway into them and we were each given one of the bottles to shake. Agasha, with her big peasant hands, managed to hold two of them at the same time.

"Now," instructed Papa, "we shake the bottles up and down until we can see little yellow lumps in the milk."

Koka and I started to shake the bottles up and down as fast as we could but Papa quickly checked us.

"Whoa there, you silly billies. Don't go so fast. You'll tire yourselves out in no time. See how Agasha does it."

So we all took our time from Agasha and for a long time there was no sound in the kitchen but the swish-swash of the milk in the bottles and the heavy breathing of the five of us as we shook the wine bottles up and down, up and down, up and down. We soon found that it was quite hard work. Koka was the first one to flag. He puffed and groaned and rested his bottle on the table for a while. The rest of us just glanced at him and smiled at each other but nothing was said and, when he'd had a little rest, he picked up his bottle and started to shake it again and also to puff and groan. Mama was the next one to go.

"Oh, dear. This is taking a long time, Karloosha."

"Never mind, Lilichka. Just keep going a little longer."

One after the other the four of us subsided into chairs, but we still kept on shaking. Agasha was still standing, shaking steadily away with her two bottles.

"Why don't you sit down, too, Agasha?"

"No, thank you, Barinya. When you stand you're nearer to Heaven," she replied, not breaking her rhythm. Swish-swash. Swish-swash.

"Look! Agasha's got lumps!" Koka shrieked. "Can I finish one of your bottles, Agasha?" She smilingly exchanged one of her bottles for his. He shook vigorously for another minute or two and then crowed in triumph,

"Look, I've got butter. I've got butter. I'm the first!"

"No, you're not, Koka. That's one of Agasha's bottles. Agasha did it."

"Now, now, Moossia, no squabbling, please," Papa warned. "Look, mine is getting lumpy, too."

As the milk separated we studied the miracle lumps of butter floating in the bottles with the greatest awe. Agasha produced more muslin. The lumpy liquid was strained. The strainings were pressed and we finished up with a lump of butter about the size of a small apple.

"Can we try some now?" Koka and were drooling with impatience to sample the miracle butter. Papa looked hesitantly at Agasha. I think he was reluctant to see the meagre results of his midnight expedition and so much heartache, time and trouble disappear so immediately. But Agasha nodded her head firmly.

"I think there's just enough bread to spread it on, Barin." She produced a cloth and unwrapped the end of a loaf of black bread. "God has been merciful," she said, and gave Papa a knife to cut the precious bread and to spread the even more precious butter. With great deliberation and ceremony he carefully carved five very thin slices of bread, counting as he did so,

"One for Koka, one for Moossia, one for Mama, one for Agasha…"

"Oh, no, Barin. Leave me out of it. Give it to the children."

"One for Agasha," he repeated, very firmly, "and one for me."

"Can I spread the butter, Papa?"

"No, Moossia, we'll let Agasha do that." Agasha spread the butter with the same care and ceremony Papa had used to cut the bread. Finally, there on the plate, were five slices of bread and butter. Papa picked up the plate and held it out to us in turn in a most polite manner. We held the slices in our hands, hesitating to break the spell of anticipation by actually eating the bread and butter. Koka started the ball rolling and rather spoiled the atmosphere by avidly licking the butter off his own slice. This was too much for Mama.

"Really, Koka, whatever happened to your manners? I've never seen such a thing!" Papa was more tolerant.

"Never mind, Lilichka. It's a special day today. Let's find out what the whey tastes like."

The bowl of nectar was passed round like a loving cup with many oohs and aaahs and smacking of lips from Koka and rolling of eyes from Agasha who tried to hang back modestly at first but was urged on to drink of the cup by Papa so strongly that she couldn't refuse in the end. We ate the bread and butter in tiny bites to make this exceptional treat last as long as we possibly could. Koka capped the situation and made Mama choke so that she had to be patted on the back to make her better when, after carefully licking a final crumb from his fingers, he turned brightly to us all and said,

"You know, it didn't taste like mice at all."

Chapter 32

September 1917

It must have been the loud rumbling noises in my tummy which woke me up early one day in the late autumn. It spent a lot of its time nowadays rumbling away, complaining because it was given so little food, no doubt. Looking out of our bedroom window I could see that we had had our first powdering of snow during the night. The earth under the trees was still brown, though, and so was most of Papa's radish plot with its last few straggling bits of greenery. We had been eating a lot of radishes during the past few weeks and I think they had a lot to do with the noises and gurglings in my tummy.

"Oh, do be quiet!" I slapped myself gently on the site of all the noise but it didn't make any difference.

There were voices coming from the dining room.

"The Swodskys have no papers, none whatever." It was Papa. "They don't even have a residence permit."

"How could they have one?" This from Mama. "They came over 'black'",

There was that word again, "black". The first time I had heard it was when the Tartar came and took away Mama's lovely furs. Now the Swodskys – they were the Poles who were living in the upstairs part of the cottage – they had come over "black". The world we were living in seemed to be getting blacker and blacker. Agasha's voice joined in the conversation in the dining room.

"What are you going to do then, Barin?"

"I don't know, Agasha. I haven't the slightest idea. If they have no papers they'll get no rations."

Mama was resolute. "We shall just have to give them a share of our rations, Karloosha."

"It's quite impossible, my dear. There's not even enough for us."

"How much are they letting us have this time, Barin?"

"Ten kilos."

"Only ten kilos?" Agasha was incredulous.

"Ten kilos of potatoes. Not enough to live on and too much to die on."

"Isn't there anything else, Barin?"

"No, that's all. Only potatoes." In sudden alarm he burst out, "Oh, my goodness, what did I do with the ration slip? I thought I'd put it just there, on the table."

"It's all right, Karloosha, don't upset yourself. I put it in the Bible so that it wouldn't get lost. Here it is. What does it actually say?"

"It says that the rations of potatoes will be available at the village shop on Thursday. If we don't pick them up before nightfall we don't get any. Our ration for the family is ten kilos, just ten kilos."

"We can't share that, Barin. That's hardly enough for the children."

By now I was observing them through the open dining room door.

"When shall we get the next ration, Karloosha?"

"Who can say, my dear?" There was a very gloomy silence broken only by the sound of Papa's fingers drumming on the table. Mama and Agasha watched him hopefully. He studied the ration slip from every angle and cocked his head slightly as he did so.

"I wonder? I wonder? I wonder?" He was lost in thought.

I dodged back into our room and started to put my clothes on. When I went into the dining room a little while after, nothing had changed. Papa was still studying the all-important slip of paper and Mama was sitting at the table and not taking her eyes off him.

"Good morning, Papa. Good morning, Mama." Mama returned my greeting and bent down to kiss me. Papa stretched out his free hand and stroked my head absently.

"Good morning, my little chick. You're up early, aren't you?" He spoke so softly that I could hardly hear him.

"Is Koka still asleep, Moossinka?" Mama whispered.

"Yes, Mama. Shall I go and wake him up?" I followed suit.

"No, no. Let him go on sleeping."

"I've got it!" Papa jumped to his feet and fairly shouted out the words and waved the ration slip above his head. His chair fell back with a crash. Agasha ran in from the kitchen, white-faced. Koka must have jumped right out of bed at the sound of the crash. His little frightened face popped round the edge of Agasha's skirt a few moments later.

"What was that bang, Papa? Have they started shooting again?" Papa didn't even hear him and almost shouted, "I've got it, Lilichka, I've got it." Poor Mama was confused and alarmed.

"It's all right, Kokochka. It was only Papa's chair. It just fell over. Karloosha! Be careful! Don't do anything silly! Kokochka, go into your bedroom and get dressed. Agasha, will you bring us some tea in a few minutes."

All we had for breakfast were some small slices of what was supposed to be black bread but which was really a kind of dirty grey, and the scrapings of some very unsweet strawberry jam which Agasha had unearthed. Papa was still walking up and down muttering to himself when the three of us had sat down at the oval table. Agasha always thought that the oval table was safer to sit at than the square one in the kitchen. If you sat at the square one there was always the danger that you might find yourself sitting at one of the corners and that was dreadfully unlucky. It meant that you were in for seven years of unrequited love.

Papa became aware that Mama had poured the glasses of tea out for us and belatedly sat down to join us. He sipped the hot tea and leaned across the table towards us. What he had to say seemed a complete anticlimax.

"Now listen, everybody. I need a pencil. But it must be an indelible pencil. It must be indelible. It doesn't matter how small it is. There must be one in the cottage somewhere."

"What's an inde- indel-ible pencil, Papa?"

"It's one you can't rub out, Koka. It's the kind which makes purple marks when you lick it." Koka nodded wisely but said no more. Mama spoke up,

"I know we had one in St. Petersburg but I don't think I've ever seen such a thing down here at the cottage."

"Well, I want you all to look everywhere you can think of as hard as you can and see if you can find one. It doesn't matter how small it is, remember." Agasha took us both by the hand.

"Come on, you two, let's see what we can find." As we left the room I heard Mama say to Papa in a low, urgent voice,

"Please think what you're doing, Karloosha. People are getting shot for the slightest thing these days. If it's dangerous, please, for God's sake, for all our sakes, think twice." Papa was not to be deflected. He spoke to her kindly but firmly.

"There's no other way, my dear. This ration is too small for all of us. It's a matter of life and death. Do you want me to let the children starve?"

Although Agasha and Koka and I searched in every imaginable place in every drawer, in every cupboard, under every bed, right through the verandah, and rummaged through our toys and even combed the garden just on the off-chance, but not a sign of an indelible pencil did we find. After a tiring search we went back to report to Papa who had been busy with Mama at the same task in the dining room and their bedroom.

"I'm sure we did have one." Papa combed his wavy hair desperately with his fingers. "We simply must find it. It's a matter of..." He broke off when his eyes fell on Koka and me. "We must look absolutely everywhere. Now think, everyone, is there anywhere at all where we haven't looked?" We all thought hard with no result and heads were shaken in deep despair. Just as we were leaving the dining room, Agasha had an idea. She bent down to Koka who was just behind her.

"Koka, what about your 'bogey hole'?"

"What about what, Agasha?"

"There's a hole in the wall behind the pedestal, in the lavatory, Barin. Koka is always posting things into it."

It was true. Koka had been squirreling away all sorts of little treasures in this hole in the wall – knives, rubbers, tiny toys – and there had been several times when Agasha had had to fish about in the hole with a piece of wire to recover a pair of small scissors which Koka had gone off with.

"Very well, Agasha. We mustn't leave any stone unturned."

The four of us crowded into the lavatory; Mama had stayed behind in the dining room. Agasha got down on her hands and knees, supporting herself with one arm on the pedestal and prying with two or three fingers of her other hand into the hole in the wall. She had no success to start with.

"I shall have to tear the wallpaper off, Barin, and probably some of the plaster and a lath or two if you want me to make quite sure."

"Go ahead, Agasha, go ahead. Do whatever you think is necessary. She tugged at the paper and a great piece of wall came away. She proceeded to hand back to Papa's cupped hands the contents of Koka's treasure trove. Amid the jumble of knives and rubbers and acorns and tiny toys and red pencils and blue pencils and crayons was a tiny two-inch stub of pencil with all the paint scraped off.

"It this what we're looking for, Barin?" She held it up.

"It might be. Give it to me. I'll just try it." He put the stub of pencil to his tongue and drew a line on the back of his hand. It was deep purple. He showed it to us all joyfully and ran off excitedly to Mama who was still in the dining room. Naturally, we all followed after him. He was like a little boy.

"Look, Lilichka, look. We found it. Just the very thing." He licked the top of the pencil again and drew another purple line on the back of his hand and showed it to her and to the rest of us.

"I think you're all very clever. Well done, Koka."

We were all pleased at this outburst of praise from Papa but none so much as Koka who, up to now, had always got himself into trouble with his postings in the "bogey hole". He grinned from ear to ear and glanced up at Agasha in a rather "I told you so" way.

"What do you want it for, Papa?" I wanted to know. He looked rather caught out and replied hastily, "Oh, oh, it's for a special drawing I want to do Moossinka... er... it's nothing very important. I just needed that particular colour. Agasha, will you please take the children out for a little walk?"

It was obvious that the three grownups were involved in some sort of conspiracy to hide something from us which was very important and, perhaps, dangerous. Agasha took her cue from Papa and almost frogmarched us into the kitchen where our outdoor things were hanging up to dry by the kitchen range. Her behaviour made me even more suspicious especially when I heard Mama, who wasn't a very good plotter, say to Papa in the most anxious tones,

"Karloosha, are you quite sure you know what you're doing?"

We were bundled out into the garden and Agasha closed the door firmly behind us. We even had to finish doing up our buttons outside in the garden. It wasn't a very suitable day for a walk. Although the sun was shining the wind was blowing hard and cut through us like a knife. A lot more snow was clearly on the way. We walked hand in hand, hunched up against the cold and in the direction of the pond, which had begun to ice over. My curiosity was thoroughly aroused.

"Agasha, why did Papa need that very pencil?" She looked straight ahead of her and avoided my glance.

"How can I answer such a question? Your Papa needed it. That's all, my little soul." But, cruelly, I wouldn't let her off the hook.

"But why that very one?" Agasha improvised wildly.

"Look at the sky, Moossinka. It's blue, isn't it? Well, to draw the sky, we need a blue pencil. Look at the grass. That's green. To draw the grass, we need a green pencil." Then her invention gave out. "And your Papa needed this special pencil to draw something… special."

Before I could ask the next, obvious question, Koka broke in. He was pulling on Agasha's hand and trying to drag her back to the house.

"I don't want to walk about any more, Agasha." Agasha played for time.

"But we've only just come out, Koka." He started to whimper.

"I want to go indoors. It's too co-o-old."

"I tell you what we'll do. We'll just walk quickly round the house and then we'll go in."

"No. I want to go back now. You and Moossia can go." Before we could stop him Koka broke away from Agasha's hand and ran back through the kitchen door. There was nothing to do but follow him through the kitchen, along the passage to the threshold of the dining room. Agasha tried to stop us but we were too quick for her. She whispered desperately, "No, Moossinka, no. you mustn't." Seized by a kind of panic, I took no notice of her at all and the result was that the three of us finished up at the dining room door still dressed in our outdoor clothes.

We were confronted by a most extraordinary tableau.

The tension in the room was almost unbearable. Our parents were so preoccupied that they were unaware of our presence. They didn't even glace in our direction. All the efforts at discretion and secrecy completely went by the board.

Mama was standing on one side of the oval table holding the ration slip in one hand and making as if to keep him from it with the other. There were tears on her face. Her voice was agonised.

"No, Karloosha, no, I can't let you do it. It's too dangerous. I couldn't endure it if anything happened to you."

Papa moved towards her from the other side of the table with an unutterably tender expression on his face. He spoke coaxingly and reasonably.

"There's no other way, my dear. I have to risk it. It it works we may, with God's help, pull through for a while. It I don't, it could be the end of us all."

He put his arm round her and tenderly kissed her tear-stained face. Then he tugged gently at the ration slip she was holding.

"Give it to me, Lilichka, let me have it. I must try."

She let Papa take the piece of paper on which so much depended and sank, exhausted, into a chair. Papa squeezed her round the shoulders, kissed her on the forehead and sat down at the table. He spread the paper, somewhat crumpled by now, flat on the cloth and smoothed it out as much as he could by stroking it a number of times with the flat of his hand. Ferreting about in his waistcoat pocket with his right thumb and forefinger he produced the tiny stump of indelible pencil, the point of which he held up to the light and studied carefully. He had the piece of paper stretched out by the fingers of his left hand. Visibly holding his breath, he lowered the pencil and drew two short strokes horizontally, one below and shorter than the other. The pencil was tucked back into the waistcoat pocket and he breathed out slowly and shudderingly. The silence in the room was so heavy that it pressed down on my head and shoulders like a leaden weight. It was like the stillness in the forest before the breaking of the biggest thunderstorm you could imagine. The leaves in the forest began to stir and that sound turned into someone muttering the same three words over and over again. It was Papa.

"One into seven. One into seven. One into seven." He gave a little laugh, picked up the piece of paper and waved it at us. "There, you see, it was quite simple. I've done it! Not ten kilos, but seventy kilos! You see?"

His whole frame sagged.

"Why do I feel like a criminal?"

"No, Barin, no, you're not. It was God's hand. He wouldn't let the little ones starve."

"Well, I must be off." He folded the piece of paper carefully and put it in the inner pocket of his jacket. "I'll go and get Aino to take me in his cart. I'll need his help if I'm lucky." His mood kept changing. He was by turns solemn, tender, excited and even quite elated.

"Agasha, you will stay with Barinya and the children, won't you? I give them into your care." He added, quite lightly, "Just in case." This was too much for Mama. She burst into tears and rushed over to Papa, embracing him fiercely.

"Karloosha. Karloosha." It was all she could utter.

"Don't upset yourself, Lilichka, please. Remember the children."

"God is merciful," reminded Agasha, and knelt down and put her arms tightly round us with the result that we began to cry, too. Mama and Papa exchanged a long embrace. Papa swiftly gave us both a hug and a kiss and went out into the passage to get his coat. We tried to follow him but Agasha waved us back and closed the door behind her. All three of us listened to the small sounds of Papa's departure until we could hear no more. As the garden gate banged to, Mama gave a wince of pain. Agasha came back. Her first glance and her first words were for Mama.

"God is wise and merciful, Barinya." Mama gave her a wan half-smile and nodded her head. Agasha went over to the side table, picked up the family Bible and placed it carefully in front of Mama. Their eyes met and Agasha bent forward slightly in an encouraging manner. Mama understood her meaning, pulled herself together and opened the Bible at random. Koka and I and Agasha all sat down round the table. Mama found a chapter heading with her forefinger and began to read in a shaky voice,

"Bless the Lord, O my soul; and all that is within me…"

She broke down and appealed to Agasha.

"It's all wrong, Agasha. How can I bless…?"

"Barin is trying to save us, Barinya. We must do all we can to help." Mama turned back to the Bible with new resolution and started again,

"Bless the Lord, O my soul; and all that is within me, Bless His Holy Name…" Soon the words began to flow more smoothly as if she were glad to have found her voice again. It grew firmer and more assured.

After the pulverising emotions we had suffered I found it difficult to listen all the time to the words of the Psalm. My thoughts were very much with Papa. This much was clear to me, that he might not come back from his shopping trip, that we might never see him again. In my mind's eye I followed every stage of his journey. Now he would be tramping over to Aino's cottage.

"The Lord is merciful and gracious…"

Now he and Aino would be slowly jogging along towards the village.

"As for man, his days are as grass; as a flower of the field…"

Now Papa would be at the shop. There would be a lot of other people… soldiers… with guns pointing at him.

"Bless the Lord, all his works
In all places of his dominion;
Bless the Lord, O my soul."

When she came to the last words of the Psalm and looked up at us again, Mama seemed quite calm. She closed the heavy volume, got up and walked about the room and peered at the clock.

"It seems ages and ages…"

"It isn't so long, Barinya. I doubt if he's got there yet."

"Agasha, I'm so frightened for him."

"All in good time, Barinya. He's got to take his turn in the queue, after all."

"What is Papa doing, Agasha?"

"He's gone out with Aino, Moossinka," Mama intervened.

"Why is Mama so scared, Agasha?" She was lost for a ready answer but did her best on the spur of the moment.

"It looks as though there might be a lot more snow, Moossia." This was an absurd answer. It didn't begin to make sense. Something warned me not to pursue this line of questioning.

"Tell us a story then, Agasha."

"Why don't you tell me a story for a change? Why does Agasha always have to tell all the stories?"

"All right, then. Let's count to see who will tell the story, then. Will you join in, Mama?"

"Yes, yes, count me in." She and Agasha laughed. They knew exactly what I was up to. I always did the counting and they knew I had long since worked out just where to start so that I could get the result I wanted. They didn't mind my cunning little ways at all. It was all part of the game.

"*Amongst-us-fools-there-is-one-big-one-1-2-3-it-is-you.*

1-2-3-4-5-it's-you.

1-2-3-4-5-6-7-8-it's-you-again.

1-2-3-4-5-6-7-8-9-10-the-czar-ordered-him-to-be-hung.

He-hung-for-a-while-and-then-flew-to-heaven.

There you are, Agasha! We knew it would be you!"

Everybody roared with laughter at the success of my little trick and Koka and I gathered round the table at one end with Agasha while Mama opened the Bible again and sat silently reading. All the time our ears were tuned to pick up any sound which might tell us that Papa was back. Agasha began the story in a sinister whisper,

"Once upon a time there was a Baba Yaga, a witch, who lived in a forest. She had a little house that stood on chicken legs. If she didn't want to see you, the chicken legs kept shut, so that you couldn't get in at the door."

197

"Agasha, did you know that if a black cat crosses his path when he's going hunting or somewhere, Papa always turns back?"

"And I should think so too, Moossinka. He's quite right. Black cats belong to witches. They're very unlucky."

"Don't keep interrupting, Moossia," Koka complained.

"She had a black cat…"

"Sh… sh… Listen…" Mama was very agitated. "Did you hear the sound of a cart coming across the lane?" We all stopped breathing and listened intently. Agasha shook her head.

"I don't think so, Barinya. It's probably something creaking in the barn." She got to her feet. "Shall I go and make some tea?"

"But you haven't finished the story yet, Agasha."

"I know I haven't, Koka, I know. What a wicked thing I am. All I think of is my own enjoyment. I'll finish the story later on. You come and help me light the samovar. And you can put out the glasses, Moossinka." Agasha found it difficult to settle, too.

Mama closed the Bible and went over to the door leading onto the verandah. She shaded her eyes with one hand, looking through the reflections in the glass out into the garden. We stopped to watch her. She turned round and flew down the passage into the kitchen. We followed quickly and found her standing stock still in front of the kitchen door, wanting, but not daring to open it. We could hear slow, heavy footsteps approaching, not like Papa's at all. We didn't even dare to look out of the window but stood there, half in hope, half in fear. Someone knocked their feet at the side of the door to get the mud off their feet. The door opened and there stood Papa with the widest of grins on his face and a heavy sack on his back. He was staggering cheerfully under the weight. All he said was,

"I took the short cut through the gap in the hedge."

Pandemonium broke loose. Koka and I and Mama pressed forward to embrace him and to pull him in through the door. Mama's face was wet with tears. Agasha was blinking furiously.

"What happened, Karloosha?"

"Nothing happened. Nothing at all. No questions asked. All went well. Here they are."

He went to swing the dirty old sack down off his shoulders but, as he did so, there was a ripping sound, the bottom fell out of the sack and the potatoes rolled in all directions over the kitchen floor. There was a hysterical burst of laughter and then we were all down on our hands and knees scrabbling around for potatoes and putting them into buckets and bowls and any kind of container we could lay our hands on.

Chapter 33

September 1917

When Agasha hauled us off into the kitchen "to help me light the samovar" or "to help me grind the dried potato peelings to make the bread", or when she insisted that we go out in the garden "to make the most of the sunshine", I knew very well that some crisis had occurred or that some disagreeable news had arrived and that she or Papa or Mama or all three wanted to spare our young feelings. But although they did all in their power to shield Koka and me from the hard facts of life, their efforts were rather spasmodic and muddled, so that I got to know a great number of things I was supposed to be ignorant of. Sometimes the grownups would imagine that the very words they were using were incomprehensible to me but I could often understand meanings even if I didn't altogether understand the actual words. Sometimes they would lower their voices and imagine that I couldn't hear what they were saying. Sometimes they would tell themselves that I couldn't hear because I was far too engrossed in what I was doing. Last of all, although I didn't quite go so far as to listen at keyholes, I did share a lot of the general anxiety; we were living rather on top of one another in the cottage, the walls weren't in the least soundproof, and so I was aware of a great deal more than I was supposed to be aware of. But it was often much later, even years later, that I realised the full importance of what I had learned.

We had had no breakfast on the day of the battle in the village, and our meal was further delayed while we were sheltering in the icehouse. So we were very hungry by the time Agasha laid before us our meagre repast of boiled potatoes which we dipped in salt and ate with our fingers, and some very thin tea the colour of pale straw. Koka and I were ravenous and the others were too occupied with their thoughts to have anything to say. Several times Papa was about to speak to Mama but glanced in my direction and he thought better of it. When Agasha was clearing the plates and pouring more tea he took advantage of the distraction to say to Mama in a low voice, which I wasn't supposed to hear,

"They set fire to Liova's house... take your tea, Moossia... nobody's seen him since."

"Did I hear Aino say that Nini's missing, too?" Papa nodded. She went on, "I couldn't make out all that Aino was saying." She paused and passed a glass of tea to Koka. "Do you think it will be safe to go down there yet? It seems to have been very violent while it lasted."

"Apparently our people beat them off and are still in control." The almost inaudible murmur went on.

"I don't really want to go, Karloosha."

"You don't have to, my dear. I'm quite willing to go by myself." But the more they lowered their voices the harder we had been listening.

"Where are you going, Papa? Can I come with you?"

"Moossia, drink your tea. Papa wants to take me for a walk, that's all." I lost interest and took my tea off to a nearby armchair and curled up with a book of fairy stories I had been reading. Koka wasn't going to be left out if he could help it.

"Can I come, Mama?"

"No, Kokochka, not this time." She made a pleading gesture to Agasha and looked towards Koka. Agasha grasped her meaning at once and went over to Koka with great cheerfulness,

"Koka, why don't you come into the kitchen and help me start the iron up. You can put all the pieces of cold charcoal in and I'll do the red hot ones from the range. Shall we?" He took her offered hand without a word and trotted off happily without another word. Mama and Papa glanced in my direction, saw that I was deeply immersed in my book and continued their low-toned conversation which I wasn't supposed to be able to hear.

"What do you think, Lilichka? We shall have to go before it gets too dark to see anything."

"I don't know that I want to go and see the corpses of my friends."

The word "corpse" froze me. I knew what a corpse was well enough. There were plenty of corpses in fairy stories. These I had always taken for granted. They represented no danger because they were invariably in distant or imaginary places. These new corpses were an entirely different matter. To think that there were corpses down in the village, bodies of people we had known, chilled me to the marrow. I sat there, looking at my book, but couldn't read a word. Through the haze Papa was speaking again.

"Believe me, I know how you feel. All right, I'll go by myself."

"No, Karloosha, no. I couldn't let you do that. I'll come."

"Dress warmly then. It'll be very cold by the time we get back."

Hiding behind my book, I spied on them as they went into the passage to get their outdoor clothes. Mama wrapped a warm, grey shawl over her little hat. Papa turned up the collar of his fur-lined overcoat so that it met his fur hat.

"Karloosha, my booties aren't high enough. I shall get them full of snow."

"You'll be all right, it isn't very deep yet. Just follow on in my footsteps."

They hesitated, looking in my direction, wondering whether to say anything more to me. But I had lowered my eyes to my book just in time. When they went down the passage to have a word with Agasha on their way out, I quickly closed my book and stole after them. They didn't see me.

"We hope we shan't be too long, Agasha."

"Don't worry about the children, Barin, I'll take care of them." As they opened the kitchen door she added, "I shall be praying that you don't find anyone you know." The kitchen door closed and Agasha prepared to do the ironing. She murmured to herself,

"O Merciful God. When will it all end?"

"When all the soldiers are dead and they haven't got any more bullets," chirped Koka with ruthless logic. Agasha was deeply shocked.

"Koka, how can you say such a thing? All the soldiers dead. I never heard such a dreadful thing. May God forgive you!"

"But, Agasha, I'm not fighting; you aren't fighting. They are the ones who are fighting."

"Yes, I know, Koka, I know. All the same… oh, it doesn't begin to make sense." She caught sight of me standing in the doorway. "Moossinka, come in and shut the door. Now, both of you, pull up two chairs by the fire. I'll open the range door for you. I'll tell you a story while I do the ironing."

"Agasha, you told Papa you would be praying. When are you going to pray?" She stopped spreading a blanket over the kitchen table for the ironing and looked at me in genuine astonishment.

"Moossinka, my little soul, Agasha is praying all the time. While I'm doing the ironing, when I'm doing the washing up, even when I'm telling you a story, I never stop praying in my heart." She finished laying out the blanket, spread a sheet on top of it and started her ironing.

It was a long afternoon's work. Agasha had time to tell us story after story. The cold bright light reflected off the snow outside the window was slowly vanquished by the spreading warm glow from the fire as darkness fell. After the story of the War of the Mushrooms, halfway through the story of the Swan Brothers, lulled by the warmth of the fire, by Agasha's soft voice and by the regular thud, thud, thud of the iron doing its work, we began to nod off, and she paused and looked over at us. Koka was at once alert and demanded, "Yes, Agasha, and then... what happened then?" So she finished the story of the Swan Brothers and told us the story of Father Frost.

"I feel hungry again."

"We shall have to wait until your Papa and Mama come back, Koka."

"Why are they taking so long? It's getting dark outside."

"I'll light the lamp and then I'll tell you the story of Alyonooshka." She lit the oil lamp but only turned the wick up halfway so as not to break the glass funnel with too much sudden heat. The light the lamp gave was still quite dim.

"Once upon a time there was an old man and an old woman. They had a little daughter, Alyonooshka, and a little son, Ivanooshka. The old ones died and Alyonooshka and Ivanooshka became orphans. Alyonooshka went to work and took her little brother with her. They walked and they walked and they walked. 'I want a drink of water, little sister,' said Ivanooshka. 'You must wait until we reach a well, little brother,' said Alyonooshka. And they walked and they walked and they walked. The sun stood high and it was very hot. Soon they came upon a cow's hoof, full of water. 'May I drink from the cow's hoof, little sister?' asked Ivanooshka. 'No, no, you mustn't' replied Alyonooshka, 'You will turn into a calf if you drink from the cow's hoof, little brother.' And they walked and they walked and they wa..." She broke off and raised her head from the ironing. "Listen, your Papa and Mama are coming. Now, listen to me. You must stay in the kitchen until I call you. Your Mama and Papa will be very tired after their long walk." She spoke very sternly so that we knew better than to think of disobeying her. We didn't even get up from our chairs when they came in. They didn't even look at us, which was most unusual. Mama hurried across the room with a handkerchief up to her face. Her voice was very shaky as she spoke to Agasha who had gone at once to her side.

"Oh, Agasha, it was dreadful, dreadful. They've just left them lying out there in the snow. So many of them. So many." Her voice rose, "I couldn't go there again. I couldn't." Agasha ventured,

"Barinya, was there anyone…?" Mama understood and answered with a note of surprise in her voice,

"No, no-one. There were so many of them but none of our people, thank God." She was standing now in the doorway and began to shudder uncontrollably. Papa joined them hurriedly.

"Agasha, take Barinya to her room. I'll make tea." He closed the door into the passage and saw us for the first time. He looked dead tired in the dim light. His eyes had lost every trace of their old sparkle. However he did his best not to impart his sadness to us, and asked in as cheery a tone as he could manage,

"Hello, you two. And what have you been doing all this time?" He perched wearily at the end of the table and forgot all about making tea.

"We've been waiting for you, Papa."

"Was it cold in the woods?" He shivered and replied absently, "Yes, Koka, it was. Very cold."

"What were you looking for out there?"

"Oh, different things, Moossinka… we thought we might meet some friends." The idea that he might be making some tea crossed his mind briefly and he started to put some tea into the pot, put it on the table and forgot it again, and resumed his seat on the edge of the table.

"Did you find them?"

"What…? Who…? Oh, no… they weren't there… thank God…"

"Will they be there next time you go?"

"I hope they won't, my dear… I don't think we shall go again, Moossinka… even if they might be there."

"Wouldn't they be waiting for you?"

"They'd forgive us, I'm sure." His voice had become more and more distant and it was as if he had forgotten our presence altogether. "We're sure to meet them again…one day." There was a long silence. A coal dropped through the bottom of the fire into the ashes… "It was so cold, so white, so still. Even their faces… as white as the snow."

Agasha came back into the room and turned the lamp up. Our eyes were so used to the dimness that it made us blink. Papa came to the surface again.

"Oh… Agasha… How is she?"

"I think she'll go to sleep, Barin."

"Ah… good… just as well… I'll go in and have a look at her." Agasha was making the tea he had forgotten about.

"Would you like some tea, Barin?" He hesitated at the door.

"Mm-m-m…? Oh, yes, thank you, Agasha." He caught sight of Koka and me, managed to summon up a smile for us carrying a pale memory of its usual warmth, and came over to us.

"Goodnight, Koka, old chap. Goodnight, Moossinka, my dear. Sleep well." I was moved to throw my arms round his neck and hold on to him tight. He was so dazed that he barely returned my hug and more or less waited for me to let him go. When I did release him he made another attempt to leave the room. This time Agasha stopped him.

"I'll find something for the little ones to eat and put them to bed, Barin. If you are still up, could I have a word with you?"

"Yes, of course, Agasha. I'll be in the dining room. I'll just have a look at the Barinya first." He finally escaped, giving Koka and me a questioning look as he went.

All that Agasha could find for our supper was some thin soup with a few porridge oats floating about in it and a slice of hard potato bread. We were speedily undressed, tucked in, kissed and each blessed with the sign of the cross on our foreheads, and Koka was asleep in no time. But my mind was in a whirl. All sorts of unanswered, unanswerable questions buzzed in my brain. What did Agasha want to talk about to Papa so specially? Was it about Koka and me? By the odd look he gave us as he left the kitchen Papa clearly thought so. But Agasha never told tales about us and it wasn't as if we had been naughty. When I heard Agasha go along the passage towards the dining room where I knew Papa to be, I was in such a state of turmoil that I couldn't restrain myself. I slipped out of bed and stole to the dining room door which was still ajar. I could just see Agasha who had her back to the door. I couldn't see Papa at all.

Their roles seemed oddly reversed. Papa was unsure, without his usual authority, and spoke in an uncertain, agitated way. Agasha was speaking quietly but with great firmness.

"No, Agasha, no. I couldn't agree to that. It's far too dangerous. It really is. You might be arrested at any number of points on the way."

"Nonsense, Barin. Everyone can see and hear that I'm just another peasant woman. Nobody will take any notice of me. Nobody will ask me any questions. I'll be able to go where I like."

"It's not your responsibility, Agasha. It's my responsibility. I'm the one who ought to go."

"You wouldn't stand a chance, Barin. They'd pick you up in no time. They'd shoot you before you got halfway there. I'm the only one who can go."

"It's so far to go in these conditions, at this time of year. It isn't as if it was summer time. How on earth will you get there?"

"No problem about that, Barin. On my own two feet. I'll walk. It may take me a long time but I'll get there. Don't you worry."

Papa groaned in an agony of doubt.

"I don't know, Agasha. I really don't know. How can I possibly agree to your going?"

"Barin, we simply must find out what has happened to the old Barinya. We can't just leave her alone in Petrograd to take her chance. Heaven knows what's going on there. I pray for her all the time. How can I honestly go on praying for her unless I do something about it? You know how Barinya feels about her mother, Barin. She's sick with worry." Words poured from Agasha's mouth in an unwonted flow. There was no mistaking the urgency of her feelings.

"That's all quite true, Agasha, but I must think about the danger to you. I really must. I could never forgive myself if anything happened to you... How could I look Moossia in the eye? Suppose you get caught by one of the patrols out of St. Petersburg?"

"I'll just tell them I'm going into the city to join the army. A peasant woman like me will come to no harm. It's not the danger to me we should be worrying about. It's the danger to the old Barinya."

"We'll talk about it again in the morning. Sleep on it, Agasha. Sleep on it. We shall never be able to persuade the Barinya. If you change your mind, remember, I shall quite understand. Barinya will never agree to your going."

"I'm not going to change my mind, Barin. Other people have crossed the lines. I'm not any more stupid than they are. The next dark night I'll be off."

She terminated the conversation by reaching out to pick up the empty tea glass which had been before Papa. I flew back to bed before she came out and caught me listening in and pulled the bedclothes right over my head. My head was in an even greater whirl than it had been before. Two things stood out clearly in my extreme mental and emotional confusion. Granny was in danger, and Agasha was going to leave me to walk all the way through the snow to find her in St. Petersburg.

Chapter 34

November 1917

I sat up in bed, rumpled my hair, rubbed the sleep out of my eyes, stretched my arms above my head and yawned loudly in my early morning ritual. Then I glanced round in alarm at the window. Surely the light was much brighter than when I usually woke up? Had I overslept? Why hadn't Agasha come to wake us up, then? Perhaps she had gone down early to the village on one of her many foraging expeditions. Then why hadn't Mama or Papa come into us instead? Koka? Koka was still just an indistinct lump under the bedclothes.

As I scrambled out of bed something else caught my attention and I stood stock still in the middle of the room. I began to feel frightened. Except for the odd creak in the woodwork, and the faint distant ticking of the clock in the dining room, all the usual little noises from people in the cottage were completely absent. I ran down the passage and pushed open the kitchen door, hoping against hope.

"Aga…" Her name died on my lips. The kitchen was empty. She obviously had gone down to the village early. I shivered with cold, hunching my shoulders, and went over to the kitchen range to warm myself but as I rubbed my hands together I felt hardly any warmth at all. Strange! The fire was usually blazing by the time I got up. When I squatted down to look I could see only a few glowing embers at the bottom of the grate. I looked about me. There was no water in the well bucket, and the samovar was still unlit.

My rising panic sent me running to the dining room. The cloth and the breakfast things were on a tray on the table but the table was still unlaid. I realised that I had heard no sound of movement or muted voices customary

207

at this time of the day from Mama and Papa. I stood at their door, my hands to my heart which was pounding rapidly. The door was slightly ajar and I pushed it first a little wider to peep round the edge, then wide open.

Mama and Papa weren't there either. The bed was unmade, the bedclothes hastily flung back and their night things cast across the bed. This was so completely unexpected that I began to tremble all over and dashed to Agasha's room. Her bed was unmade, too, although her nightgown was folded and placed on the pillow. Just as I was on the point of screaming in total terror I heard the sound of someone knocking the snow off their boots outside the kitchen door. I raced to the kitchen just in time to see Mama come in from the garden in her outdoor clothes. I burst into tears at the sight of her and she hurried over to me and took me in her arms.

"Whatever's the matter, Moossinka? What are you crying for? It's all right, my dear; it's all right. Sssh now, sssh."

"I thought everybody had gone away." I could hardly get the words out.

"I'm sorry, my dear. I thought we'd get back before you woke up."

"I thought you weren't ever coming back. Not ever."

"I just had to go and see Aino for a few minutes. I wasn't very long."

"Agasha wasn't here and you weren't here and Papa wasn't."

Agasha and Papa came in at that moment. Agasha was carrying an empty shopping bag. At the sight of her the floodgates opened again and I tore myself from Mama's arms and buried my face in Agasha's skirt. Mama rose to her feet and stood helplessly clasping and unclasping her hands.

"I thought Aino would be off somewhere in his cart," she explained. "I was only away for a few minutes."

"I thought you weren't ever coming back."

The three grownups gathered round me making soothing noises and I began to control my sobs. Koka's voice broke chirpily into this highly charged scene.

"Look at me, everybody. I dressed myself this morning. All by myself."

He had, too, though he still looked as though he had been dragged through a hedge backwards. His shirt was only partly tucked in; his collar was half in and half out, and one of his socks was very much at half-mast.

"And I remembered to clean my teeth."

There was no doubt about that, either, for a two-inch rim of toothpowder was still surrounding his mouth. His appearance was so unexpectedly ludicrous that I couldn't help myself. I began to giggle through my tears and this particular crisis was over. All became bustle and briskness as we shared the task of preparing a very scant breakfast. Koka was hurriedly straightened up and had his face wiped clean of toothpowder. Papa made the fire up. Mama prepared to light the samovar and Agasha went outside with the bucket to get some water from the well. There were snatches of low-keyed conversation between Mama and Papa as all these activities went on.

"Did you have a word with Aino, then, Lilichka?"

"Yes, I caught him just in time. He's coming in to talk to Agasha when he gets back."

"And Agasha showed me the ropes down in the village."

"Did they have anything this morning?"

"Not a thing. We went early enough, Heaven knows."

"What times we live in."

"Agasha has a lot of courage, I must say."

"What do you mean?"

"Well, a lot of them in the queue looked pretty rough customers to me."

"Were they unpleasant?"

"No-o-o, I can't say they were. They all seemed to know Agasha. They obviously liked her."

"That's not surprising, is it?"

"Of course it isn't. But it was a very great help to me. They seemed to accept me so it won't be so bad when I go on my own. At least they won't tear me limb from limb."

"Do you mind very much?"

"I can't afford to mind, Lilichka. Of course, I shall be careful not to open my mouth more than I absolutely have to."

Breakfast was over in no time and I got up from my chair. "Please may I leave the table?" Koka followed suit at once, "Leave the table?" To our astonishment Papa didn't give us his usual smiling permission. He spoke sharply to us and rose quickly from his chair.

"No, no, sit down again." He saw that he had frightened us and continued more softly, "I'm sorry, my dears; I didn't mean to upset you. You see, well, I'm not cross with you. I've got a lot on my mind at the moment. Just sit down there for a little while." With his napkin still in his hand he went over to the door and called to Agasha.

"Agasha, I think you'd better come into the dining room. I must tell the children. I think you'd better be here." There was the sound of Agasha putting a bucket down on the floor. Her voice called, "Yes, Barin, I'm coming." She walked briskly along the passage, wiping her wet hands on the corner of her apron. Papa was hovering by his chair as she came into the room and his eyes met those of Agasha. They held the glance for a moment and he went to sit down.

"I think you'd better sit down, too, Agasha. Get yourself a chair."

Agasha made no move to sit down, folded her hands across her apron and stood ready to listen to what Papa had to say.

"I think I'd rather stand, Barin, if you don't mind." There was an anxious note in her voice. Papa glanced up at her and smiled wanly but understandingly.

"No, no, of course, Agasha. Just as you please." He looked round at the rest of us. Mama didn't say a word. Koka and I, forewarned, sat bolt upright. He coughed into his hand and cleared his throat, almost at a loss to know how to begin what he had to say. "You see, my dears…" Mama clasped her hands in front of her as if she were praying. Papa tried again. He stood up as if that would make it easier for him to speak and the words came with a rush.

"You aren't babies any more. You can understand what I have to say. Of course you can. The fact is, I have to tell you that Agasha is going away from us for a while, a little while," and then quickly, before we could interrupt, "but she will be back again very soon. She won't be away very long."

Koka and I sat in chilled silence, quite numbed by the terrible news.

"And there is something I have to ask you." Papa moved along the table and bent down towards us confidentially. "While Agasha is away from us she doesn't want us to talk about her being away, you understand?" We nodded, dumbly. "It's a secret, you see?" We nodded again. "We must all do what Agasha wants us to do, mustn't we?" We nodded more vigorously. He had more to say to us.

"Now comes the most difficult thing of all. You must promise to do as I ask, children." He paused and waited for our reply. Eventually we found our voices and responded in thin, scared tones, "Yes, Papa."

"I don't want you to tell lies, of course. You know that, I'm sure. But, if anyone asks you where Agasha is, don't say anything, you see, not a word. All you have to do is… just… shrug your shoulders." He demonstrated to us, turning up the corners of his mouth and raising his eyebrows at the same time.

Almost mesmerised by these extraordinary instructions, we imitated him as precisely as we could. "That's right, that's all you have to do. Just shrug your shoulders." There was another exchange of shrugs. He reached out and ruffled our hair lightly.

"I always knew I had two clever children." He backed away towards his chair, smiling at us and glancing at Mama and Agasha for their approval. As he sat down our faces began to crumple and Agasha moved round and knelt with her arms round us.

"It won't seem very long, I promise you. Agasha will be back in no time at all. Now you be good children and just do what your Mama and Papa tell you to do, won't you?" Papa's seriousness and the air of mystery and the slightly comic quality of the instructions he had given us had held my tears at bay but Agasha's gentleness totally dissolved me. I was overwhelmed by panic.

"When are you going, Agasha, when?" She hesitated.

"I don't know, my little pigeon. I'm not sure yet. Maybe in a few days. Maybe quite soon." She was breaking the bad news as gradually as she knew how.

"Today?" When she smiled and stroked my hair without answering, Agasha underlined my worst fears and I burst into tears again. She had to abandon her hold on Koka to put both arms round me. Koka, deserted, began to whimper and crept round for comfort to Mama who had sat through the whole episode without speaking, her hands still clasped in an attitude of prayer. Agasha tried to still my fears.

"Don't cry, my precious, don't cry. Try to be a good girl while I'm away. Just think how much that will help me."

"Are you going a very long way, Agasha?" I managed to get out through my tears. For some obscure reason the shock of her imminent departure had quite erased from my mind the significance of the conversation between her and Papa which I had overheard. I just didn't relate the two.

"No, no, my sunshine. I wouldn't go a long way from you, of course I wouldn't. Just tell yourself that Agasha is going for a long, long walk. That's all it is. You'll see. I shall soon be back." She rocked me to and fro and made little inarticulate noises to calm me. They were the only sounds in the room for a while until Papa stirred and spoke to Koka.

"Koka, bring me the Bible, will you?" Koka obediently went over to the side table and managed to pick up the big, heavy book. Nobody thought to help him and he staggered over to Papa with it clutched tightly to his chest.

Papa located the blue ribbon which served as a marker and opened the book at a familiar place. As he read the familiar words his voice seemed deeper, more resonant than usual.

"Bless the Lord, oh my soul; and all that is within me, bless his Holy Name. Bless the Lord… who forgives all thine iniquities." His eyes scanned the text of the Psalm until he found the telling phrase he was looking for and his voice was completely assured, "For as Heaven is high above the earth, so great is His Mercy… Bless the Lord." He continued to contemplate the words he had just read to us, his eyes fixed on the Bible between his hands.

Agasha brought us all down from Heaven to Earth. She became her old, practical self. She got to her feet rather awkwardly because I was still holding on to both her hands.

"You will find everything in order in the kitchen, Barinya. There is enough wood for the kitchen range until the morning. Aino will bring in some more water from the well and some more logs when he comes over later." She had quietly withdrawn her hands from mine as she spoke and moved over to Mama. Mama understood that she was saying goodbye, and came to life. The two women embraced warmly and Agasha made the sign of the cross on Mama's forehead and moved round the table to Papa.

"I think I'd better go down to the village first, Barin. I want to find out as much as I can what's going on before I set off. The sooner the better, now that the nights are dark. That'll be a great help." Papa took one of her hands in both of his and shook it warmly. He was totally unable to speak. I had never seen them shake hands before. She made the sign of the cross on his forehead and turned to Koka and me. We were unable to move at that point. The circumstances were beyond anything we had ever experienced. We couldn't believe it was all happening. When she bent down to kiss us and to bless us her resolution wavered in her eyes and there were tears in them.

Papa found his voice.

"Agasha, I can't let you go. I can't…"

"How could I sleep in my bed if I didn't go, Barin?" He fell silent again. "Don't worry about me. I shall be all right." At the door she gave us an unforgettable smile. "God keep you all safe. Pray for me."

I began to run after her but Papa leapt after me and caught me by the arm. Agasha had closed the kitchen door and was moving about in there.

"No, no, Moossinka! Don't! Don't make it more difficult for her. Let's go to the verandah window and wave to her as she goes down the path." But it had started to snow again and it was quite dark outside. I glued my nose to the window but there was no sign of Agasha. Papa touched my shoulder.

"She must have gone the other way. Through the gap in the fence."

This disappointment was the last straw. I rushed into Agasha's room, refusing to believe that she wasn't there. I came face to face with her ikon of the Madonna and child. The Madonna's smile was the same as Agasha's but, at that moment, I only wanted Agasha. I threw myself onto her bed and buried my head in her pillow in a paroxysm of tears. I was dimly aware that Papa was standing in the doorway behind me. He made no attempt this time to quieten me but pulled the door softly to and left me to cry my grief away.

This was the very first time in my life that I had to be separated from my own, my very own Agasha.

Chapter 35

November 1917

After Agasha had left us I lost my appetite almost completely. Our sparse diet of the past few months had not been at all nourishing and we had all been getting thinner and thinner, almost as gaunt as Frau Tremer had been just before she died. When I pushed my plate away from me at mealtimes regularly Mama and Papa were very anxious and would stand over me trying to coax me or even force me to eat more. But I had no interest in food and just closed my mouth obstinately when one or other tried to get an extra spoonful of thin soup or porridge or potato past my lips. I took to going out in the garden and standing stock still looking up at the sky fixedly. Sometimes I had my outdoor clothes on, sometimes I didn't bother. I was just looking up into the sky for evidence of Agasha's presence just as she would look up into the sky for evidence of the presence of God Himself. Papa would come out of the cottage and find me there, quietly lead me back into the warm kitchen, sit me down and rub my hands and feet to restore the circulation.

Day followed weary day as if we were living in a vacuum. The cottage, without Agasha, became, for me, a large, empty echoing box. And yet, paradoxically, the whole place was full of her presence. As I grew weaker this became stronger and stronger. When the kitchen door opened from the outside I would run towards it with her name on my lips. More often than not it would be Aino with a bucket of water from the well or an armful of split logs for the kitchen range. He would invariably smile kindly at me with his wrinkled face and nod his head agreeably. He had no idea of the black abyss of misery into which I fell when I saw that it was he and not Agasha. I would sit on her bed for hours upon end gazing at her ikon of Mary and the Baby Jesus. If I waited long enough it would actually turn into Agasha's face and smile down on me. Sometimes I would hear her voice calling me and I would run happily towards the sound of it, into the dining room, the kitchen, her bedroom, the garden, only to sink back into despondency again when I found nobody there and was obliged to realise that her voice had only been in my imagination.

In self-destructive moods I took to sitting out in the verandah. It could be dangerously cold out there at this time of the year. I didn't care if I lived or died. At night, in the small hours, I would steal in there regardless of the time of day or night, with my eyes glued to the garden path and my nose pressed to the frost-free circle I had breathed away on the window pane. I could see images of Agasha through the falling snow and the fitful light of the late-rising moon. Mostly she would be wading through deep drifts of snow or striding through the woods. Sometimes she would be hiding from her enemies. Occasionally she would turn and walk straight towards me. I'd get to my feet ready to open the door and let her in, but her image would fade just before she reached me.

It must have been about the fourteenth night some time before dawn that Papa, who was awake, too, came into the darkened dining room in his dressing gown and saw the door into the verandah slightly ajar. He instantly knew the reason because he had found me in there several times before. He softly came to stand behind me.

"She won't be coming tonight now, my dear. The moon is rising. Look how bright it's getting in the garden." He led me back into the dining room, sat me down and started to rub my feet, which were like ice.

"How long have you been sitting in the cold out there, Moossinka?"

"I don't know Papa. Not very long, I think."

"How cold you are."

"I don't feel cold, Papa." He examined my face anxiously.

"T-t-t-t. I didn't hear you get up."

"I was ever so quiet. I… I… crept." He smiled and nodded. "Ah, I see. And, of course, I'd closed the kitchen door."

"Haven't you been to sleep at all, Papa?" He touched me on the cheek.

"Don't you worry your little self about that, my dear."

"Have you been in the kitchen all night?"

"Part of the night. I've just made myself some tea. Look." There was a half empty glass on the dining room table. The tea looked more like hot water. He had obviously brought it in with him a few minutes before because the "tea" was steaming.

"Were you sitting in the dark, Papa? I didn't see any light under the kitchen door."

"It wasn't all that dark. There was the fire. I turned the lamp right down to save the oil. There's hardly any left." We were still talking together in whispers. "And the moon was just beginning to shine in through the window." It never occurred to Papa to be cross with me for not being in bed. There was a complete understanding between us. We were both intensely worried about Agasha and very much on edge waiting for her return, almost like two conspirators.

"Would you like some tea?" I nodded.

"Come on, then, let's go back into the kitchen." He led the way down the passage. We both went on tiptoes. He pointed to the two rooms where Mama and Koka were sleeping and put his fingers to his lips, smiling mischievously. I imitated him and almost giggled. We went into the kitchen and closed the door behind us, which made me feel very secret and rather naughty. This was a very peculiar time of the day, of the night, for us to be half in the dark, drinking tea together. I took charge and poured some of the watery tea out for myself and filled Papa's glass up.

We had just settled down comfortably at the table when there was a curious scuffling noise outside in the garden. We looked at each other wonderingly and then at the outside door. The latch half lifted and then clicked up the last little bit. The door swung open and a bulky, indistinct, snow-covered figure slid carefully through the door with its back to us. We got up, almost but not quite sure who it was. The figure carefully closed the door and dropped the latch and turned round with gloved hands ready to brush off some of the snow clinging to it. It was… yes, it was… Agasha! She jumped when she saw us and then her face broke into a beaming smile as she held out her arms to us. Papa took one of her hands in his and just shook it and shook it and shook it. All he could say was,

"Agasha, thank God, thank God", over and over again.

As for me, I simply shrieked her name and hurled myself forward into her embrace. We both hurried her to a chair and, although she protested, just made her sit down and rest. As Papa was turning the lamp up Mama, hastily putting on her dressing gown, and Koka in his pyjamas and with bare feet, both no doubt wakened by the loudness of my cry, came running in, wide-eyed and breathless. Mama put her hands up to her cheeks in disbelief at seeing Agasha there safe and sound, and hurried over to kiss her as she sat there on the kitchen chair, still liberally peppered with melting snow. Koka practically pushed Mama to one side in his eagerness to throw his arms round Agasha and nestle against her bosom without saying a word. The other three of us became very busy. Papa went over to the range, removed the top, stirred up the fire and started to heat some soup. I took Agasha's snow-covered shawl from her head and shoulders, shook it thoroughly, which drew laughing cries of protest from the rest, and draped it, in best housewifely fashion, over the back of another chair which I set near the fire. Mama was now on her knees removing one of Agasha's soaking felt boots and I knelt down to help with the other. The whole room was glowing with sheer joy.

"When I saw the moon was rising, I gave you up. I didn't think you'd come tonight."

"I was so near I decided to chance it, Barin. I couldn't wait to see you all again." She stretched her arms out in front of her in sheer weariness. "I'm so glad to be home."

"Here's some hot soup for you, Agasha." Papa was pouring it into a bowl as he spoke. "Let's all go into the dining room."

He led the way carrying the steaming bowl of soup; Koka and I each took one of Agasha's hands and pulled her along the passage with such force that she stumbled at one point and protested laughingly. Mama brought up the rear, naturally impatient to hear what Agasha had to tell us. Koka and I stayed so close that she had some difficulty in raising the spoon to her mouth. Mama and Papa sat at the table across from her, waiting anxiously.

"Did you manage to see…?" Mama couldn't control her feelings.

"Let her drink her soup first, Lilichka. There's no hurry for a few minutes. Agasha will tell us all her news in good time."

At last she pushed her soup bowl away. "Thank you, Barin, I don't know when soup tasted so good." She picked me up and affectionately rubbed her cheek against mine.

"Yes, yes, I did manage to find the old Barinya in the end."

"What did you do? Did you go to the factory?"

"I went there to start with. But I didn't dare go inside. The old Barinya's house and the apartment were still there but a lot of strange people were going in and out and she didn't seem to be living there any more."

"What did you do?"

"I didn't know what to do at first. Then I thought that, if I went round Petrograd to all the friends of the Barinya I knew, I might find her that way. And I did in the end. I found her staying the night at the Repins."

"Staying the night?"

"Things are very difficult for property owners there now. They are all in danger. She has to sleep in a different place every night for fear of being recognised and arrested."

"How is she in herself?"

"You'd never believe it but she's really fairly well. You know the old Barinya. She's dreadfully thin, of course."

"What about Aunt Dorothea? Did you see her, too?"

"She's dead, Barin."

"Dead? How? Why?"

"She just gave up the ghost. It was all too much for her. She just didn't wake up one morning. The little dog died too… Kroshka… almost at the same time. … Barinya had no end of time and trouble burying them." There was a horrified pause from Mama and Papa at this somewhat matter-of-fact statement.

"What do you mean, Agasha?" Papa eventually got out.

"Nobody would help. Nobody would have anything to do with her. One of the rich, you see. When they looked at her clothes and heard her accent… Nobody would agree to bury Aunt Dorothea. Nobody would even agree to take her to the cemetery. Not for love or money."

"Dear God… What did she do?"

"She wrapped Aunt Dorothea in a blanket and managed to get her onto a little sleigh. And she wrapped Kroshka up, too, and strapped them both on so that they wouldn't fall off on the way. She tied a rope to the front of the sleigh and pulled them all the way to the cemetery herself. She said she had to stop every hundred yards or so. It took her nearly three hours."

Mama put her hands to her brow to steady her spinning head. Tears ran down her cheeks. Papa jumped to his feet and walked about the room agitatedly.

"What a world we live in! Good God! She's an old woman… I'm sorry, Agasha. Go on. We'd better hear it all. What happened when she got to the cemetery? Did she just leave them there?"

"How could she do that, Barin?" There was some reproach in Agasha's voice. "No. She tramped all round the cemetery trying to find someone to help her. In the end she came across an old man who told her where there was an open grave which hadn't been used. He said he would help her... but only after she had promised him one of her rings", she continued levelly.

"How despicable! What are people coming to?" Papa was aghast at this terrible narrative. Mama made no sound but was weeping all the time. Koka and I didn't fully understand the full import of what Agasha was saying but the charged atmosphere kept us still as mice.

"The old Barinya loved Aunt Dorothea very much. They'd been together for many years. She was very fond of Kroshka, too. It broke her heart to put them into the grave without even a coffin for Aunt Dorothea... When the old Barinya told me how she threw a lump of hard frozen earth onto them she just cried and cried. I thought she'd never stop."

"We can't leave her in St. Petersburg, Karloosha, we can't"

"What can we do, Lilya? We aren't in a position to get her out, are we?"

"I'm not so sure about that, Barin." Agasha very deliberately looked Papa straight in the eye. There was a deep meaning in her tone which Koka and I couldn't hope to understand.

"But the first thing I'm going to do is to put these two sleepy things back to bed. Some little ears have heard too much for their own good, I think." She began to lead us out of the room. In the doorway she turned back towards Papa and repeated with even greater emphasis, "I'm not so sure about that, Barin."

Chapter 36

November 1917 – Agasha

I got up earlier than usual and went about my usual chores as quietly as I knew how. I laid the fire in the range ready to start when the Barin came down. I got some water in from the well and laid the table for breakfast. Any moment I expected one of the children to wake up and come in to question me. That was the last thing I wanted. I couldn't bear the thought of Moossia's tears.

But all went well. I listened at the door of the children's room and heard only the sound of heavy breathing and of Koka turning over in his sleep.

So I managed to put on my valenki and the warmest clothes I had, opened the door and closed it carefully, and made off down the path without disturbing anyone.

As I made for the road I was oddly light-hearted. Of course I knew it might be dangerous but I also knew that God was watching over me and would protect me. How many people had had the luck to pass their lives with people like the Dvorskys? Thinking of their kindness and their care for me brought tears to my eyes. Of course, Moossia wouldn't like me being away but when I got back to Kelomakki, as I was sure I would, she would get over it and be her usual self again.

It was a lovely morning. Everything was still except for the distant sound of old Petrovich's dog howling after his master. Eighty years old! Whoever killed him must have been out of his mind. He had never done any harm to anybody. Who did it? Was it the Reds or the Whites or the Bandits? Nobody would ever know. His pockets had been emptied so perhaps it was just ne'er-do-wells who had done it.

Of course, dead people had been found in the woods before, but no one we knew so well, no one we saw every week. We were more shocked than we had ever been when the Barin found him. Aino helped Barin to bury him where he had found the old man, in the woods which he had loved and where he had spent so much of his time.

The days were short and the sun didn't come up until nine o'clock in the morning but the waning moon helped me on my way. The snow had gone but there had been a hard frost for several days and I could hear the sound of my footsteps echoing along the road. There were occasional showers of snow which went into my eyes like tiny knives and I was blinded for a little while and had to duck my head and shoulder my way forward.

I passed through Kanorva and didn't see a soul. Everyone had stayed indoors, keeping out of the cold. I didn't blame them. I would have done the same but I had something important to do. The whole world seemed deserted but when I was about two versts from Kuokalla a little cart just like Aino's joined the road from a track coming up from the sea, about thirty paces in front of me. The horse had been a beautiful creature with a dark mane and tail, the colour of my own hair, but now it had become a mere skeleton. The driver had seen me out of the corner of his eye and he pulled up. He didn't turn round but gestured with his right arm inviting me to join him on the cart. I ran after the cart, slipped on a patch of ice and almost fell over. As I got up and brushed my coat down he still made no move. I hesitated because I was uneasy about travelling alone with a man.

"Want a lift?" he asked in a harsh voice.

"Yes, please sir." I thought it best to be very polite. He sounded as though he could be very bad tempered. As I still hesitated he said very crossly,

"Come on then. I don't want to be here all day."

So I climbed onto the cart and sat beside him. After all, I wouldn't be on the cart with him for long. I was tired and Kuokalla wasn't far. For the first time I got a good look at him.

I didn't like what I saw. It was a shock. He looked just like Lev Wenzerul, a rogue in the village I was born in. The likeness was uncanny. The same grey straggling beard; the same swollen nose; the same red face; the same bleary eyes: the face of a typical drunkard. He flicked the horse's back with his whip and the poor creature slowly pulled the cart forward towards Kuokalla. After a few yards,

"Where you come from?" The voice was low and rasping.

221

"Kelomakki, sir." I recognised his type at once. I'd met it before. I like to think the best of everybody but I took an instant dislike to this man. Lev Wenzerul had been a pest. He got roaring drunk every night; staggered down the middle of the street singing rude songs, and chased every girl in sight. We despised him but were really afraid of him. You never knew what he would get up to next.

"That hole! I can't stand it."

I said nothing. I think Kelomakki is a very nice place.

He flicked the nag on its back and it plodded on its weary way. After a few yards the man fished a half-empty bottle of vodka from a pocket. I had been right. But then, it was obvious from the start.

You could see he was a heavy drinker. Where did he get the vodka from? I almost changed my mind and got off the cart. I felt I was in a dangerous situation, but I sat tight. After all, I thought, I was strong enough to cope with this drunken lout; it wasn't far to Kuokkala and I could always jump off the cart if I needed to. He kept up a desultory conversation.

"Where are you going?"

"St. Petersburg… sir."

"You must be mad." He slurped some more vodka. "You're much safer out here. Far more getting killed in Petersburg. Sure you won't have some vodka? It'll keep out the cold."

I kept silent. Then I saw something I'd not noticed before. He was wearing a complete officer's uniform. Peaked cap, greatcoat, knee-length boots, everything. There was a dark, sinister stain on the greatcoat's right shoulder. Up to then I'd been uneasy at sitting beside him. Now I was really alarmed. He was too old and too much of a sot to be of any use in any fighting group. Obviously he had gone into the woods and stripped a dead man of his clothes. The cart trundled on. But he wouldn't leave the subject of St. Petersburg alone.

"What are you going to Petersburg for?"

Was he a spy? Better be careful. "Going to see my aunt," I lied.

"Where she live?"

"St. Basil's." He whistled.

"She rich? You better be careful."

"Not rich at all. She's a cook," I lied again.

"She'll be all right then. Here we are. Don't go no further. You'll just have to keep on walking." I was very glad to get off the cart.

"Thanks for the lift."

"That's all right. I can see you're one of us. I don't go giving lifts to anyone. Specially to those rich bastards who started all this trouble. If they weren't so bleedin' greedy, we'd a' left 'em alone. Good luck."

He went round the corner of one of the buildings on the left and I heard a door open and close, the horse neigh, the sound of voices, and that was the end of that. I didn't see him again, thank goodness.

I was a bit stiff after sitting on the cart but it soon wore off and I went on my way to Ollila. In the middle of the village there was a rough barrier and two men, one tall and thin and the other short and fat. They weren't in uniform but looked very comical together and I smiled. But when the short one levelled a rifle at me and demanded to see my papers the smile left my face. Fortunately my papers were in order and they let me pass but not without the inevitable questions and answers. Where was I going? What for? Where did she live? Was she rich? I gave the same lying answers I had given to the man in the cart. But they left me with food for thought. They would never let Mrs Sturm pass. Her papers would not be in order and if she opened her mouth they would recognise by her accent what class she belonged to, and they might shoot her on the spot.

I went on turning these problems over in my mind as I walked on to St. Petersburg. Just before I crossed the bridge over the Neva which led to St. Basil's a tram had come off the rails. Three engineers were struggling to get the wheels back on the track, swearing out loud and using words you'd never hear from the mouths of the Dvorskys. Two students stopped for a few moments and exchanged comments with the engineers. They were muffled up to the eyebrows and stamped their feet on the ground to keep the circulation going. They didn't stay on; it was too cold. And then they moved away, laughing and joking.

I wasn't sure where to look for Mrs Sturm. In those days the well-to-do tended to move from place to place for safety's sake. So I decided to start looking in the most obvious place and made for the factory. It was a lucky guess.

When I passed our old apartment I looked up to see if there was anyone living there. There was a light in the living room window and a sort of red flag draped outside it.

The lock of the gate into the factory grounds had been broken and I walked round the frozen pond where we had all had such fun the previous winter, feeling more and more anxious. When I rang the bell there was a pause and then the sound of someone sneezing over and over again. The lock clicked and there stood Mrs Sturm, her eyes streaming with tears. She sneezed again before she spoke.

I was surprised to see her in person. Dunyasha usually opened the door but, obviously, she had gone since I was last there. Mrs Sturm must now be entirely alone.

"Agasha, my dear, what a surprise, how nice to see you. What brings you here?"

"I've come to take you back to Kelomakki, Barinya."

"Come in out of the cold. What an angel you are! Come into the kitchen. I live there all the time now. It's the only place where I can get a bit of warmth. I'll give you some tea. Tea! Well, that's what I call it. I haven't had a decent glass of tea for I don't know how long. I've only just this moment lit the samovar. Luckily Pavel brought in a good supply of logs before he went off. Don't ask me where he went. He just wouldn't talk about it. But I have my suspicions."

I didn't ask her what her suspicions were. It was none of my business. So we sat down sipping our hot water as near to the stove as we could get and talked things over. Clearly my plans had to be changed. I had hoped that we could set off back to Kelomakki straight away but that was clearly out of the question before Mrs Sturm's cold had got better. To take her back now would be disastrous.

We chatted for a while, mostly about the children and other members of our different families. Then I thought I'd better get to the point.

"Barinya, if you don't mind me saying so, I think we have some problems. I walked straight along the road. Of course, I was stopped and asked for my papers at Ollila. It was all right and they let me through. They could see that I was someone of no importance. But, if you had to show your papers, well…" I trailed off.

"Of course, you're right my dear. What do you think we ought to do?"

"Well, I thought we ought to walk along the railway track."

"What about going through the stations? There are bound to be some nosey parkers there. Wouldn't that be dangerous?"

"I'd thought about that. We'd have to go round the villages through the fields."

"Hmmm."

"Another thing. Don't mind me saying this. I walked here in a day. But I'm much younger than you..."

"You mean to say that I'm much older than you are?" She laughed out loud and then sneezed three or four times. "How tactful you are, Agasha. Anything else?"

"Well, yes." I began to feel very self-conscious. "We must do everything we can to make you seem like an ordinary peasant, as if you are my aunt, for example. That's what I shall say you are. You'll need to look as though you might be my aunt. Your clothes..."

"I don't think there's any problem about that. Olga left some clothes behind her when she went away. I think she found what she hoped was a better job. After all, it was very dull for her here, cooped up with an old woman and Dunyasha. She needed something livelier. I hope she found it. She was taller than I am of course but we can easily cut a bit off the skirt." The Barinya was entering into the spirit of things. "Anything else, Agasha? Don't be afraid to say."

"Well, yes, I'm afraid there is." It was getting more and more awkward. "If you speak like you usually do, they'll know you're one of the well-to-do..."

"No problem, Agasha. I'm not a bad actress. I think I can manage that." She thought seriously for a few moments then her face brightened. "I know what, I'll pretend to be the village idiot." She lolled her head and let her mouth go slack and said something I couldn't understand. It was very funny and I laughed.

So that was all settled. All we had to do was carry it out. We spent the next three days preparing. I went out to the markets to see if I could get some food. I began to worry about Moossia. She wouldn't like me being away so long, but it couldn't be helped. There was almost nothing in the market, not much more than there was in the shop at Kelomakki and I had to pay through the nose for it. But I did manage to get a loaf of rye bread and a few potatoes. We ate the potatoes very sparingly and kept some of the bread back for the journey. We spent all our time in the kitchen and slept there, too. Mrs Sturm slept on the stove and I slept in an armchair which I pulled as near to the stove as it would go.

Chapter 37

November 1917

The one oil lamp we had been able to use lately and which had to be carried at great inconvenience from one room to another because of the extreme shortage of paraffin was finally reduced to its last thimbleful of fuel, and sputtered out in a swirl of smelly black smoke. Papa knew that this was going to happen and had managed to unearth an old carbide lamp and a supply of carbide from the barn. The lamp hadn't been used for years and had to be taken apart, cleaned and put together again before he dared to light it. I was sitting on Agasha's bed late one afternoon, leaning with my back to the wall. I had just woken up after dozing off. I spent a lot of time in this room sleeping on Agasha's bed. I could hear Papa wrestling with the lamp on the other side of the partition. Mama was in the kitchen, too, preparing the soup for supper because this was our first, main and only dish in the evening, more often than not. There were metallic clinks as bits of the lamp rolled off the table and fell to the floor, and exclamations of annoyance at his own clumsiness as Papa struggled to put the lamp into working order.

"Do you think you can get it to go, Karloosha?"

"Think so… think so. I got that last bit on the wrong way round. If I can just get this last screw, bolt, whatever it is… There, that should do the trick. Now, I'll just fill the reservoir with water…" The conversation veered.

"Does Agasha stand a chance, Karloosha?"

"If Agasha can't do it, I don't know anyone who can."

"Will they really have to walk all the way, every step?"

"They might be lucky. They might be able to find someone who would give them a lift for a part of the way, some peasant like Aino who hasn't got round to eating his horse. But it could be too dangerous to do that. Everybody is so unpredictable these days. I expect they'll prefer to walk. Don't worry. Leave it to Agasha… we've got to leave it to Agasha… Here comes the gas… now… I'll just get a light from the fire… that bit of paper. Let's see… what about that?"

"What a cold blue light it gives. It'll make us all look like ghosts. Nothing like as pleasant as lamplight."

"It's better than no light at all, my dear."

"Yes, yes, of course it is. Don't think I'm complaining. I think it's very clever of you to make it work after all this time."

"Thank you for that kind word. Mostly common sense, you know… and I didn't think for a moment that you were complaining. Agasha knows the ropes far better than we do. She can talk like a real dyed-in-the-wool peasant when she wants to."

"I know she can. But what about Mamochka? Do you think she'll be able to stand up to the journey after everything she's already been through?"

"Never underrate Mamochka, Lilya! And you know what Agasha says, 'Even a flea can tackle a lion when the need arises.' We mustn't lose hope. It won't be long… Mustn't waste the carbide. I'll turn it off until we really need it." Then, as an afterthought, "The moon is on the wane."

"The moon is on the wane." Papa's words pealed in my head like a chime of cathedral bells. "The moon is on the wane" rang over and over in my heart for days on end. I clenched my fists as hard as I could to control my impatience. "The moon is on the wane." I sat under Agasha's ikon and prayed, "The moon is on the wane, please let Agasha and Granny come soon."

To "get some fresh air into our lungs", Papa used to take us for a brisk walk across the garden and along the edge of the wood before we went indoors, drew the curtains and settled down for the evening. We would always turn round at the kitchen door and scan the sky. The day came when Papa took longer than usual to do this.

"It's getting dark very early tonight. Look at the clouds. How low they are."

"Is it going to snow again, Papa?"

"Perhaps, perhaps. There'll be no moon at all tonight." We looked at each other and the same thought was in our minds. Would it be tonight? Papa started to bolt the door when we were inside and then had second thoughts and drew the bolts back again, deliberately, first at the top and then at the bottom of the door. Koka and I paused as we were taking our coats off and Mama turned away from her work at the kitchen range. He answered her unspoken question. "I'm going to leave the back door unbolted from now on. They could come at any time."

"Won't that be dangerous? There are all sorts of dangerous characters wandering about in the woods."

"Don't worry! I'm going to sit up until it gets light. I'm hardly sleeping these nights in any case. I'll get a rest during the day."

"Let me take turns with you."

"We'll see, my dear, we'll see. It may not be necessary."

"You think they'll come tonight, don't you?"

"Yes, I do." He was lighting the carbide lamp.

"What makes you think so?" He shrugged.

"I don't know… I just feel it in my bones." Koka clowned about, shaking his arms and trying to feel his finger bones. Papa playfully cuffed him about the head. But I think we all felt it in our bones. I certainly did. I felt it in my whole being and a great weight was lifted from my shoulders. This had to be the night when they came back. It was unthinkable that any of us should go to bed.

"Can we stay up tonight, Papa?"

"Well… all right. You can stay up for a while, just in case. If you fall asleep, of course…"

"I'm sure I won't!"

"Very well, then. We'll see."

"The soup is ready, Karloosha. Shall we have it now?"

"I'll light the way for you." He went to pick the lamp up and had to speak firmly to Koka, "Koka, don't get so near the lamp. You'll set your hair on fire." Koka was still in a funny mood and jumped into the air like a shot rabbit so that we all laughed at him. We went in a little procession into the dining room. Papa showed us all the way by the cold blue light of the gently hissing carbide lamp, followed by Mama carrying the tureen of soup. We all settled at the table and Mama picked up the ladle and held out her hand towards me.

"Moossia, pass your plate, please."

Chapter 38

November 1917 – Agasha

There had been a heavy fall of snow overnight. So early on Friday morning we cut the bread up in pieces and stuffed them into our pockets. When it began to be light we set out for Kelomakki. There were still occasional showers of snow. It was very uncomfortable but we couldn't do anything about it.

All went well until we reached the outskirts of the city. Then there was the first test. We were stopped by guards who wanted to know all about us. The guard who asked us the questions was a jolly, rosy-faced young man who looked as though he needed a shave. Fortunately for us he wasn't very good at his job.

"Papers?"

I handed over my papers and he examined them carefully then returned them to me.

"Where are you going?"

"Kelomakki."

"There aren't any trains running."

"We know."

"You might get a lift, of course."

"We might. If we don't we'll just have to walk it."

"That's a hell of a long way for the old lady." He held his hand out vaguely towards Mrs Sturm. I tensed: this was it! Then she did something very clever. She leaned over towards me and said something that was complete gibberish. She pointed towards the guard, examined the buttons on his coat, laughed like an idiot and looked into his face in a come-on way.

"Who's this, then?"

"My aunt."

"She all right?"

I tapped the side of my head. All this nonsense made the guard forget to ask for Mrs Sturm's papers and he waved us through. It had been a very clever performance and a very close shave.

When we had got to the edge of the city we made for the railway. I started to climb the embankment and held out my hand to help the old lady.

"It's all right Agasha. I can manage."

Just as we got to the top of the embankment we heard the sound of the armoured train and flattened ourselves on the ground. It wasn't the time to take chances.

We walked along the track steadily. Of course Mrs Sturm couldn't walk as fast as I could. I knew she wouldn't be able to and that we would have to find somewhere for the night and it would have to be in the open. By early afternoon we were halfway between Ollila and Kuokkala and it was starting to get dark and mist began to form. I was beginning to despair and then I saw what looked like a deserted church about three hundred paces on our right hand. There was nothing for it. We staggered across the frozen field. To make matters worse, Mrs Sturm started to sneeze again. There was the sound of gunfire about a verst away but it was nowhere near us.

When we came up to the ruin we did find some shelter against the wind. We set up camp at the west end of the church, which was the least exposed bit. We couldn't lie down, of course. But I gathered a handful of icicles from a bush and shared them between us. They were our only source of water. The Barinya was exhausted. So we sat down with our backs to the wall, sucked on the icicles and ate what was left of the bread.

"Agasha, how long shall we have to stay here?"

"Until the moon rises, Barinya."

"God help us."

"I'm sure He will, Barinya."

We said our prayers, sat close together with our knees drawn up to our bodies, our arms folded, our gloved hands under our armpits, and our chins buried in our scarves, trying to keep in as much warmth as we could. We didn't expect to sleep but hoped to rest and make ourselves fit for the rest of the journey. We had reached about halfway. I did doze off a bit and then a small animal ran across my feet. I nearly jumped out of my skin and was wide awake again. I think it was probably only a mouse looking for its supper.

Chapter 39

November 1917 – Agasha

Two more hours passed. The moon showed over the horizon. It was time to move. I roused the old lady and helped her to her feet. We were both very stiff and stamped our way across the field towards the railway to get our feet warm. We'd gone about two versts Kuokkala when we felt a rumbling noise coming along the rails. We got off the track and hid behind a bush, but it was only two railway engineers on an open truck pumping their way towards Kuokkala. Up and down, up and down they pumped, in turn. They didn't have guns and they were making a huge effort to get to wherever they were going.

There must have been a breakdown further along the line. I felt very sorry for them to have to turn out in this bitter cold. They weren't any danger to us. We walked on in silence. There wasn't anything to talk about.

The old lady started to breathe very heavily. It was a huge effort for her. It was an effort for both of us. I caught her arm and made her stop.

"Barinya, would you like to have a rest?"

It took a few seconds before she could speak.

"No, no, Agasha. Don't want to waste time. Must get there as soon as we can. They'll be worried. Sooner the better," she puffed, and started to walk ahead of me.

"They'll wonder where we've got to. I'm sure they expected to see us long before this. Goodness knows what they'll be thinking. If it hadn't been for my wretched cold we'd have been there three days ago." She was unstoppable.

The rest of our journey was just routine. We walked and walked and walked. When the armoured train was coming we knew in advance from the sound in the rails. We would take cover till it had passed and then walked and walked and walked. We walked round Kuokalla and Kanorva by the fields. No one saw us. No one asked for our papers. We sucked on icicles and ate the last crumbs of the bread. At last, in the evening, we reached the little station at Kelomakki and walked along the track to the cottage, footsore and weary. Aino had spread ashes on the path as he usually did when it was freezing. I let Mrs Sturm through the gate and walked towards our journey's end with a great sense of relief. She'd only gone a few steps along the path when the door of the verandah was wrenched open and the Barinya came running down the path. She hadn't stopped to put on a coat and was wearing one of my cook's aprons.

"Mamochka, Mamochka, we wondered what had happened to you. Oh, my dear Mamochka! We thought the most terrible things. We thought you'd had an accident. Mamochka, oh, my dear! We thought you might have been shot!"

The Barinya and her mother fell into each other's arms, hardly able to speak. They laughed and cried at the same time. I stood there, my face streaming with tears, and I was laughing and crying at the same time too.

Never was there such a homecoming.

Chapter 40

November 1917

We were all laughing and talking and shouting at the same time. Granny looked very strange to us wrapped in her heavy woollen skirt and with the peasant shawl draped over her head. When she threw the shawl back so that we could kiss her more easily we could see that her face was cruelly pinched by cold and hunger and she seemed incredibly small and fragile. But her spirit was as indomitable as ever. She embraced us all in turn, clinging for a long time to Mama who was crying out of sheer happiness. I was already hanging on so tight to Agasha that she could hardly move. I was kneading the folds of her skirt with my hands to reassure myself that she was really and truly there, like a cat testing its claws in a cushion. Her big, gentle, work-worn hand stroked my head unceasingly.

"Sh... sh... Moossinka. There's nothing to be upset about. It's all over. I'm back. Agasha is back with you again. Calm down, my sunshine. Calm down."

Koka was bewildered. He stood right in the middle of the group, turning to look at one face after another, completely dazed by the hullabaloo. When she went to embrace Papa in his turn Granny's surge of vitality momentarily ebbed. She tottered and gave a little gasp of dismay. She would have fallen if Papa hadn't stepped smartly forward and caught her. He lifted her almost bodily and, followed by the rest of the family, carried her into the house, settling her into the nearest chair. Mama hovered over her anxiously for a few moments, saw that she was unharmed, and went over to Agasha and kissed her warmly.

"Now you must tell us all about the journey, Agasha."

"Lilya, Lilya, what can you be thinking of?" Papa interrupted. "They must have something to eat first. I'm afraid it will only be soup, Mamochka."

"Thank you, Karl, but I couldn't get a thing past my lips at this moment. I'm much too excited. Lilichka's quite right. There's so much to talk about."

"Very well, Mamochka, whatever you say. Let's all go into the dining room. We shall be more comfortable there. Let me help you, Mamochka." But the amazing old lady pulled herself very upright.

"It's all right, Karl. I think I can get that much further on my own two feet. For heaven's sake, anyone would think I was a hundred." Granny's customary energy was already fast returning and her little outburst provoked a ready laugh as she had intended it should. She herself led the way back into the dining room. She had noticed that Agasha was hanging back modestly in the kitchen.

"Come along, Agasha, you must come, too. I should think so, indeed." Papa steered her to the most comfortable chair in the room and tried to get her to sit down but she resisted and firmly pushed him to one side.

"Before anything else and before I even sit down, there's something I have to say. Where's Agasha?" Her rather imperious tone softened. "Please come here, my dear. Moossinka, let go of Agasha for just one minute." She took Agasha's hands in her own and was clearly very moved. "As long as I live, Agasha, I shall never be able to thank you for all you have done for me. And that goes for everyone in this room. We shall always be in your debt."

Agasha was extremely embarrassed. She would have liked nothing better than to run out of the room and hide somewhere. Surprisingly, she stood her ground. Her eyes were modestly lowered and her lips twitched as she tried to find the right words. At last she spoke, almost inaudibly,

"I did little enough, Barinya... God... God was merciful."

Their eyes met and a smile passed between them, a smile which bore witness to the bond which their hazardous journey had forged between them. "Nobody has any debt to me." Her eyes dropped again. "Love is a ring. A ring has no ends. I know you love me. I love you... all of you."

She broke away from her position, took my hand in hers, and went over to the doorway and stood there uncertainly. Everyone was choked with emotion. The silence grew deeper and deeper in a happy, serene way. Granny tactfully ended it by sinking down into her chair with a sigh of great physical relief and brought us back into the light of common day, sounding more like her usual self.

"What a welcome change it is to be allowed to have my wits about me!"

She looked round from one to the other of us, enjoying the nonplussed look on our faces. "I should think it is. You see, I had to be Agasha's dotty old mother on the way." She began to loll her head to one side and let her eyes roll up in her head in such a way that we all had to laugh. All of us except Mama, that is, who was a little disconcerted, especially when Granny garbled her next words as if she had a mouthful of hot chestnuts. "When anybody asked me a question I couldn't give them a proper answer."

"But why, Babooshka?" I didn't understand at all. To keep everything proper and ladylike, Mama jumped in and offered two explanations at once.

"Granny wasn't feeling very well... she was tired." Papa laughed and brushed away her scruples.

"It's all right, Lilya, nothing to be ashamed of. Quite the contrary. Tell them, Mamochka."

"You see, my dear, it was just to be on the safe side. If I'd spoken the way I usually speak, someone might have realised what class of person I was. It might have been dangerous. It was all Agasha's idea and a very clever idea it was, too. If anyone had found out what sort of person I was Agasha could have been in terrible trouble."

"So could you, Barinya." Agasha had found her tongue again.

"It doesn't matter so much about me, I'm an old woman. I've had my day. But what would the family do without you, Agasha? What would Moossinka do?" She confided in Mama, "I almost refused to come. In fact, I did, at first. I thought it was suicidal to make the journey. Honestly, I didn't want to take the risk. But, luckily, Agasha wouldn't take no for an answer and here we are! Come along, Lilya, help me to get out of these frightful clothes. It's all right, I've got some more of my own underneath. Let's go into your room. Oh, just a minute. I almost forgot. I've brought a little present for the children." Koka, who had been sitting on Papa's knee sleepily sucking his thumb, jerked into life. "A present, Babooshka? What is it?"

"Yes, my darlings, a present. Don't get too excited, Koka, because it's only a little present and it's not an ordinary sort of present because, well, these are not ordinary sorts of days, are they?" She rummaged about prolongedly and teasingly in the folds of her peasant skirt and stealthily drew from her pocket a very small package knotted into a piece of torn rag. This she placed with a flourish on the dining room table. "It is for you both to share." She painstakingly undid the knots and spread the rag flat to reveal one lump of sugar. Our eyes popped and we licked our lips. Sugar was an unheard-of luxury!

Granny picked up the sugar lump between her thumb and forefinger and considered it. "How are we going to share it out?"

"Break it in two, Babooshka."

"Have you ever tried to break a lump of sugar this size in two, Moossia? There's bound to be a big bit and a little bit. That wouldn't do, would it?" Koka and I agreed wholeheartedly. "Now, let me see."

"I know," Papa had the answer. "Can you find me a piece of strong cotton, Agasha? About a yard long… Now then…" He carefully and securely tied one end of the cotton round the sugar and broke a generous length off the reel. Next he stood on the chair near him and tied the free end to the base of the oil lamp above the table and now no longer in use because of the total lack of paraffin. He adjusted the length of the cotton so that the sugar lump dangled about a foot above the tabletop, and tied the cotton off. Clambering down off the chair he waved triumphantly at the sugar lump.

"There you are, you see. That's the perfect answer. When one of you has been particularly good Agasha will allow you to come in here and have a suck at the sugar lump. No cheating, mind you. No biting!"

"How disgusting, Karloosha!"

"I don't think it's in the least disgusting, Lilichka. I'm sure the children don't, do you?" We most certainly did not. "It's a perfectly simple and sensible answer to a most difficult problem. Does anyone have a better solution?" There was no reply to this question.

Fortunately, or unfortunately, we must have been unusually well behaved for the next two or three days and we must have sucked at the sugar lump with exceptional ferocity because it disintegrated on the third day and we had a great bargaining session dividing up the fragments between us. But the sugar lump affair passed off quite amicably and was very enjoyable while it lasted.

Chapter 41

November 1917

The question arose after Granny's arrival as to which room she should occupy. Agasha, of course, offered her room and said she would go upstairs and use one of the rooms in Aunt Fanya's part of the cottage because Aunt Fanya had gone abroad and the Poles had left long since. Granny, independent and forthright as usual, wouldn't hear of it.

"I never heard of such a thing! I didn't come here to turn the whole house topsy-turvy. Turn you out of your own room after all you've done for me? Certainly not! Besides, your room is right next to the kitchen and the children's room. What if they call you in the night?"

There was no arguing with Granny in this mood and a room was speedily prepared upstairs; another stove was lit and that was that.

Although she didn't actually take over the running of the cottage, partly because she was too tactful and partly because she wasn't very well after the terrible experiences she had endured, all the same the atmosphere changed considerably after her arrival. Koka and I were on our best behaviour under Granny's eagle eye and this improvement even extended to the grownups to some extent. When she arrived on the dot at the breakfast table, remarkably neatly dressed considering that she had worn her entire available wardrobe under her peasant disguise all the way from St. Petersburg, and with her hair well brushed and neatly piled on her head, she had from the first day what can only be described as a "bracing" effect on us all. By far the largest part of her energy must have been spent for the benefit of us all on more public occasions like mealtimes. Then she put on a very convincing front as the Granny we had always known and been in awe of. But she would also be found at other odd times of the day dozing off in an armchair for an hour or so. That was when you could see how tired-looking and lined her face had become.

For Koka and me it was a halcyon time. We didn't begin to understand the dreadful fate Granny had been rescued from but it was greatly reassuring to us that she was now safe with us. The nightmare days and nights when Agasha had been torn from us were obliterated from our minds even in the short space of a few days. Agasha was comfortably with us again, our rock, our touchstone, the very centre of our existence. Our spirits, which had fallen almost to zero when she was away from us, now soared to an almost exaggerated extent. We were in a state of euphoria. We still received only very little food and we were hungry most of the time even though Papa and Agasha went off on foraging expeditions nearly every day, were often away for hours at a time, and then only to come back empty-handed. Strangely we discovered that you could be hungry and happy at the same time.

The weather had got colder again and the snow was firm so we were able to go about the garden and the nearby wood on our small children's skis. Papa came back from one of his expeditions with a "Suomi Kelki" or small, children's size, Finnish sleigh. Our pleasure knew no bounds. It was just the right size for us, rather like our Russian chair sleighs but much lighter and smaller. Indeed, I always thought they must have been invented by a gifted, intelligent child. You stood on the backboard with one foot and held onto the back of the chair holding your partner and then pushed yourself along for all you were worth with the other foot. It was something like riding a scooter. And then you coasted deliriously, the wind whipping your cheeks until they burned and almost took your breath away.

One of the best places was in the lane where the snow had been packed down. There was a bit of a slope at one point and you could race down this and get up such a speed that the sleigh would carry you round the bend and out of sight of Papa, who always insisted on being close at hand and would run after us calling out not to go too far and to be careful and not to fall off and all the other things Papas call out in such circumstances. We even managed to persuade him that the best, the most exciting, the most delightful place for us to sleigh would be down on the railway line which was so much more level than the bumpy surface of the lane. This was exhilaration beyond our wildest imaginings. We had wings; we simply flew down the tracks. Of course, it was quite safe from traffic because no train had passed through Kelomakki for weeks and weeks. Where we got our strength from, heaven only knows. The only limit to our exuberance was the length of the day and Papa's stamina. He would keep good watch over us, stamping his feet, clapping his hands and running up and down to keep himself warm. When he had thoroughly tired himself out we were the ones who had to pack up and go home, although we would have been happy to go on sleighing all night. Paradise!

Perhaps we did overdo it. Perhaps it was inevitable after months of poor food. Perhaps it would have happened in any case... Koka caught a bit of a cold and Agasha kept him in bed for a day. That wasn't very much out of the ordinary. I woke up in the middle of the night and thought there was a dog in the room, barking. When I paid proper attention I realised it was Koka making that peculiar noise. I told him not to play silly jokes but he didn't answer, so I put the pillow over my head and went to sleep again. In the morning Agasha and Mama were standing at his bedside. Koka was barking again. The back of Agasha's hand was laid against his forehead.

"No doubt about it, Barinya. He has a temperature."

"Dear God. I hope it's not pneumonia again. We shall have to keep him in bed and keep an eye on him. Perhaps it will pass."

It didn't pass. It got worse and worse. Koka not only went on barking but he developed a ghastly wheeze as well and difficulty in getting his breath. Mama and Agasha were in to watch over him.

"Wheeze, bark, bark. Wheeze, bark, bark." The noise went on hour after hour. I had got up but began to feel unwell, too.

"Agasha, my chest hurts. I want to cough but I can't."

"You, too, Moossinka. You'd better get back into bed."

I got back into bed and began to bark too.

"Merciful Heavens, Agasha. It's whooping cough! It's whooping cough!"

There was no question of sending for a doctor at this hour. There weren't any more doctors left in the district. Mama and Agasha went off to break the news to Papa. A short while later they returned with a steaming bowl of yellow porridge and our ordeal began. Unfortunately the yellow porridge wasn't something good to eat. That wouldn't have been very nice at all because the porridge was made of mustard. It was spread liberally with a wooden spoon onto a large piece of torn sheeting and then slapped, smoking hot, onto our chests. On top of this went a sheet of rubber and a thick pad of blanket, and the whole bulky parcel was bandaged round with more strips of torn sheeting and fastened with an English pin. The porridge was very hot and painful when it was first slapped on and it didn't improve when it began to do its work which was to make us sweat profusely. By the time that happened we had been trussed like chickens and tucked up firmly in our beds to cook for the allotted time.

Protests were loud and long especially but by no means only from Koka.

"Please don't do it, Mama, please don't. Agasha, please don't." He died a thousand deaths as soon as he caught sight of the bowl of steaming porridge and tried to roll himself into a ball so that it would be impossible to put the plaster on him. "I'll be good. I'll take the medicine. Really I will. I promise! I promise! Don't put it on me. Don't. It burns. A-a-a-ah!"

Agasha, with tears streaming down her face, had to help Mama to hold him down. They would both keep up a consistent accompaniment to his cries of protest.

"Kokochka, we must do it. You and Moossia are ill, very ill. We must try to make you better, mustn't we? Come along now, be a good boy," over and over again. Through my own tears I would plead, "How long, Mama? How long?"

"Only ten minutes, Moossinka, only ten minutes. Be a big girl and we'll take it off in ten minutes." It was an agonising, searing ten minutes. We would cry, we would claw at the bandages to get them off, but Mama would sit on one bed and Agasha would sit on the other to restrain us until the allotted time was over and the horrid plasters taken off. We would be rubbed gently with a little warm oil, cocooned and bandaged again and, with a warm shawl wrapped round our shoulders and chests, propped up in bed to wait for the next ordeal. These took place every morning and every evening, remorselessly, without let-up, until the barking stopped and the whooping petered out.

No sooner were we on our feet again and more or less in circulation than another, worse blow fell on the family.

"Where's Mamochka this morning?" Papa asked. For the first time since her arrival at Kelomakki Granny was not at her place at the breakfast table. Mama rose from her chair and hurried anxiously upstairs. We had nearly finished our thin tea and potato bread by the time she came down again.

"I'm afraid she's very poorly, Karloosha."

"Delayed reaction, I expect. I'm surprised she's been able to stick it out so long. I told her she ought to have a few more days in bed."

"No, Karloosha, no, it's more serious than that. She hardly slept at all last night. Her face is flushed. She obviously has a high temperature and she's been sick several times."

"What do you think it is then?"

"I don't know. We shall have to wait and see again. I only hope it isn't what it think it may be."

"May we go up and see her after breakfast, Mama?"

"No, Moossia. She really isn't well enough for visitors." Mama became very brisk and businesslike. "In fact, I don't want anyone to go upstairs for a few days. Koka, are you listening to me? And I'm going to make a bed upstairs and stay with Granny." Agasha had come into the room to clear the table and had heard the end of the conversation.

"Can't I come up and give you a hand, Barinya?"

"No, Agasha. When I say no one, I mean no one. At mealtimes I want you to leave me a tray halfway up the stairs and call up to me."

"But what in the name of goodness is it, Lilichka?"

"There isn't any point in alarming you all. I may be wrong but please do as I say."

We all nodded dumbly and she disappeared upstairs.

We carried on as normally as we could for two or three days. On the third morning she came down just as were finishing breakfast. She was transformed, dressed completely in white, a white skirt, a white blouse, an all-enveloping white apron and a white kerchief bound round her head. Koka and I got up and went towards her but she raised her hands to fend us off and spoke sharply, "No, Koka, no, Moossia. Don't come near me! You never know!" She called Agasha from the kitchen and then stood as far away from us as she could get.

"I'm afraid I have some very bad news for you. Granny is very ill indeed. She has smallpox." There was a general gasp of dismay.

"Agasha, have you been vaccinated?"

"No, Barinya."

"Fortunately we all have but you can never be a hundred per cent sure. No one must come near Granny and no one must come near me, especially not Agasha. Karl, from now on, it would be much safer if you put my trays on the stairs. Luckily we still have some carbolic. I shall rinse all the dishes before I send them back and I'm going to hang a sheet wrung out in carbolic at the top of the stairs. I'm afraid the whole place is going to reek of carbolic but I can't help that."

"Are you sure you can cope with all this by yourself, Lilya?"

"As we have no doctors now I shall have to do my best. Providing I don't catch it myself I'm sure I can manage and I shall be as careful as I know how."

"How do you know all this, my dear?"

"I wasn't wasting my time at the nursing classes last winter, you know. I'm not just an idle, silly woman." Papa waved the suggestion away.

"Of course you aren't Lilya."

The change in Mama was astounding. Her delicate, rather languid self was completely submerged by the needs of the moment. If we had ever had any least doubt about her devotion to Granny, here was proof positive that we were totally mistaken. Now there was no doubt but that she was her mother's daughter. Indeed her whole manner was uncannily like that of Granny. She went on, incisive but calm.

"Above all, don't breathe a word to anyone about Mamochka having smallpox. Say nothing at all, if you can, otherwise, some busybody will start a scare about an epidemic and Mamochka will finish up in the isolation hospital. In the present state of affairs we know very well how that would end up. They would probably take Agasha too, as she hasn't been vaccinated. Don't worry, I'll see you all again when Mamochka is better." She turned on her heel and went straight upstairs.

We were all thunderstruck. Papa and Agasha went out to the kitchen together to confer. Koka was very agitated.

"Moossia, do you think Granny is going to die?"

"Don't be idiotic, Koka. Why should she?"

"People do. The postman died."

"That was different. Agasha said he died from too much starch."

"How can you die from too much starch?"

"You get all stiff and you can't move and then you die."

"What about us? Are we going to die?"

"Don't be silly. Agasha won't let us."

Koka and I had gathered a number of titbits of information about smallpox. There were frequent outbreaks of the disease and it was very much feared, and much talk on the subject and evidence of its ravages on the faces of people we knew. Aunt Olga, Papa's sister in Estonia, had had smallpox. She had a beautiful face but it was marked all over and forever as a result. We knew that, if you placed cloths soaked in spirit on the sufferer's face it was supposed to minimise the pockmarks. If you were a girl and caught smallpox and were badly marked as a result your chances of marriage became much smaller. Altogether it was a very frightening hazard in life. Vaccination had become very popular but not everybody believed that it was effective. On the other hand, it was widely held that a wet nurse who had had the disease and recovered from it carried an antidote in her milk which protected her nurseling. Unfortunately for me, if not for Agasha, she had never suffered from smallpox.

The household moved into yet another phase. One of the most immediately noticeable effects was the change in the smell. Mama had been only too right. The whole place did smell of carbolic. It penetrated everywhere, not just upstairs where we never went now and where all our thoughts were concentrated on Mama's battle to save Granny's life.

We only caught an occasional sound of Mama moving about upstairs and the muted murmur of her voice as she attended to Granny's needs. There was no sound at all from Granny whose voice had hitherto been quite penetrating. She must be very ill indeed if she couldn't talk at all. When we were out in the garden, which we were fairly often as the weather began to improve, we would stand underneath the upstairs window trying to catch a glimpse of Mama. We would wave frantically to attract her attention whenever we saw any signs of movement behind the curtain. Occasionally we were rewarded. She would come to the window, move the curtain aside, still in her white clothes and white kerchief, and wave to us and smile. Once and once only, when the coast was clear, we crept to the bottom of the stairs to catch sight of her as she came from behind the carbolic sheet and halfway down the stairs for her tray. But she saw us as soon as she started to pull the sheet to one side and waved us off and wouldn't come out any further until we went away. As she looked rather cross on this occasion and didn't smile we didn't try that again.

Aino was very kind at this time. We saw much more of him and he showed us where the early primroses were coming through; where the sparrows, already in possession of the bird box in the lime tree, were having a battle royal with the starlings who were bullying them and trying to take over. It looked as though the starlings were bound to win the day because they were so much bigger. But the courageous little sparrows fought them to a standstill until the starlings gave up and went away. But, best of all, Aino brought Pikko back to us.

Aino was some sort of dog doctor and had been looking after Pikko for most of the winter because he had had some sort of doggy fever. He must have been a very good dog doctor because Pikko's coat was very shiny and he was full of life. He barked and crouched and jumped and pounced so joyfully that Koka finished up flat on his back at the first meeting. Pikko scratched at him with his paws and began to lick at his hands and his face and any bits of Koka he could get at. Koka lay there waving his arms and legs in all directions and alternately shouting and giggling. Aino and I pulled Pikko off before it all went too far but Koka continued to lie there, wriggling and giggling and very pleased that Pikko had recognised him and taken notice of him. From now on Pikko assumed his role as our watchdog and was tied up on a long lead just outside the barn so that he could creep into it for shelter when he needed to.

Mama wouldn't speak to us on the stairs but she would to Papa and so we got news of her and Granny that way. It was a long drawn-out business. Mostly we were able to guess how things were going by other small signs. For a long time the only voice we ever heard from upstairs was Mama's. Now there began to be two voices. One of them was faint and quavering but there were, distinctly, two voices. Later on, the amount of food taken upstairs increased. Instead of one tray going up there were two. Finally, when we were playing in the garden with Pikko, we heard the upstairs window opening and a white bundle was thrown out onto the ground. We ran over to investigate and Mama leaned out of the window and shouted,

"Go away, Koka! Go away, Moossia! Go right away! Don't you dare touch those things!"

We could now see that Mama was no longer dressed all in white and more bundles of sheets and things came flying out of the window. We went to what we thought was a safe distance and, after a while, Mama came out of the cottage, rolled all the things she had thrown out of the window into a sort of ball, dragged it all down the garden and past the pond, and proceeded to set fire to the whole bundle. When we went indoors later the smell of carbolic was overpowering but it must have done some good because, a few days later, Granny came downstairs for a short while. She was using a stick and had to be helped down the stairs one by one. Her face was very pink both from the exertion and from the remnants of the smallpox. It took hours to get her back upstairs again to her room. But, even now, she had insisted on getting fully dressed and, although she was physically very fragile, the spirit in her eyes was already shining through and you could see that she would soon be a force to reckon with again.

Moossia

Chapter 42

May 1918

Dear Mrs. Dvorsky,

I wonder if you will remember me? We met at the Laikannen's about a year ago on Easter Day. I am inviting a few women friends in to lunch next Friday and I hope that you will be able to join us, say, at about two o'clock. We are now living in the old Razumovsky house. I expect you heard about poor Mr. Razumovsky. His widow went to live with her daughter on the other side of the village. If you go down the right hand lane just before you come into Kelomakki you will find us on the left about a hundred yards further. I do hope that you can join us. Please don't bother to answer this note. Just arrive.
Yours sincerely,
Elena Rügen.

"What do you make of that, Karloosha?" Mama passed the note she had just read aloud to him across the dining-room table. It was written on a sheet of very elegant paper quite out of key with the harsh life we were living at the time. Papa sniffed at it before reading the note. Mama laughed out loud.

"I half expected it to be perfumed," he explained, "It's very informal. When did this arrive?"

"Quite early this morning. A small boy came through the gap in the hedge and gave it to Agasha when she was hanging out some washing."

"I don't remember this Elena Rügen, do you?"

"Of course you do! You were there with me. I distinctly remember you having a long conversation with her. Medium height, rather thin, very vivacious, flaming red hair." She was teasing him.

"O-o-o-oh, that one." Papa coughed modestly and lowered his eyes to the note in his hand. He enquired, rather too casually, "Is there a Mr. Rügen?" Mama laughed again and said, archly,

"Why do you ask, I want to know?"

"Oh, it's just that I don't remember meeting one."

"You wouldn't, would you? She seems to live with her sister. They're very dashing, reckless kind of women, rather bohemian. Two for a pair, I'd say."

"Will you go, Lilya?"

"By myself? What do you think?"

"I don't see why not. They won't eat you. You might be lucky and get a square meal for once. I'm all in favour of that."

"It would make a nice change." She broke off a piece of hard potato bread and chewed it with difficulty. We were sitting at the table in the garden for the first time that spring. It was getting much warmer and the snow had almost completely gone except for a small obstinate lingering patch here and there in a sheltered place. This note from Elena Rügen was a most unusual event. People had hardly enough food to keep themselves alive let alone enough to entertain their friends. With winter over and nothing much yet growing in the gardens, supplies were more difficult than ever. You often came across peasants picking green shoots and nettles and digging up roots to add to their larders. They weren't the only ones, either, because Agasha knew a lot about wild plants, too, and used her skills on our behalf. We were all thinner than ever and the grown-ups in particular had pinched faces and dark circles under their eyes.

"Somehow I feel uneasy about it, Karloosha. Do you think they're dealing in the black market?"

"Chance would be a fine thing, my dear. There doesn't seem to be any black market at the moment."

It became clear that Mama had decided to accept the invitation when Agasha got several of her summer dresses out of the trunk where they had been stored all winter. There was a good deal of detailed and animated discussion over them.

"I don't want to overdo it, Agasha. I don't want to be too dressy, do I? But, after all, it is a sort of party, isn't it?" Finally they set to work with their needles taking the lilac dress in because Mama had lost a great deal of weight during the last starvation winter. The dress was washed by Agasha's careful hands, hung out to flutter in the breeze and tenderly pressed. The mauve kid shoes were brought out and given a vigorous brushing and, one way and another, there was a whiff of peaceful, happy times in St. Petersburg in the air.

When the moment for her departure to the Rügens' arrived we had all gathered in the garden waiting for her to emerge. She stood on the step of the verandah almost sparkling in the lilac ensemble with the lilac gloves, kid shoes, ribboned straw hat and with the parasol in her hands and we clapped our hands in pleasure. Papa offered her his arm and squired her down the garden path as far as the garden gate. Koka and I followed at an awed distance and Agasha watched admiringly from the front of the cottage. Mama gave us all a little wave and set off in the direction of Kelomakki. Papa's eyes were riveted on her in pride and affection. As she went out of sight he turned reluctantly from the gate, still smiling tenderly, and held out his arms to us. We ran gaily to meet him. Agasha watched the three of us coming up the path together. She was positively glowing with satisfaction. Then she quietly went round the side of the house towards the kitchen to pick up the threads of her day's work.

It had been quite an occasion in its small way, the like of which we hadn't witnessed for many, many months. For a few hours we were wistfully happy. Perhaps life could be again as it once was. We were dreaming of the family life all together at the dining table in our apartment on Fourteenth Avenue, of the Christmas parties, of dear, outrageous Uncle Fedya, of cross Aunt Olga. Perhaps, one day, it would all be the same again. Perhaps... perhaps...

The party at the Rügens' turned out to be a long drawn out affair and it wasn't until early evening that we heard Mama's cry, "A-a-a-a-ooh, A-a-a-a-a-ooh," as she walked back along the lane. Koka and I ran down to meet her and clung to the skirt of her dress. Papa appeared from the verandah door and we sat down round the garden table to be joined a little later by Granny agog to hear all the news of the party. Mama was tired from her long walk back from Kelomakki and we had to wait in patience while she sank gratefully into a chair and methodically peeled off her gloves, took out her hatpins, removed her hat, stuck the hatpins back into the hat and arranged gloves and hat neatly on the table.

"Did you have a nice party, Mama?" I couldn't wait.

"Yes, thank you, Moossinka. It was very pleasant."

"Tell us all about it."

"There isn't much to tell, my dear." What a disappointment.

"Did you play games?"

"No, Moossinka, we just sat and talked about our families and our friends and what had become of them. We talked about what it used to be like in St. Petersburg, and we had lunch. The Rügen sisters have a wild sense of humour." She laughed to herself reminiscently.

"Was it a good lunch?"

"Very good, Mamochka. Half the time I didn't know quite what I was eating. The sisters have a very clever cook. They actually had some black bread. Then we had some meat, real meat! It tasted rather sweet. What do you think it was, Agasha?"

"I expect it was horsemeat, Barinya." Agasha replied without pausing for thought. Mama wasn't in the least put off.

"I must say, it was very good."

There the matter rested for several days.

Koka and I were swinging from one of the lower branches of the lime tree when a smartly dressed lady, about the same age as Mama, looked over the garden gate and called out to us.

"I'm sure you must be Moossia… and Koka."

We dropped to the ground and went over towards her. I couldn't understand how she knew our names because we had never seen her before. She came through the gate.

"You are, aren't you?" We nodded without saying anything and she very strangely uttered a peal of quite meaningless laughter. "I knew you must be. You see, I met your Mama at the Rügen sisters' the other day. What a lovely lady she is, your Mama, I mean!" She was a very talkative lady. "Now, tell me, are you both feeling better now?" She was moving up the path with us trailing after. "Your dear Mama told me you had this dreadful whooping cough. How perfectly awful for you." Koka started to cough obligingly but I finally found my tongue.

"Thank you very much. I'm better now. So is Koka."

"What splendid news! Perfectly splendid." She gave vent to her extraordinary laugh again. "You know, I quite took to your Mama and I told her I would call in and see her one of these days. It's such a lovely day I thought I'd take a tiny walk and keep my promise. Is she at home, by any chance?"

"Yes, she's in the dining room." By now we'd advanced as far as the verandah.

"And where is the dining room, my dear? Would you be very kind and show me? Or perhaps you'd go and tell your Mama that Mrs. Antonov has called to see her?" I opened the verandah door and Mama must have seen us because she appeared from the dining room and greeted our new acquaintance with outstretched hand.

"Oh, Mrs. Antonov, I thought I recognised your voice."

"I hope it isn't inconvenient for me to call now."

"Not in the least. I'm delighted to see you. Do come in."

"I was just saying to your daughter... what a dear, sweet child she is... I was just saying. I said to myself, 'It's a lovely day and I think I'll take a little walk...'". The dining room door swung to and the sound of Mrs. Antonov's voice was mercifully softened. But it didn't stop. It became a distant burbling noise, rising and falling by her shrieks of meaningless laughter. Very occasionally it would pause, apparently without end. Koka and I fled back to the lime tree. Koka hit the nail on the head.

"I don't like that lady. She never stops talking."

The lime tree branches creaked above our heads. Agasha came outside to draw a bucket of water from the well. Papa's hammering at something inside the barn. Constantly, in the background, there was Mrs. Antonov's endless chatter punctuated for Mama to slip a word or two in edgewise but her voice was so controlled that we couldn't hear it and, inevitably, Mrs. Antonov's flood of chatter would sweep on again. The creaking of the branches, the sound of hammering, the squeak of the roller above the well, the sound of Mrs. Antonov's voice, were stopped dead by a piercing scream which was instantly recognisable as coming from Mama. "No! It's not true! I won't believe it!" There followed a heavy sound as of someone falling, and a deathly silence,

We let go of the branches like two shot birds. Agasha let go of the well windlass and the bucket went rattling back into the depths. The hammering stopped abruptly. Mrs. Antonov dashed out of the dining room, across the verandah and out into the garden. Her previous bright, mindless, chattering magpie manner had completely gone. She looked totally distraught. When Papa moved over towards her she retreated hastily backwards along the garden path. She waved him back away from her frantically although they were still yards apart and called out hysterically,

"I'm sorry... I didn't mean... I'm sorry... I had no idea she'd take it so... O, my God! My God!" She swung away from Papa, shot out of the garden gate and ran along the lane. We could hear her gasping for breath as she went.

Papa and Agasha sprang into action as she went and ran towards the dining room. We followed at Papa's heels. When we got there we were faced by an appalling sight. Mama was lying quite flat and motionless on the floor. Papa and Agasha were kneeling on either side of her. She stirred and made a choking sound in her throat.

"I'll go and get a glass of water, Barin." Agasha went off to the kitchen. Papa was stroking Mama's cheek with the backs of his fingers.

"What was it, Lilichka? Try to tell me. Lilichka, dearest!"

"Has Mama fainted again?" Koka did his best to be helpful but Papa didn't even hear him. Agasha returned with the glass of water and knelt again by Mama who began to stir and tried to raise herself on one arm. Her lips moved several times before she was able to speak. Her eyes dilated with horror and she managed only these words, "Karloosha… Human flesh… it was human flesh…" and fainted clean away.

"What can she mean, Agasha?"

"I've no idea, Barin, unless it's something to do with the Rügens' party the other day."

"We can't leave her here on the floor, can we? We'd better lift her onto the bed. We must keep her warm." They struggled with Mama's inert body and managed to carry her into the bedroom.

"Is Mama very ill, Papa?"

"I don't know, Moossia, my dear. I think she probably is. I don't know for sure. Now be a good girl and take Koka out into the garden to play. I'll tell you all about it when I know myself."

Mama lay motionless for several days on the bed, covered with rugs and with relays of hot bricks at her feet and sides. Papa and Agasha watched over her day and night, relieved occasionally by Granny, but only occasionally because she wasn't fully recovered from her own illness. They held her hand, tried to get her to drink something, spoke to her in a low voice, doing everything they could to communicate with her. I would wake in the middle of the night and climb out of my bed to discover one of them still at Mama's side in the light of the carbide lamp turned as low as it would go. If they did get some sleep they slept in their clothes so as to be at hand immediately if needed. Once or twice I found Papa asleep but very restless and uncomfortable on the dining room settee. Agasha, of course, now had two children and three patients on her hands. Granny still needed a certain amount of cosseting and Agasha also did her best to shore Papa up with endless cups of straw-coloured tea and as reassuring a manner as she could muster.

There were no doctors to be found anywhere and, in sheer desperation, Agasha assumed an extra burden and undertook long journeys on foot into the surrounding countryside. She brought back with her different "wise women" on whom the peasants largely relied for their primitive medical skills. These ladies came very unwillingly, were at a total loss and went away again as quickly as their feet would carry them. Maybe they simply had no advice to offer but equally possibly they didn't want to be involved with people who, they thought, might turn out to be on the losing side. Papa, at his wits end, was constantly trying to get Kóka and me to "go out in the garden and play" but we were also infected with the overwhelming feeling of intense anxiety and invariably drifted back into the house again and hung about indoors.

The last of the "wise women" to arrive I brazenly watched though the bedroom door. She was a pale, scrawny creature with a leathery face and big veined hands. She sat down by the bed and felt Mama's heart for a while and looked up at Papas if to ask, "Why have you bothered to bring me here?" Rummaging about in her ragged and none too clean clothes she produced a broken piece of mirror which she held up to Mama's mouth. She then turned the unclouded mirror to Papa, got to her feet and pulled the corner of the rug over Mama's face. I had no doubt about the meaning of this gesture and fled from the cottage to the shelter of the barn, thoroughly frightened and distressed.

During the night I woke up and heard people whispering and stumbling about outside our bedroom door but I pulled the bedclothes up round my ears and managed to go to sleep again. We weren't allowed to go into the dining room for breakfast the following morning but had it, such as it was, with the others in the kitchen. Granny and Papa and Agasha all had pink eyes as if they had been crying a lot and had very little to say apart from, "Is there any more tea left?" Whenever we asked a question we just received a pat on the head or a caress and fingers would be put up to lips. We were told to go out into the garden once more, but not to go away. So we went over to talk to Pikko. He seemed to be the only living creature who wanted to be bothered with us.

The events of the morning took a wholly strange and unprecedented shape. Agasha came out of the kitchen door carrying the samovar and took it all the way round the cottage to install it in the veranda. She then returned by the same roundabout route to get a trayful of tea-glasses. Several people came up the garden path and went into the dining room by way of the verandah. They were all people who lived nearby and whom we recognised but whom we had hardly set eyes on during the winter. A few minutes later they emerged from the dining room. Some of them accepted a glass of tea from Agasha. They shook hands with Papa and Granny and then went away again down the garden path. The men looked very solemn and coughed into their hands and the women were crying and held handkerchiefs to their eyes. Several groups arrived at intervals and exactly the same things happened. Eventually Papa came right out into the garden himself and looked round for us. He came over to where we were and squatted down beside us and scratched Pikko's forehead. He was very pale and looked very, very tired. We abandoned Pikko at once and went and put our arms round him instead.

"I'm sure you know by now, my dears..." he couldn't go on. "I'm sure you know...". I couldn't bear it any longer.

"Mama is dead, isn't she, Papa?" He nodded without speaking... then..."Yes, my dears, Mama died last night. We have put her for a little while in the dining room. I'm sure you would like to come and say goodbye to her for the last time." We were both crying by now, but very quietly, and we all went across the garden hand in hand and through the verandah into the dining room.

Here the curtains had been partially drawn and the light was generally dim. Granny and Agasha were kneeling by the dining room table, their hands together in prayer. Mama, dressed completely in white, was lying on the table which had been covered by a dark blue chenille cloth. Her hands were crossed on her bosom and in them had been placed a tiny bunch of primroses. We could see her profile only, carved and pale, from where we stood. There was a whispered sound of prayer from Granny and Agasha. Papa lifted Koka up and he kissed Mama's face and was lowered to the ground again. Then it was my turn. I kissed her cold, peaceful face, too, and Papa made to lower me to the ground. At that very moment Mama's eyes flickered slightly and she gave a barely audible sigh. Papa saw it happen and he nearly dropped me.

"Merciful Heavens! Mamochka, Agasha, look! Lilya's eyelids moved! They did! I'm sure they did! She's alive! I can't believe it!"

The two women were quickly at his side and took Mama's hands into their own. Agasha raised one hand and breathed on it. It was almost as if she was breathing life back into Mama's body. Ever so slowly she came back from the dead as it were and, after an age, was apparently ready to get down off the table. When her feet touched the ground her knees buckled and she had to be carried back into the bedroom. She tried to say something but her voice was so weak that no sound at all came out of her mouth.

We all clustered round her bed, hardly daring to believe what we had just seen with our own eyes. When she looked up at us and did her best to smile, although it was only the slightest ghost of a smile, it made us sink spontaneously to our knees and offer a prayer of thanks for her return to us.

Chapter 43

May 1918

Summer came. There was a little more to eat. Living became less fraught and slightly easier than it had been for the last eight or nine months. It's true that, with the fine weather, there seemed to be more men going through the woods carrying guns. Sometimes they wore uniforms, sometimes they didn't, but in neither case did they molest us. From time to time we could hear the sound of distant gunfire but it never came too close for comfort so we shrugged it off. It was enough to live from day to day. Koka and I spent a lot of time at Aino's tiny cottage helping him about the place. One of our chief tasks was to keep watch over the fresh batch of baby chicks, for the time had come round again. The hawk hovered, ever watchful, and there were the inevitable casualties and tears and solemn little funerals when we once or twice managed to chase the hawk off after he had pounced. But there were quite a few survivors and they grew bigger and stronger and quicker and cleverer until the hawk left them alone.

Aino was very skilful with his hands. He could make all manner of nets and baskets and even useful things like bows and arrows. He carefully instructed us in the use of the bow and presented us with a small one of our very own. We dashed off to our own cottage to show it to Agasha. Koka was greatly excited.

"Agasha! Agasha! Look what Aino made us!" We burst into the kitchen fully expecting Agasha to be there at this time of day, preparing the midday meal. As there was no sign of Agasha Koka changed his mind and led the way into the dining room.

"Papa! Papa! Look what Aino made us!" There was no one in the dining room either so we went straight through it into the verandah.

"Papa! Papa!" Look what Aino..." The words died on his lips. All our excitement evaporated and we stood stock-still. The four grownups were all together but every one of them was quite, quite still. Their attitudes were frozen. We might have been staring at a picture on the wall. Mama was sitting on one of the wicker chairs with her hands in her lap crushing a handkerchief. Granny was sitting by the little table and leaning on it with her head in her hands. Papa was motionless by the door staring out into the garden. Agasha had her back to us. She was still in her outdoor clothes and was turned towards Papa as if she had just finished speaking to him. Koka nudged me, almost giggling. He whispered, "Are they all asleep?"

Agasha heard him and turned round to face us. My breath caught in my throat painfully because I hardly recognised her. Her face was white as linen; her eyes and her nose were red with weeping and her lips trembled in the effort to suppress her sobs. She said just one word, "Moossinka," and swept me up in her arms in a crushing embrace. The tableau unfroze. Koka was still holding out the little bow, on the edge of tears, and Papa came over and picked him up. Mama and Granny got up out of their chairs. Everybody had the greatest difficulty in looking at Agasha and me. I was terrified and started to cry loudly.

"Hush, my sunshine. Hush." Agasha rocked me to and fro.

"Why are you crying, Agasha? What happened? Mama? Granny?" But Mama was on the point of fainting and sniffing deeply at a bottle of smelling salts. Granny couldn't speak and lowered her eyes. Papa, still holding Koka, came close to Agasha and me.

"Tell her, Agasha."

"It's no good, Barin! I haven't got the heart. You tell her." She held me desperately close and never stopped her rocking motion. "God forgive me! I have sinned! The Evil One moved my tongue." I leaped in to defend her from her own accusations.

"It isn't your fault, Agasha. It can't be your fault. You didn't know." I looked to Papa to support my words but he silenced me by putting his finger to his lips.

"Sh. Moossia... Moossia. We can't avoid it, Agasha. They have to be told." He stroked my cheek. "Moossia, someone found out Agasha's secret."

"What secret?"

"That she went to St. Petersburg."

But that was winter. Now it's summer. We never talk about it any more, I thought.

"I didn't tell, Papa! I didn't tell! Really and truly!"

"I know you didn't, Moossia. I know. Come into the dining room and I'll tell you all about it." We all went through into the dining room and found ourselves seats. "Agasha went down to the village again to queue at the shop. There were a lot of people in the queue talking about the war and the soldiers... Then somebody started to talk about people crossing the lines into St. Petersburg. Quite a lot of people have done it, apparently, in one direction or the other, although it's very dangerous and quite forbidden. One man said that people might have gone one way; they might have gone the other way; they might even have gone over and back again but nobody had ever lived to do it twice..." He hesitated and Agasha took over.

"And like a fool I blurted out, 'I have, I've been over twice.' May God forgive my foolish, boasting tongue!" She paused to control herself but never stopped rocking me. "And then a man came up to me out of the queue, a man with a rifle, and started to ask me all sorts of questions, 'What's your name? Where do you live? Who else lives there?' He took me down to his office further along the street. There were two more men there with guns." She keened, "God, God, what have I done?" Her whole body was convulsed with sobs. Papa tried to finish the story but now she wouldn't let him. Controlling herself with extreme difficulty,

"No, Barin, no. I must tell her myself. It's part of my punishment." But she still couldn't go on and just repeated, "Oh, Moossinka, my dove, my sunshine." Then she pronounced her own sentence,

"They told me they are going to take me back to Petrograd."

The immediate seriousness of what she was saying didn't penetrate into my understanding. I tried to comfort her,

"Don't cry, Agasha. They're going to take you back home. Don't cry. We shall all be going back home, shan't we, Papa?" He shook his head sadly.

"No, Moossinka, no. We shan't be going back. We can never go back." This was too much for Mama. She rose to her feet and stood trembling.

"Don't Karloosha, don't. I can't stand it. It's like a nightmare. I must lie down. It's too much! It's too much!" When she moved, unsteadily, Granny got up to support her and they both went out of the dining room together. Even then I simply couldn't grasp what was going on.

"You can hide, Agasha! You can run away!"

"No, no, my precious, I can't. Where could I go? If I'm not here when they come for me tomorrow they'll be very angry. They might take Granny and your Papa and Mama instead."

Papa spoke in only a little above a whisper, "How can I make you understand, Moossinka? They're going to take Agasha away from us."

"But they can't, Papa! How can they?" At last it began to sink in. Agasha took in a great shuddering breath and, with a superhuman effort, recovered her composure. From this moment she remained calm. She achieved an almost terrible serenity. Slowly she let me slide down from her arms. I was staring fixedly at Papa.

"I still have a whole day with you, my precious."

"A day? Only a day?" She put her hand round the back of my head as if to shelter me.

"Yes, Moossinka, my dove. Fate has decided that I shall be taken from you." Her face was now close to mine. "After all, you're a big girl now, aren't you? You don't really need your Agasha so much now, do you?" Far from being comforted, I was stunned.

"Don't you love me any more?" Papa was ready to crack. He burst out, "Now that's enough, Moossia! Stop it! We've had as much as we can stand." Agasha gently pulled him together as well.

"It's all right, Barin. How could you ask me such a question, Moossinka? Of course I do." She became a rather pale, muted version of her old everyday self. "Now I'm going to make some tea. I'm sure we can all do with some." She took me by the hand and led me into the kitchen as she had so many times before.

From then until her leaving I watched everything she did with manic intensity, down to the minutest detail. That was the way Agasha filled the samovar with water. That was the way Agasha lit the samovar. That was the way Agasha drew water from the well. I was trying to imprint every one of her movements indelibly in my mind for all the Agashaless days to come. When the full realisation of what lay before me welled up inside, it completely overwhelmed me and I flung myself onto her bed sobbing as my heart broke into jagged fragments.

I must have been left to sleep there because when I woke up it was morning and I was still in my clothes on Agasha's bed and lightly covered with a blanket. Not seeing her, I jumped up, panic-stricken, and rushed into the dining room.

Granny, Mama, and Papa were all sitting there at the table, calmly drinking tea. Everything looked perfectly normal except that, this time, Agasha was sitting down at the table with them. I fell upon her and held her tight.

"So there you are, sleepy head." Her greeting was the same as always. Mama was also very matter-of-fact.

"I'll pour you out a glass of tea." Everything seemed so ordinary that the day before began to seem like a bad dream. This impression was shattered when Papa asked, almost too casually, and probably for my benefit,

"What time did they say they would come, Agasha?"

"Twelve o'clock, Barin." What could he be talking about?

"Who's coming, Papa?"

"Agasha told you yesterday, Moossinka. The men are coming to take her back to St. Petersburg." So it was true. I couldn't stop them, Agasha couldn't stop them. Nobody could stop them.

"I'll kill them!" Koka was standing in the doorway in his pyjamas waving his little fists fiercely.

"No, Kokochka, no. That wouldn't help. If I go without making a fuss then no harm will come to me or you or anyone else. If I resist then there will be trouble for all of us. I'm sure you don't want that to happen, do you?" Koka dropped his fists to his sides helplessly.

"Moossinka, here's your tea." I took the glass automatically from Mama. All the grownups were weaving a web of unreal calm about me. More and more I began to feel that I was sleepwalking. The web grew wider as Mama spoke to Koka.

"Koka, I think you should go back and get dressed."

"I'll go and help him, Barinya." Agasha got up. "Why don't you come too, Moossinka?" I left my freshly poured glass of tea on the table and we all three went out of the room together.

For the greater part of that morning Koka and I sat on Agasha's bed, hardly speaking, waiting and watching her go in and out of the room. Perhaps for our sakes, perhaps because she had now accepted the inevitable, she moved about with incredible poise, a kind of heaven-sent serenity. Whenever she came in she had a smile or a caress for us. Part of the time she was getting together her very few belongings and packing them into a small battered fibre suitcase which lay open on the floor. Her heavy brown woollen cardigan lay across the end of the bed for her to pick up as the last act of her departure.

"Do you think she's going to wear her cardigan to go away, Koka?"

"Of course she is. All the rest of her things are in the case. You can see."

"Perhaps... if she didn't have her cardigan, she couldn't go?" Koka stared at me as if I were going crazy. My mind certainly had begun to work in an abnormal way. "Don't you think so?" I went on. He shrugged, not knowing what answer to give. So I picked up the cardigan and began to poke my fingers through the knitting and to pull it into holes. This time, for once, I wasn't crying. Agasha's manner had somehow dried our tears. In my strange action there was more of a fierce, demented resentment, not against Agasha, but against life, against fate, insofar as I could comprehend them.

"What are you doing, Moossia?" Koka was shocked at my destructiveness but it was quite straightforward to me.

"If she can't wear it, then she can't go."

I had intensified my efforts when Agasha came in. She understood at once what I was thinking and came over to disentangle my fingers which were hooked in the wool. She wasn't in the least cross and her voice was gentle. But her eyes were sad.

"Don't do it, my sunshine. It's no good. It won't help. Nothing can help now." She put the cardigan back at the end of the bed, sat down between us, and gathered us in her arms.

"Listen to me, children. When they come for me, I want you to stay here, right here. Then, whenever I think of you, and I shall think of you, all the time, I shall always have a picture of you in my mind."

"Agasha, don't go! Please don't go!"

"Moossinka, my dove. I have no choice. Agasha has made her porridge and now she must eat it. Don't forget, my precious, whenever you look up into the sky above your little head, it's the same sky covering us both."

"But you won't be here, Agasha! You won't be here!"

"What nonsense you talk, Moossinka! I shall always be here. You may not be able to see me but I shall always be here. Just think for a moment... When you look up into the sky on a sunny day you can't see the stars, but you know they're there all the same. Don't you understand? May God grant that this time will pass and I shall be allowed to be with you all again. We must pray for that time to come." She released us from her embrace, kissed each of us in turn and made the sign of the cross on our brows. She then took the ikon down off the wall, wrapped it in the cardigan, and packed it away among her clothes in the fibre case, which she closed with some difficulty. She took one long last look at us, smiled affectionately, and went out of the bedroom door, shutting it softly but firmly behind her. For a few moments we sat there staring miserably at the closed door and then the tears came. We clung desperately to each other and collapsed in an untidy heap on the bed.

Koka and I faithfully carried out Agasha's last instructions so we never saw her go. Neither did we see the men who came for her. There was the sound of advancing footsteps on the sandy path through the garden and the clicking of the latch on the kitchen door. Mama and Papa and Granny were all in the kitchen, too, but hardly a word was spoken. The sound of footsteps retreated and, after a long pause, the door latch clicked to.

When we picked ourselves up off the bed the whole place had changed. The whole world had changed. The cottage never seemed the same again. I wandered listlessly from place to place but always ended up in Agasha's room. I had to come to terms with the future. I had to face the hours, the days, the weeks, the years ahead without Agasha, who had held me in her arms since the day I was born.

Chapter 44

May 1918 – Agasha

Dear Barinya,

I found a small piece of candle at the back of the drawer where I keep my handkerchiefs and so I'm writing to you in the night when I'm sure not to be disturbed.

I'll give this to Aino to hand to you when I'm on my way to St. Petersburg. I couldn't face you myself because I'm so ashamed of all the trouble I'm causing. It's all my fault, of course. If I'd kept my mouth shut everything would have been all right, but I didn't.

I've always tried to get on with everybody. You know that. But during all the hours waiting in the queue at the village shop we pass the time gossiping. It's natural for women to gossip, isn't it?

And we have to wait so long for things we don't always get. Mostly we chat about our families and what we'll do when things are normal again. Of course I told them about Oleg and about you. Most of them were sympathetic about Oleg and very interested in what I could tell them about you and our life in St. Petersburg.

But there's often a maggot in the apple, isn't there? The maggot in this case has been Polya Sergeievna. I mustn't spread gossip. It's a sin. But I have to tell you that Polya Sergeievna is not a very nice person. She sneers at other people. When I told them about the Barin being all alone in St. Petersburg she said,

"I bet he has a high old time when his wife's away."

I told her she didn't know what she was talking about. She didn't know Mr. Dvorsky. She doesn't have any children of her own and is jealous because I look after Koka and Moossia.

On that particular morning we were talking about people who had got into St. Petersburg, some by one way, some by another. I didn't go into it. Then someone – I can't now remember who it was – said,

"I bet nobody has done it twice." She sounded so cocksure that I couldn't resist it and said that I had. It was very stupid of me and I bit my tongue the moment I said it.

"Prove it." It was Polya, of course. She spoke so spitefully that I couldn't resist.

"I don't have to prove it. Come and see for yourself. I went to bring the Barinya's mother back. She's there, in the cottage. See for yourself."

I hadn't noticed the two grim-faced men in the shop. They both had pistols at their belts. One of them came over to me.

"Is that true? What you said about going into Petrograd?"

"Yes," I said. "What about it? I didn't do anybody any harm."

"Never mind about that. You'll have to come back to Petrograd with us."

"I can't. I've got two children to look after."

"All right, then. We'll give you till the morning. We know where you live. We'll come for you at twelve o'clock. If you're not there we'll take the other people in the cottage."

So that was that. I shall have to be ready for them at twelve o'clock. By the time you read this I shall be on the train for St. Petersburg.

I'm so sorry, Barinya. I've caused a lot of trouble all because I couldn't keep my mouth shut. I'm so sorry. When she grows up, don't forget to tell Moossia how much I loved her, how much I loved you all. I'm sorry all this has happened. I don't know what they'll do to me. I cried a lot. I was very upset to begin with but now I feel quite calm.

It's all in the hands of God.

Agasha.

Chapter 45

May 1918

"Papa had another letter with a funny stamp on it this morning, Moossia." Koka leaned on his spade, gossiping like an old peasant.

"How do you know?"

"We-e-e-ell," he began his story laboriously, determined to make the most of it, "I heard the postman give his long whistle in the lane..."

"That always means there's a letter for us."

"I know. I know." He paddled his hands up and down crossly. "Shut up. It's my story."

"All right, then. No need to get upset."

"I sa-a-a-w Papa go out to him."

"Where did the letter come from?" A wild hope seized me. "Was it from Agasha?"

"No, it wasn't. Papa would have said. When I asked him where it came from he said it was from over the water..." He was scratching his head in puzzlement. "What's over the water?"

"How should I know?" My disappointed hopes brought me to the verge of tears. I dropped my own spade and sank to the ground, drooping my head so that my hair fell across my face and hid it from Koka.

The pain of Agasha's leaving lasted for a long time. In one sense it never stopped, and was never far below the surface. Yet, after a while, inevitably, and because we were children and fairly easily distracted by the host of pleasant things to do in the open air now that summer had come, and maybe because we were rather better fed – why, we even had an egg for breakfast occasionally – our unhappiness began to fluctuate. Sometimes, it's true, I would find myself scanning the sky for signs of Agasha's presence with tears rolling down my face but then, at other times, I could be quite content handing the seed potatoes to Aino as he carefully cut the sprouting eyes out for planting, or helping Koka launch his home-made birch bark boat with the paper sail onto the pond, or working energetically in the two pocket-handkerchief gardens which Papa had allotted to us near his radish patch. That was all Papa ever seemed to grow: radishes. What practical use our little gardens were ever going to be to us was difficult to say. We made them as pretty as we could by fringing them with large stones and we dug them and raked them religiously just as we had seen Papa and Aino tend their gardens but, when it came to growing anything in them, we were flummoxed. If Papa only had radish seed to sow, we had no seed at all. We were nevertheless content, for the time being, to go through the motions.

"Moossia, what are you going to plant in your garden, potatoes?"

"Potatoes! Potatoes! Where would I get potatoes to plant, silly?"

"Aino was planting some yesterday."

"I know he was. I was helping him."

"Well, then…"

"Don't be stupid! They're Aino's potatoes. If he gave them to us he wouldn't have enough to eat in the winter."

"Then what's the point of all this digging?" His denseness exasperated me.

"If you have a garden you have to dig it. Otherwise it's not a garden." Koka was still leaning on his spade and I was quick to point out, "You're not doing any digging, anyway. You're just leaning on your spade." But his mastery of country lore was quite equal to mine.

"When you're a gardener, that's what you do." I had no ready reply to that so I beat a strategic retreat.

"I'll go and talk to Granny and see what she says…"

Granny was in the kitchen, where she was usually busy at this time of day. She was cutting up some green shoots at the table and dropping them into a saucepan. She gave me a big enquiring smile on her old wrinkled face but I couldn't think just at that moment quite what it was I wanted to talk to her about. So I sat on a chair with my elbows on the table closely watching what she was doing. My eyes fell on a small enamel basin on the other side of the table. It looked oddly interesting. I raised myself up on my hands so that I could peep over the edge of the bowl and see what was inside it. There were a couple of handfuls of dried peas at the bottom of the basin. Peas! You could grow peas! Just the very thing. I would have to be very careful how I approached the matter.

"Bab-oo-oo-shka, do you think you could spare me some of those peas?" She looked up in some surprise.

"Peas, Moossinka, dried peas? Whatever next? They'll break your teeth."

"I wasn't going to eat them."

"Oh, weren't you…?" She thought for a while and the suspense built up. "If you weren't going to eat them… whatever would you want them for? They aren't playthings, you know."

"I don't want to play with them, Babooshka."

"There are hardly enough for the soup. We can't afford to waste good food, Moossia…" I kept carefully silent. "If you aren't going to eat them, and you aren't going to play with them, whatever else would you do with them?"

"Well, you see, Babooshka, you see… they're for my little garden."

"And what little garden is that?" Mama had joined us.

It was all getting more and more difficult. I began to wish I'd never started it all and squirmed on my chair.

"For my little garden for planting things." Granny and Mama looked at each other and I hoped that I could see the beginning of a twinkle in their eyes. I pressed my luck. I smiled my best. I wheedled.

"Please… I only want a few… just a few." Mama began to enjoy the game and teasingly pursed her lips and there was a longish pause. Granny untied the knot.

"Oh, well, if that's what you want them for, I don't suppose a few more or less will make any difference, will they? Let's give her some, Lilya." Mama reached out her hand for the basin.

"Hold your hand out, then. Here you are. One, two, three, four. There you are. Now, don't ask for any more, will you?" Triumph.

"Thank you, Mama. Thank you, Babooshka, very much." I held the four peas in a vice-like grip and scooted off into the garden where Koka was waiting, full of curiosity. As I went out of the kitchen door I heard an odd burst of laughter from Mama and Granny. I had no idea what they were laughing at.

"You've been in there for ages, Moossia. What did Granny say?"

"She gave me some peas. Look! I've got peas to plant!" I unclenched my fist boastfully and then rather wished I hadn't. Now I looked at them closely I didn't like the look of them at all. They were small, very small, a disagreeable greyey greeny colour, and even more wrinkled than Aino's face. Koka didn't think so either and lost no time in telling me so.

"They won't be any good. I wouldn't bother, if I were you."

He went off disdainfully and disappeared round the corner of the barn, leaving me to contemplate the four little waifs in the palm of my hand. I wasn't going to desert them now, and tucked them into the soil with the tenderest care. In my mind's eye I saw a forest of gorgeous flowers rising from the ground, whole bouquets of pink, red, blue and white blooms. When I told Aino about them he gave me some small pieces of broken glass which I popped over the peas with twigs to shelter them from harm. Every day, many times a day, I went to see how they were getting on. I examined the soil from every angle. I watered them regularly. I scratched the soil to make it easier for the little pea plants to get through. I even spoke encouraging, motherly words to them. So when the four tiny shoots began to show for the first time, my pride in my offspring knew no bounds. I ran into the cottage to tell everybody the good news.

"Mama, Babooshka, Koka! My peas are coming up! My peas are coming up!" But everyone took them for granted. No one showed more than a passing interest.

"Yes, dear," said Mama. "Now go into your room and put a dress on. I've laid it out ready for you. We're going to pay Masha Petrovna a visit. I don't want you to go like that, just in your shorts." That was all anybody said. Of course, Papa wasn't there. Everybody else was already dressed up, ready to go. Their total indifference to the little miracle in my pocket-handkerchief garden made me turn awkward.

"Do I have to change? Do we have to go there?"

"Now go and do as you're told, Moossia. We simply must go and see Masha Petrovna. She has been very good to us." Koka was very impatient to be off.

"Come on, slowcoach. Granny says that Masha Petrovna will give us some goggle-moggle."

They all looked and sounded unusually cheerful. That and the good news about the goggle-moggle made me forgive their hardheartedness towards my pea children and I went off obediently and put on the white dress lying on my bed. We walked sedately in a little crocodile down the garden path, through the garden gate, and turned along the lane towards Masha Petrovna's house.

"Why are we going to Masha Petrovna's today?" I asked.

"We must thank her for all she's done for us."

"What has she done for us?"

"Never you mind."

It was a fairly long walk; some time before we got as far as Kelomakki we turned down a narrow rutted lane through the forest and eventually found Masha Petrovna's house in a clearing all on its own. It was a tiny wooden house with one storey, sitting very squat upon the ground. It had a very dilapidated thatch and appeared to be entirely surrounded by chickens. Masha Petrovna was very like her little house. She was very small and old, with a pink, friendly face and her grey hair was escaping in all directions from the multicoloured kerchief she wore round her head. She, too, seemed to be entirely surrounded by chickens. She was wearing an apron made out of a sack and was coming across her unkempt garden from a tumbledown henhouse with a basket of eggs on one arm and a whole flock of chickens chasing after her. She was surprised to see us but returned our greeting in a friendly way.

"Hello, Mrs Sturm. Hello, Mrs Dvorsky. Hello, my dears. How nice to see you. Never mind the birds. They won't hurt you, Koka. Just you stand still for a few moments. Bless my soul, how you've grown! I know it's a long time since I've seen you but how you're growing. Why, Moossia, you're as tall as I am. Of course, you didn't have a very long way to grow, did you?" She chuckled away at her own little joke for several seconds. Her hens seemed to see the funny side of it, too, because they set up a flurry of cackling at the same time. Masha Petrovna was a very, very nice old lady and the first grownup I'd met who didn't have to bend down to talk to me. She turned pleasantly to Granny.

"I'm sure you must be tired and thirsty after that long walk. You sit down over there, my dears, and I'll go and get you some nice tea." As we could hardly move for the crowd of chickens all round us, she shooed them off a bit and then dived with a free hand into a pocket and scattered a handful of corn to entice them away. I got the impression that Mama was not too anxious to taste Masha Petrovna's tea. She spoke up very hastily,

"Please don't bother, Masha Petrovna. We only came…" Her words fell on thin air because Masha Petrovna had already disappeared into her little wooden house and reappeared a few moments later with two steaming tin mugs which she presented to Granny and Mama with a little bow.

By now they had found their way to a little outside table under a couple

268

of birch trees. Masha Petrovna had got rid of the basket of eggs and carried another, empty basket in the crook of one arm. Granny and Mama sipped cautiously at the steaming tea from the tin mugs. They had to go on drinking it because their hostess was watching them closely with an encouraging eye. The energetic old soul now turned to us. "Come along, you two. I've got all the eggs out of the henhouse. You two can come along with me and see if the little monkeys have laid any more in the bushes. Those birds of mine, you know, they lay their eggs in all sorts of funny places this time of the year." We searched high and low but Koka was the only lucky finder.

"I've found one! Look! I've found one!"

"Well done, Koka. Clever you!" Masha Petrovna couldn't have sounded more surprised and enthusiastic. Koka preened himself in response.

"Can I keep it, Masha Petrovna?"

"Of course you can, my dear. No, just a minute. I tell you what. I tell you what we'll do. I'll go and get another one out of the basket for Moossia and then we'll make some of this goggle-moggle your Papa has been telling me about. You wait here. I'll be back in half a minute." She trotted off into her little wooden house and returned with a basin, two forks, and another egg, and set them all down on the table.

"Now just you show me how you make it."

Granny took charge. "First of all, Masha Petrovna, you separate the whites from the yolks." She looked about her. "Lilya, empty the rest of the tea out of the mugs. Now we put the whites into the basin and a yolk into each of the mugs. Children, here's a fork. You whip the yolks in the mugs. Take it in turns, my dears. I'll whip the whites in the basin." We all set to work. Soon Koka and I had whipped the yolks up and there was a mound of stiff foam in the basin. Granny held the basin upside down to make sure the foam was stiff enough. "There, you see. That's just right. Now, children, put your mugs down on the table. Over here, please." She rapped the tabletop smartly with the butt of her fork. A born organiser, she was in her element. "Thank you. Now we share the whites into the mugs. We whip the whites and the yolks together... and there you have... goggle-moggle."

Masha Petrovna had followed every detail of the proceedings with intense and genuine interest. "Well, I never did! In all these years I've been keeping chickens I've never seen anyone make that before. I shall have to try it. Well, I never did."

We forked the goggle-moggle into our mouths and savoured it lingeringly. Then we used our forefingers to glean the remnants from the mugs and reluctantly put them down, thoroughly polished, on the table. Granny had watched our antics with an amused smile on her lips.

"Off you go, children. Go and see if you can find any more eggs while we have a chat with Masha Petrovna."

We knew this was an excuse to get rid of us for a while and that there weren't any more eggs because we'd already looked with Masha Petrovna but there was a very interesting-looking wood all round the old lady's holding so we went over towards that to have a good look at it. On the way we passed a little wooden hut which we knew was Masha's Petrovna's outdoor lavatory. As we ran a number of hens ran after us. There must have been a fence round the garden at one time because there were a number of ruined posts sticking up here and there. We took no notice of them and ran off towards the trees. There was a confused shouting behind us from Masha Petrovna which sounded like,

"Stop them going over there. Stop them going over there." We couldn't hear very clearly because we were a little way off, there was noise from the wind in the trees and the chickens following us were making quite a lot of noise as well. We turned round and obligingly started to drive the chickens back towards the garden. As we had no idea how we should do this, our efforts were far too wild; the hens got excited, flew in all directions, cackling and squawking fit to beat the band. They got completely out of control as we dashed first in one direction and then in another making more and more noise and getting more and more excited by the second.

"You run round them Koka," I panted, "and I'll try to stop them going behind the hut." We separated in hot pursuit. There was more confused shouting from Masha Petrovna as she started to come over to help us, followed by Mama and Granny.

"Moossia! Don't let them go behind the hut!" whooped Koka. I ran for all I was worth with my hands stretched out wide to reach the back of the hut before the hens did. Almost there!

More shouting and hallooing from Masha Petrovna. Another few steps! Horror of horrors! The ground gave way beneath me and I found myself up to my chest in the most awfully smelly pond behind the little hut. For some reason the cover had been left off Masha Petrovna's cesspit and I had fallen right into it! Now, too late, I understood what the dear old lady had been shouting about. It had nothing to do with the chickens. She was trying to warn me about the open cesspit!

Now that the disaster she had tried so hard to prevent had actually happened, she was quite magnificent and took control of the dreadful malodorous situation without a moment's pause.

"No, no," she called out to Granny and Mama, "don't come any nearer. You'll ruin your clothes. My old things don't matter." She edged towards the brink of the cesspit and held out both hands to me. "It's all right, Moossia. Don't lose your nerve! Here! Take hold of my hands! Both of them! Now put your feet on the edge! Right! Now... heave!"

"My shoes! I've lost my shoes!"

"Never mind about your old shoes, my dear. More important things to think about than shoes. Hang on! There we are!" She hauled me up onto dry land by her own unaided efforts. There I stood, wet, bedraggled, feeling very sorry for myself and smelling to high heaven. Granny and Mama stood a little safe distance away. Mama's face was puckered in extreme distaste but Granny was remarkably cheerful.

"Thank goodness it wasn't any deeper, Moossia. Then you would have been in the soup!" She was almost laughing.

"Mamochka, I think I'm going to be sick."

"Go away from here then, Lilya. Go and sit down by the table. Masha Petrovna and I will cope with Moossia." Koka provided a cheerful little unending refrain a few yards off.

"Moossia, you do smell! You do smell! Ugh!" He held his nose and danced around our little group in circles. Granny came towards me resolutely.

"Turn round, Moossinka. With your back to me. Hold your hands away from your sides." With her own arms held out to their fullest extent she seized my dress at the neck opening and ripped it from top to bottom and gave the sleeves a hearty tug so that the entire garment fell in a nasty little heap at my feet. Masha Petrovna was already hurrying back to the little wooden house, calling back over her shoulder, "I'll fill the tub with water." Granny led the way over with her hands held out fastidiously in front of her. I followed, dripping with slime, my arms held out like a scarecrow's. Koka continued to dance round us, keeping up his delighted chant, "Oo-o-oh, Moossia! You do smell! You do smell!"

Further trials and tribulations awaited me when we got to the little wooden house. Before she would even allow me inside Masha Petrovna's dwelling, Granny insisted that I have several buckets of water poured over me to remove the very worst of the slime. The water was very cold and left me gasping for breath and speechless with the shock. When I was taken inside I was put into the big wooden bathtub and scrubbed until I felt I had hardly a square inch of skin left on my entire body. Bit it didn't appear to do any good at all. When I was allowed to escape from the washtub, coughing and spluttering, the smell was just as bad as ever. By now I had lost my knickers in the tub and was stark naked. So Masha Petrovna very kindly brought me a long woollen vest of her own which reached down to my ankles and a big woollen shawl which she tied right round me and knotted at the back. As she stepped back to have a good look at me, her eyes met Granny's. They were both trying to keep their faces straight but there was a twitch on their lips and a sparkle in their eyes which told me how very peculiar I must look. The dear old lady knew how I was feeling and even apologised,

"I'm sorry, my dear, but it's all I've got. There's nothing else that would fit you at all." Granny came to the rescue.

"That's perfectly splendid, Masha Petrovna. Thank you very much indeed. I'll see it's all sent back to you; now I think we'd better take her home before anything else happens." We had moved into the garden sunshine by now. "Come along, Lilya. I think it's time we went home. You know, Masha Petrovna, we really came to thank you for all your kindnesses in the past. Now, it seems, we must start to thank you all over again."

"Don't you give it a thought, my dear. Goodbye, children. Give my kind regards to your Papa!" Mama shook her warmly by the hand.

"Goodbye, Masha Petrovna, and thank you very much for… everything. I don't suppose we shall see each other again." I was still wondering why Mama had said that when Koka came up to me sniffing like a dog and broke my thoughts.

"You still smell, Moossia. You still smell." Granny clapped her hands at him and chased him away.

"Never mind all that nonsense, Koka. We'll give her another tubbing later."

I couldn't wait to be safely back home and led the way several yards in front of everyone else, practically running all the way. I felt very silly indeed in Masha Petrovna's long vest and shawl and hoped and prayed we wouldn't meet anyone on the lane. We only did meet one young woman with a child in her arms and I saw them before they saw me and was able to dash behind the nearest tree and hide until they had passed by. Granny kept her promise about the extra tubbing, not once, but over and over again. Although I must have been cleaner than I had ever been before, the smell persisted and it was almost a week before I became a tolerable member of society again.

Chapter 46

May 1918

So for several days I was virtually cut off from the rest of the family. The grownups were never deliberately unkind to me but they clearly didn't want to be too close. Koka, on the other hand, made no bones about it. He ran away from me pointedly and held his nose whenever I got near him. It was just a naughty game to him but, as he had been my constant playmate for as long as I could remember, his conduct made me feel very lonely. I went down to Aino's cottage to talk to him but he was away. He sometimes went off for several days at a time to stay with his son who lived in a nearby village. Mostly I spent the time with Pikko, who didn't seem to mind the smell, or looking after my pea children. They were growing up fast now and I had to take away the pieces of glass Aino had given me to shelter them, and give them some larger twigs for them to climb up. I'd spend hours prodding the soil round them with an old kitchen fork, picking out minute weed seedlings and watering them. Koka would be at a safe distance sailing his homemade boat on the pond or throwing stones to get it to move when it was becalmed in the middle of the pond, which it very often was. As I was stroking the heads of the pea children one morning I felt little buds coming between the stalks and the leaves. This was immensely exciting and I ran the risk of going over to Koka to tell him the news.

"Koka, Koka, come and have a look at my peas."

"Why, what's happened to them?"

"I think they're growing buds."

"Lots of plants grow buds."

"Buds to make flowers. They're going to make flowers." Koka was totally unexcited and went on throwing stones towards his boat in the pond. "I'll come later on when I've got my boat back." I tried to coax him,

"It's all right. I don't smell any more. Papa said."

"I know you don't. I've told you. I'll come later."

I went back to contemplate the little miracle of creation the four pea-children were showing me. I squatted before them, stroking their heads and singing them a little song without words and, be it said, without much of a tune either. I was dreaming of the armfuls of lovely flowers I would be able to pick in perhaps a few days' time when I heard Papa's voice calling us to the verandah. He was in one of his serious moods.

"Sit down for a moment, children. There's something I have to tell you." As he and Mama and Granny were already sitting on the only available chairs, we sat cross-legged on the floor.

"I expect this will be quite a surprise to you. As a matter of fact… we are going away tomorrow."

"Going away… tomorrow?" This was more than a surprise. It was a bolt right out of the clear blue sky. Mama elaborated.

"Yes, we have to take the opportunity and go away tomorrow morning." A wonderful thought occurred to me.

"Are we going home and will Agasha be there?" Papa took up.

"No, Moossinka, we aren't going home. We're going across the sea to another country."

"But won't Agasha be waiting for us there?"

"No, my dear. Agasha knows we aren't going home."

"Not ever?"

"Not ever."

"But where? Where are we going?"

"I told you, Koka, across the sea. First we shall be going in a train and then on a ship." Koka couldn't have been more pleased.

"Hurrah, we're going on a ship!"

I still couldn't take it in. Tomorrow? Tomorrow morning? It wasn't in the least convincing. To start with, there were none of the usual signs that we were going away. None at all. I could see Papa's chessboard and Mama's embroidery, for instance, lying about on the table as usual.

"But you haven't done any packing, Mama."

"No, Moossia, I haven't done any packing." She looked at Papa and wiped her eyes with her handkerchief. Her voice was very odd.

"It's all right, we'll help. Come on, Koka." We hurried off to our room and started to get together a collection of our favourite toys on Koka's bed.

"Koka, we haven't got a case to put them in."

"Never mind, I'll go and get one."

"No, Koka, don't bother. You aren't going to need a case." It was Papa speaking. He and Mama were standing at the door.

"But how can we do our packing, Papa, if we haven't got a case?" He came and put his arms round us.

"It isn't any use packing, my dears. They won't allow us to take anything with us."

"Not anything?"

"Not anything." Koka wriggled free and went to pick up the homemade boat he'd brought indoors with him from the pond. It was his pride and joy of the moment. "But my boat, my boat?"

"Come here a moment, Koka, there's a good chap." Papa knelt by the bed on which we had started to pile our precious belongings ready for packing, and he picked up the toys one after another.

"Now, what's this, Koka?" Koka didn't know at all what was going on; neither did I. He wrinkled his forehead in puzzlement but accepted Papa's question as the beginning of some new sort of guessing game.

"That's my hobby horse."

"And what's this, Moossia?"

"That's my fat fairy story book."

He picked up one thing after another and got us to identify them: books, boat, spinning top, dolls, teddy bear, bow and arrow, Vanka Vastanka, the tumbler.

"Now I want you to look at all these things very closely and now... close your eyes, both of you, both of them... tight... Can you still see them?"

We nodded with our eyes still tight shut.

"Now they belong to you for ever and ever. No one can ever take them away from you. You can open your eyes now."

We looked up at him in some bewilderment, only half understanding what he was driving at. Mama came forward and picked up the teddy bear, looking at Papa pleadingly. He shook his head sadly but firmly.

"No, Lilichka, no. I'm sorry. They said nothing, nothing."

"But Teddy must go with us. He must!" Koka was on the point of tears.

"I'm very sorry, old chap. Teddy will have to stay here."

276

"But he belongs to Koka." Papa didn't answer me directly. He did his level best to soften the blow and gently took Teddy from Mama and sat him up at the head of the bed on Koka's pillow.

"You see, Koka, after all, this is his home. This is where he lives. I'm sure he will be very happy here with all his friends."

"But what will happen to them all?"

"No doubt some other children will come and look after them. So be sure and leave them all ready." He began to move towards the door.

"But who will they be, Papa? What will they be like?"

"Ah, who can say, Moossia? I don't know, my dear. What will they be like? I'm sure I don't know." He stood for a moment or two in bemused thought, shook his head perplexedly and went out of the room.

The carbide lamp burned very late that night in the dining room. Granny heard us tossing and turning in bed and talking to each other and came in from time to time trying to get us to go to sleep.

"Babooshka, is it really true that we're going away tomorrow?" She sat down on my bed and I tucked my legs up under me to make room for her.

"How can we go away? We haven't done any packing." Koka sat up in bed indignantly.

"Hush, Koka, hush, it's getting very late. Yes, my dears, I'm afraid it's true. They won't let us stay here any longer."

"Why won't they?"

"It's because of the war, you know."

"Why can't we go home to Agasha?"

"…because of the war, too."

"Have you done your packing, Babooshka?" Koka couldn't get the idea of packing out of his mind.

"No, Kokochka, no, I haven't. Nobody has done any packing. They won't let us take anything with us, anything at all."

"How can we go away if we haven't done any packing?" He yawned hugely in the middle of his question.

"You'll understand one day… Now snuggle down and I'll tell you both a goodnight story. Try to go to sleep. It's awfully late and we're all so very tired, aren't we? There was an old man called Masai who lived by the river. He used to go out fishing in his boat…"

"Papa says I can't take my boat." Koka's voice was getting quite faint.

"Then we must all do as Papa tells us, mustn't we? One day the rains came and there was a big flood and all the rabbits ran up to an island in the river to get out of the way of the water..."

"But tomorrow..." Koka wouldn't let go but his voice was getting fainter.

"Tomorrow will take care of itself... When he saw all the rabbits huddled on the island, Masai was very sorry for them and he got in his boat... he got in his boat... he got in his boat..."

Granny and Mama and Papa weren't in their ordinary, everyday clothes when we went in to breakfast in the morning. They were already dressed for the journey. Papa was wearing a suit with a high stiff collar. Mama studied me as she poured the tea.

"You'll have to go and change your dress after breakfast, Moossinka. You can't go in that one." This perfectly ordinary remark came as a terrible shock to me. It was only at that moment that our departure ceased to be a kind of fairy story and became hard, brutal fact. We were actually leaving and, what is more, leaving that very day. My first thought was for my pea-children.

Abandoning my breakfast untested, I ran out of the dining room, across the verandah, and down to the tiny garden where my little ones were growing. The buds were now showing clearly but they were still green. There was no sight of the riot of colour I had been waiting for all these weeks. Now I would never see them in their full glory. I squatted down and pinched one of the buds to look inside it and see what the colour was going to be.

"If you squeeze them like that, Moossinka, you'll kill the buds. I'm sure you wouldn't want to do that, would you?" Granny had followed me out into the garden and was standing just behind me.

"I did so want to see, Babooshka. I did so want to know. They're my children... my children."

"I know, my precious, I know. But if you love your children as I'm sure you do, you wouldn't want to hurt them, I'm sure." She picked up the watering can which I had left lying nearby. "Here's some water. Now sprinkle some water on them and give them your blessing." I dipped my fingers in the watering can and sprinkled the little pea plants one after the other. Tears poured down my face for the children I would never see again.

"That's right, my dear. Now they'll live and blossom and be happy. Think how grateful they will always be to you." She put her arm round my shoulder and guided me back towards the kitchen door. As we went I saw Papa walking from the verandah across the grass towards the barn with his shotgun under his arm.

"Is Papa going hunting again, Babooshka?" I asked innocently. She was at a loss for words. Her face paled. She looked at me and then at Papa and then at me again.

"It's nothing for you to bother your little head about."

She grabbed my hand and swept me indoors right through into the dining room, closing the outside door, the kitchen door and the dining room door as we went. When we were in the dining room she went and closed the door onto the verandah as well. She seemed confused and anxious. Mama, who was still sitting at the breakfast table, added to the sudden rise in tension by starting to talk non-stop. She took no notice at all of my tearstained face.

"Moossinka, what can you be thinking of? You went right out into the garden and you haven't even touched your breakfast. Just look at your tea. It must be cold, stone cold. Now sit down and eat your bread up and I'll give you some fresh tea. I'll just pour your old tea into Papa's glass. Now there's some nice hot tea for you. Drink it up. And when you've finished your breakfast I want you to go and wash your face and hands and change into your sailor suit for the train. Mamochka, let me top your tea up for you, too. Yours must be cold as well."

"It's all right, Lilya. I don't mind. I quite like cold tea. Cold tea makes you beautiful." There was a note of desperation in their voices which made no sense to me at all. They both nearly jumped out of their skins when Papa brusquely opened the door from the verandah and came into the dining room still carrying his gun. He was in a very pent-up state, too, and breathing heavily. He stood inside the door for a moment and then broke the gun and extracted the two unfired cartridges. Koka chose that moment to burst into the room from the direction of the kitchen. He was already dressed in his sailor suit ready for the train. He stopped dead when he saw Papa and gave him a fierce, accusing look and clenched his fists as if he was about to attack someone. Papa understood the meaning of the look and held out the cartridges towards him to show that they hadn't been fired. He explained to Mama and Granny,

"It's no good, Lilya, Mamochka. I couldn't do it. I couldn't. We shall have to leave him behind."

"If only we'd had a chance to talk to Aino."

"They've given us so little time to leave. If we don't go now there may never be another chance. I went down to talk to Aino first thing but he still isn't back yet. Give me another glass of tea, will you, Lilichka? Koka... what have you done with your sailor hat?" Koka shrugged uncomfortably and studied his feet.

"I don't like it."

"Whoever heard of a sailor without a hat? Go and get it, will you, there's a good chap?" Mama joined in.

"And, Moossia, you must go and get washed and dressed, too."

In our bedroom, Koka gripped me fiercely by the arm and whispered, "I saw."

"What are you talking about?"

"I saw Papa with his gun."

"So did I."

"He was going to shoot Pikko. I saw him through the window, going over to the barn with his gun. He was putting bullets in it."

"Cartridges."

"Oh-o-oh, cartridges, then."

"Papa would never shoot Pikko. He wouldn't. I just know he wouldn't. I think you're just being silly. Now go away and let me get ready." He shrugged his shoulders again and flung out of the room.

When I had washed my hands and face and changed into my sailor suit I found everyone sitting out on the verandah waiting for me. Papa's greeting was quite cheerful.

"Oh, there you are at last, Moossinka. Now we can all go and see if everything is as it should be. Lilichka, will you please lead the way?" Granny stayed on the verandah but the rest of us trouped after Mama into the kitchen. She took a long, lingering look round, made a little "Tchk, tchk" of annoyance and swept a few crumbs from the kitchen table, and led the way to her and Papa's bedroom.

"Now, who left the wardrobe door open?" she complained rather crossly. "That's how the moths get in at your clothes." Papa was patiently amused and murmured in a calming way, "Lilya, Lilichka!" She realised that she was being rather silly and smiled back at him, "I know, Karloosha, I know."

We found ourselves face to face with the door of what had been Agasha's room. It had been closed ever since she had been taken from us. No one made any move to open it and look inside. It would have been too heartbreaking. We stood for a few moments, not looking at each other, each occupied with our own loving thoughts of Agasha.

Mama became almost gay when we reached our own room. Teddy had fallen flat on his face and she propped him up again on the pillow so that he was looking down again on all the other toys. She wagged her finger at him playfully.

"Now, Teddy, remember you're in charge. You must look after your friends for us and just you take good care that they don't get up to mischief." At that moment Teddy's head lolled forward as if in answer to Mama, so we were able to laugh a little.

Everything that could be said had now been said and Mama moved round the dining room in silence. She looked at a picture here and touched a piece of furniture there. The table had been cleared but the samovar was still in its place at the head of it. She put her hand on it as if it were a magic charm and turned towards the verandah. Papa quietly resumed command, ushered us all gently onto the verandah and closed the door behind us. We had said goodbye to the cottage.

"Sit down everybody, please." We all understood what the real meaning of this was and went to our familiar places and sat in quiet for a while, preparing to leave in peace and to leave the cottage in peace. Nobody said a word. We could hear the birds singing in the garden; a cockerel crowed a short distance off and Pikko barked three or four times from where he was tied up in the barn. He ended in a plaintive, grumbling, yawning sort of whine. We were all unwilling to take the first step and Koka and I stole a quick look to see how the others were taking it. Papa got up.

"Time to go, Lilichka." We all rose to our feet. A moment of panic from Mama.

"Have you got the food, Karloosha?" He showed her the shopping bag he had just at that moment picked up, and opened it so that she could see what was inside. There were some pieces of potato bread, a few cold potatoes, a few hard-boiled eggs and a bottle of water. This was all the luggage we were taking with us. She nodded, reassured.

"Lilichka, you take Koka's hand. Moossinka, give me yours. Mamochka, will you go first, please?" We went out of the verandah door into the garden. Papa closed it behind us, finally. Another, sudden, urgent thought from Mama.

"Karloosha, have you locked the kitchen door?" Papa laughed outright and shook his head humorously.

"Whatever for, Lilya? Someone would only break it in."

It was sunny and peaceful. Everything looked more familiar, more friendly than it had ever done before. Pikko must have sensed that we were going away for good because he barked and whined furiously and pathetically after us as we went down the garden path, through the gate, across the lane, over the ditch by the little plank bridge and through the wood on the way to Kelomakki Halt. The ground on the other side of the wood was dry and sandy and it took us quite an effort to trudge through it onto the squeaking planks of the platform.

There were no other passengers waiting for the train, but two men, not in uniform but with guns slung over their shoulders, came towards us out of the shelter of the trees. Without saying a word they gestured to Papa. He calmly produced papers and tickets. One of them looked the papers over carelessly, returned them and made another gesture at the shopping bag. Papa obligingly showed him what was inside it and the two men went away again and stood in the shade of the trees watching us.

We didn't have long to wait. The train appeared in the distance, huffing and puffing and hissing and groaning.

"I don't know what we shall do if it doesn't stop for us." Papa was anxious and tense.

"It's bound to stop when it sees us." Granny was soothingly calm and phlegmatic.

She was right. The engine stopped with a terrible clanking noise as if it were about to collapse into tiny pieces. The guard didn't get out but hung crossly from his place, already prepared to wave the train on.

"Hurry along there! Get in. This isn't a proper stop."

Papa practically lifted Granny up onto the train. Mama followed close on her heels; Koka and I were bundled aboard and Papa jumped up last. Just as he joined us a furious barking approached like a whirlwind down the path through the wood along which we had come. Papa was just in time to close the carriage door and prevent Pikko from joining us on the train. He had broken loose from the barn and trailed a long piece of rope with a broken end behind him. The engine made a tremendous hissing noise and let out a huge cloud of steam. Pikko was startled by this and ran for his life. He sat on his haunches and barked back at the train. We ran to the nearest window, Koka and I, and pressed our noses to the glass to see what was happening. When the train rumbled and wheezed its way forward, Pikko started to run after it but, in a very short time, the train was going much too fast for him and soon he became only a small, barely moving speck in the distance.

Moossia

Moossia

Afterword

Agasha made it back to St Petersburg, or Leningrad as it was renamed, and survived there until the Second World War. She disappeared during the siege of Leningrad sometime between 1941 and 1944.

The Dvorskys reached Denmark, and eventually England, where Dagmar/Moossia settled down. She died in 2006, survived by two children.